to the lion
THE CHRISTIAN IN TENSION
OR AN UNPOPULAR BOOK

renownhouse
PUBLISHING

www.renownhouse.com

To the Lion: The Christian in Tension – First Edition
Copyright © 2008 Renown House
www.renownhouse.com
www.therenown.com

All rights reserved. No part of this publication may be reproduced, stored in a retrieval system, or transmitted in any form or by any means—electronic, mechanical, photocopy, recording, or any other—except for brief quotations in printed reviews, studies, and promotions, without prior permission of the publisher.

ISBN 978-0-9817830-1-7

Cover Art and Photography by Steve Stanton
www.stevestantonphotography.com

Printed in the Unites States of America
07 08 09 10 · 10 9 8 7 6 5 4 3 2 1

For my older brother.
For my bride.

Rich —

What a grace it is to keep finding you! Thank you for all your encouragement and your friendship!

Grace
Heath
therenown@gmail.com

~Contents~

Preface
Introduction

Passages	Part 1	Pages
P1-11	The Lion and the Irony	13
P12-18	Paradox/Tension	33
P19-23	What is wrong with the World/Exposing My Heart	40
P24-30	On Being *Good*?	50
P31-42	The Pride	62
P43-49	Mystery of Technology	77
P50-65	A Message of Fools	85
P66-77	Why there is Religion	100
P78-85	Heart Reasonings	112
P86-97	And Trembling…	121
P98-118	Sovereign of Good	131
P119-134	The Beautiful Standard/Acceptance	151
P135-152	Disciples of Life	163
P153-160	Triune	176
P161-177	The Beautiful Correlation	184

	Part 2	
P178-182	The Keystone	199

	Part 3	
P183-201	All Hail the Mediator	207
P202-212	Unity	225
P213-221	The Culture of Death	237
P222-242	Denying Humanism/Embracing Man	246
P243-260	Worth of Worship	265
P261-269	…the Church	285
P270-279	Moral Treasons	294
P280-287	The Spectacle	305
P288-296	Media Fools	325
P297-306	Humility of History	334
P307-312	The Poiema	345
P313-319	On Being "At One"	355
P320-330	The Naked Ache	363
P331-341	Rest/Paradox	374
P342-359	The Lamb and The Lion	384
Appendix		399
Graces		402

"That night, that year
Of now done darkness I wretch lay wrestling with
(my God!) my God."
~G.M.Hopkins

"The stone the builders rejected has become the keystone"
-Jesus of Nazareth

"We only live, only suspire
Consumed by either fire or fire,"
~ T.S. Eliot

~Preface~

This is not a book for amusement—though it is a book about joy. I have written this book of joy because of a great gathering of sad circumstances: Because many of us *Christians* are more concerned about the trend of our clothes, the increase of our careers (often disguised as ministries, let us not be fooled), and feeling the blind rush of sentimentality, than we are about holding a Christian worldview and living out the implications of grace and truth.

We are at an awkward shadow in the road where it is fashionable to speak of God, but not to live in accordance with who He is. Many have mistaken truth for that which merely amuses, and sadly, many cannot see the great joy in "the fear of the Lord." We have lost our sense of wonder, and this is unreasonable. I hope you too have felt the swelling desire for something more pivotal, more meaningful than social *Christian* niceties, than hollowed out religious motives and glassy-eyed mottoes. And so, this was written to answer certain questions, but more so to question certain *answers* that keep us pacified and "lingering in the shadow."

Now, a primer to what is ahead, because it is good to count costs. The subtitle to the philosopher Nietzsche's famed book *Twilight of the Idols* is: *How One Philosophizes with a Hammer*. Now that is a good subtitle! The book you now hold is no hammer; but if I were to gratuitously add yet another subtitle it would be this: *"How One Worships Upon an Anvil,"* for its purpose is ultimately to be a medium which we are broken upon, that truth may be acknowledged, and worship forged.

Yet, I have not the power nor love nor skill to break and re-forge an unwieldy human heart—that only God can do. God's Word alone is the true hammer to sound out idols. When Nietzsche tried to swing *his* so-called philosophical hammer to demolish all idols, he only brandished a more powerful idol—the idol that made all other idols to begin with—man himself!

With great irony Nietzsche only validated all forms of idolatry by upholding man as god. Man himself was Nietzsche's hammer and savior, and through these gates of thought he opened a flood of desolation upon the modern world—and for that, within the church as well. Yet, here in this book, man is upon the anvil and in dire need of one greater than himself—and for that, so too is the *church* upon the anvil. Now, as an anvil needs a hammer for any creative action, this text needs a context—and that context is the Word of God. Without the Word of God this book is an absurdity. That being said, this book is primarily for the *Christian*.

This book is not written for the scholar, though it is written for the thinking person; and as Christians we all ought to be thinking persons, for we are people with hearts. It was not written for ease or for "intellectual autopilot;" it is a difficult read. It is not *technically* difficult, as though it were an academic text for a doctoral student, but it is difficult *spiritually*—and by spiritually I mean *acknowledging and living the truth*— not the vague but vogue spiritualism that is simply a justification to act any selfish way we want.

The medium of this message is intentional; do not think it haphazard or unimportant. There is an order in all of this; there is a center, and from it comes meaning. This book's form is not smooth; it is written in stark and staggering passages rather than flowing narrative. It comes at you with *strokes of light* (like brief sparks from a hammer's stroke, or movements of a brush on canvas) and it comes at you fast—this necessitates the reading being slow and deliberate, punctuated and dwelled upon—something very unpopular in our frenzied and tightly scheduled age; yet this is something greatly needed, and so the book's form (being written in numbered passages) asks it of you the reader.

This book does not move in a neat straight line (such as: *here is the argument, here are its points, have a nice day*); rather, it jumps about meaningfully, and is concerned about the cumulative effect of all the so-called *strokes*. It encourages odd leaps and unusual connections between *seemingly* disjoint passages. This is because it aims to form not a small pinpoint of thought in your brain, but to paint a wide constellated portrait on your heart and mind. Its aim is not mere information transmission, but internal transformation. Though it is concerned with reasoned arguments it is equally concerned with affections, for the heart is directed by its desires. Now, I must say, this is an angular book that is meant to challenge you, to affect you, to question *you*.

So let us see what reactions come; let us see what type of light is sparked—of frustration or celebration—maybe both…

~Introduction~

I once heard a story about a wise ruler from a beautiful and exotic kingdom—an isle of seventh heaven somewhere beyond the seven seas. It was a strange and wonderful place—romantic and real, both ancient and modern like an advanced civilization from a science fiction film. Imagine Atlantis meets Camelot.

Both wise and good, the kingdom's ruler sent an ambassador out to the far countries to show the world his goodly wisdom. Time passed, and the ambassador returned to the good ruler. "What did you learn, my friend?" the ruler asked with high hopes and an inviting smile. The ambassador slumped, scratched his high brow, and looked confused; then he grew insulted. He said tersely, "Are you not going to ask me who called me teacher; who I taught—how many, and where?" The good ruler sadly put his head in his hands. "You are still blind," He said, "I sent you to discover obedience, not to be obeyed. You were to teach because you had much to learn. You were to serve to know the wisdom of serving." The king's heart weighed heavy as he sat upon his throne. The scholar scowled.

If this is a true story (and I know it is) it is a sad one. It is sad because someone who thought they had *it all* figured out had not. That seems sad to me—not that they had not figured *it all* out—but that they *thought* they had figured it all out. It is sad because it speaks so simply to the fatal cut of our nature—the dark wound of pride: the wound of pride that sinks us into self-deception as Atlantis sunk into the sea, as Camelot sunk into the waves of war. This silly story should be a serious warning to us all, for we are all this arrogant ambassador at some time or another. It is in our heritage to scowl at *The King* and think we know better.

So, a word of caution: when someone thinks they have it all figured out, they have little figured out—this is a good thing to figure out. This being so, it would do us all a great deal of good if we took a *new* trail amidst our *know-it-all* generation by walking an *old* trail—let us follow the way of the one who truly does have all the answers, who really does know the way—for He is the way. Rather than making new dead-ended trails of our own while pretending we know the route, let us follow a path already blazed and marked for us by Jesus. For when we make new trails of our own we are only trying to carve our own name into the jungle green of life with a machete we call theology or philosophy or talent; we are only self-promoting, selling our wares of ego. When we do this, we get lost in the swoops and jogs of our own gigantic signature! So, reasonably, it is much better to walk the path that God has laid before us, no matter the narrow or incline.

Lost in the insane swoops of my own name, God rescued me, hounded me through the jungle's winding green; and so I have come to write about it in this book. This book is about abandoning the quest for one's own dizzying name and being found by the one named Jesus.

~

At one time, I had wanted to write a book of great thoughts that would revolutionize Christianity; one that would turn the mediocrity of modern *religion* on its soft drooling head—start a fire—maybe ignite a modern Great Awakening or some fantastic revival that would blow like a clean wind, whisk over the seas, and sweep the far countries and polar icecaps. Sadly, I was only trying to cut my name into the landscape. I was foolish, and so Jesus turned me on my head because it was soft while my heart was hard.

It turns out that *genuine* Christianity is already a revolution—and if I revolved it anymore it wouldn't be revolutionary to the world!—rather, it would turn worldly and that is the last thing the world needs. It turns out that I was not to begin a revolution, but to fully join one. Not to make a name, but to learn a name. Not to draw up new colors, but to stand under an already raised and flying flag. I was not to launch a thousand ships to chase down beauty, but I was to laud a thousand praises because the beauty had hunted me.

In time, I realized that what I was to write down was what I was truly coming to believe, what had captured my thoughts *and* my affections—but not what I had captured or mastered—for it was not even what I had sought out! In fact, this faith was often the very opposite of what I had searched for! It was all more daring than I had the courage for; all more wonderful than my heart had hoped. In an immense irony, it turned out not that Christianity was not revolutionary enough, but true Christianity was too revolutionary for what I had wanted!

I admit, I had wanted to write something innovative, and blaze a stunning new trail; yet I have only gazed on an ancient pearl, journeyed known currents, and been guided by the same stars sailors have read every night for thousands of years. Pride had driven me. I wanted to be the first to discover a great buried treasure, but when I had found that treasure chest and opened it, it opened with a shout not a creak—and there inside were the children of God, all weeping and laughing together about the obvious secret of the Gospel. It turns out that what I thought was a tucked-away secret was really an expansive reality, a wide open world; and it was my world that had been small and claustrophobic all along. Pride had dizzied me. I was so upside down that at first I thought I was peering into a confined treasure chest when, in reality, I was really looking out upon a paradise from the inside of a coffin!

What was once a secret I too have seen as obvious and inviting. The whole world seems like a secret when your eyes are closed; life is a secret to a dead man! Life is a secret to most, though it remains evident as the light and the blur of the afternoon sun.

And now, I am writing in order to teach what I have learned, and to learn, for I am a pupil because I am a pilgrim. I have found myself set upon a rutted and ancient path home—

but it has shown itself to be dazzling and new to me, with innovative turns and virgin foliage sweeping *and* slapping across my face as I rediscover what has been traveled before; for there is no new mile when Jesus is your leader. Every danger has been faced; every oasis and glen has been rested in. One need only trust, endure, and enjoy.

These are the writings of someone traveling; and sometimes it is difficult to write when you are in motion (if the thoughts seem to bounce about, it is because the road is not always smooth—mostly it is not). Yet, it is easier to write honestly when you are in motion than when you are stationary; there is more to see, more to learn, more to catch you off-guard, more to rattle loose your silly armor and more to confront your dishonest beliefs. So if I jump about, jump with me—good things can come from rough roads, from odd combinations, sudden recurrences, punctuated refrains, and strange sights.

~

Now all this started with a pressure in my chest that, after some powerful fracturing of the heart, eventually made its way to my head like some kind of precious oil oozing up through the depths of the earth. You must understand that I was starting to get a headache—and it was no ordinary headache.

That mirthful genius, G.K. Chesterton, once said that it was chess players who went mad, not poets: *"the poet only asks to get his head into the heavens. It is the logician who seeks to get the heavens into his head. And it is his head that splits."* Well, I use to write poetry with what God placed in my soul, but for some reason I had started to only play chess with those things instead, moving them about coldly and competitively—hence my headache. I had replaced sprawling wonder with spiritual equations. I had traded the depth of water and the shine of fire for flat dogmatic concrete and religious asphalt. I felt a little like I was going mad; like I had taken the first thin step on the spiral stair case of insanity. Yet, by some intervention, my heart broke, and again poetry flooded into my mind to mix with logical prose—and as water seeks its level, the logic in my mind also poured into my heart.

It was a mistake to "*exchange* poetry with formulaic prose," to divide the head from the heart. It seems it is best to hold them together. It is silly to think a man's heart or head would still go about *living* if they were cut apart from each other—the one simply needs the other. And so, it is best to keep mystery *and* reason held in beautiful tension.

Now, in the hardening of my heart, I had gotten a headache from trying to cram is contents and the earth's horizon into my mind—not to mention this solar system, the unknown galaxies of the Creator's hand, and the Creator Himself! (Trying to cram God into your head will make you feel like the devil, and trying to cram heaven into your brain will make you feel like hell!)

Somewhere in the wake of my *headache* I realized I was to write this book as a type of catharsis—a working out of the dissonance of what my rebellious nature had desired to be true and what the truth of God's Word really says about who we are, who God is, and what is the meaning of all this madness called existence. I was to write it as an expression of sanity in a world gone mad; as a weaving together of heart and mind in a happily dismembered age.

Essentially, it was to be preaching to the preacher about this wonderful gift of a harmonized heart and mind that found trust in God, not man. That being said, if at any point of this journey you feel that I am standing tall on my paper pulpit and am being too preachy, I most surely am, and it is my intent—because I am preaching to myself—reminding myself of the wonderful things God has revealed, for I am prone to forget! Yet I am preaching to you too, and that is fine; after all, preaching is a very noble word like *sacrifice, marriage*, or *repentance*—we just don't realize it because of all the fashionable absurdity that is about. Though many have taken up the repulsive habit, I won't apologize for an apology of the Christian faith, or for speaking the Good News.

    Now, a warning and a hope: For me, paper and pen, computer and type, are an excruciating detailed mirror. Sometimes, when I look in the bathroom mirror I half expect to see *Times Roman Numeral* font looking back at me. Rather, I see my gray-blue eyes and my jaw's scruffy shadow. If you find yourself reading these reflections and you catch a vague glimpse of some strange face fading in and out of the text, some image of a tired looking young man who has worn himself out trying to be good on his own strength, trying to be what he by himself cannot be, it is because this is a portrait of sorts—a portrait of a man going sane. As the pages turn on, I hope it is a portrait that looks more like the face of love than my own. I hope by the end of these numbered passages, a bolder color devours the muted gray-blue of my own image, and the golden face of a Galilean carpenter who divided all of time and all of the cosmos is vividly seen. I hope that these words lead to at least one disciple mirthfully weeping at the feet of the Lion—the Lamb of God, Jesus the Lord, who takes away the sins of the world.

    Now, let us begin where every good story begins—at the crossroads. In doing so we will find ourselves beginning with the Scriptures, for they say "Stand at the crossroads and look; ask for the ancient paths, ask where the good way is, and walk in it, and you will find rest for your souls" (Book of Jeremiah 6:16). And in asking for what is good, we are quickly ushered back to the beginning!

In the joy of fear *and* trembling,

Heath Hardesty

www.therenown.com

PART ONE
(1-177)

~The Lion & the Irony~

01. *To the lion—all the Christians to one Lion!*

"Christians to the Lion!" When I first heard these words something sounded inside my chest and made its resonant way to my head—though, as a warning bell or wedding bell, I could not tell. "Christians to the Lion!" it tolled again—yes, that is it! If only we were to go to the Lion! To the Lion!—all else is not Christianity!

Yet, what is Christianity? Is this the right question? *What* is Christianity? This *what* just might be where *we* error.

Here, right at the start, we have come to a breakpoint; a divide in the road of how one views the world. We must expose a popular deception; we must poke our fingers through this smiling papier-mâché mask: **It is not always negative or pessimistic to speak about *error* or what is *wrong*, for we are seeking truth and benevolence, not ease and self-safety.**

To address error, in fact, is positive for it acknowledges a standard and recognizes the meaning of what is to be called *right*.

More often than supposed, it is positive to address the negative. Wrong turns caught early are good turns. And by *early*, I simply mean *before it is too late*.

Shining brilliantly behind the joy of good turns is the joy of again acknowledging *right* and *wrong*, *good* and *evil*—the joy of living in a universe that is not a wash of gray opinions, but one that turns brilliantly upon a standard; a universe worth living in and worth dying for.

To again speak of *right* and *wrong* is to have a looming stone statue, a horrible gargoyle, fall off from one's back—then we can again run, jump, kneel, and are no longer terrorized by its heavy grimace—by creepy ideologies of man-made relativity. When this absurdity falls away we are free from the superstition that all is equal, that a gargoyle is an eagle, that all should be tolerated, and that there is no difference between man and beast.

So, with this acknowledgment that there *is* reality, that there is that which is right and that which is wrong, we go forward—anything else and we melt into a swamp devoid of both reason and heart.

Yet, this book is not about right and wrongs, and not about absolutes; for these are second order things. This is about The Absolute. In The Absolute all things find their place.

02. Now, into the fray—and please, wrestle through these next few passages (if they are struggled with here at the beginning we will have more freedom in the end—so let us not surrender truth to what is easy).

"In the beginning God created..." (Genesis 1:1). God is our Creator, our origin. All problems come from an original (relating to our origin) act of judgment: *trusting our own knowledge of good and evil rather than trusting the Word of the Creator, the Word of the one who truly knows.*

"To the self!" we say, and reject the order of creation in which we are to live through and by God. "To the self!" we say, and are now disunited from God like a thin branch estranged from its fruitful oak trunk. Ironically, by judging right from wrong for ourselves, we have set ourselves against God; this is the significance of that famed tree in the center of the ancient Garden—the *tree of the knowledge of good and evil.*

At the center of our existence is the pivot of trust: this tree or that one; the Sovereign God or the autonomous man.

Humanity has chosen the tree of the knowledge of good and evil; in its fruit, the self-defeating fruit of self-reliance, we established our own broken origin. From here the world crumbles.

Entropy was introduced when man thought he could hold the universe together; when he reached to hold the weave it came unraveled like a slack ball of yarn. Man is no God.

We *error* because *we* judge God; because *we* judge all things "out of our self" rather than living through God as we were meant to— rather than trusting His perfect knowledge.

Rather than trust the infinite Creator, man has placed his trust in the finite creature. In doing this, our propensity is to define and separate what *we* call good and evil—but, and this is the rub, since we do this on our own accord, living out of our own means and no longer knowing God, we judge in distrust of God and therefore unravel good even from good. We simply warp all that we judge merely by judging! We work against all established order and reason by ordering ourselves as the source of reason and ruling.

Now it follows that because we are *the created* and not the Creator, we are necessarily limited in strength, perspective, and understanding—as said before, man is no God. This being so, we disunite unions and attempt to do away with intended tensions that would live naturally in God-ward faith. This is because reality is simply greater than us; we cannot hold it together; and so, we try to control it by compartmentalizing it, dividing it up, by gripping tightly what we can hold at the expense of what we cannot. Better to grab at something than lose everything— right?!

We tear the universe into pieces because of our unbelief. The evidence of *original* (regarding our origin) unbelief is entropy; the wages of sin is death.

In other words, man has crowned himself *god*, but he is a lousy *god*, an absurd *god,* and he cannot keep his *self* together let alone the throbbing world he was set within. And now, trusting absurdly in himself, man attempts control (the maintaining of his god-delusion) by ordering the pieces he has torn into *manageable* bits— *this vs. that, either/or, etc.* This is to say, he sins: he contradicts reality by masquerading as God though he is merely a creature; and from behind his bawdy god mask, he attempts to remake reality for himself—*this star here, this atom over there, this tradition, that religion, do this—not that!* Absurd!

Man has shattered the mirror of reality and now sees in abnormal divisions rather than designed union. He is held captive by the fractures; he has shattered his own vision and his original power of will. See Genesis 2 and 3.

Imagine a muscle rebelling against the body that bears it; imagine a disease that makes the hand into a fist to beat against the very head and chest that give it the life to do so. Is this not the essence of all tragedy? Man destroying himself?

Man's irony: he tries to synthesize his world by making false antitheses; that is, he attempts to unify reality by breaking it all to pieces. And we as heirs of Adam find ourselves pitting justice against mercy; cracking apart God's sovereignty from human moral responsibility; ripping the perforation that we have run between truth and grace, reason and faith. As Adam's kin, we tear good from good just as we tear good from evil—and we do it even within the very sanctuaries built for worship of the one God.

It is not our judgments that are wrong; it is that we stand as judge that is wrong. What? Doesn't this go against all that is Christian? No; it goes against all that is religion; all that is of man who trusts in himself. When I refer to religion, I men man's attempt at control under the guise of trusting in God—we will look into this in various ways.

Man is like a judge who releases the innocent and sentences the blatantly guilty; yet, each judgment was a grievous wrong for he was no judge at all, but an imposter who killed the judge, stole his wig and robe, and has no authority for the seat he sits upon—each judgment is invalid for the gavel was in a criminal hand.

Until we trust in God we do not live in accordance with reality; rather, we live according to our self-reduced version of reality; a reduction that is violence to truth. We mince the truth, lop off its arms, head, and legs by forcing its greatness into our narrow, truncating perspective; we call a lie truth, and then mediate all life through this lie.

We are unable to hold truth in tension.

What does this mean? Why talk of tension, and where does all this meet with Christianity? This tension brings us to what is called *Sola Fide—faith alone.* Why do Christians speak of *faith* incessantly? Why, or how does salvation hinge upon faith—for *the righteous live by faith.* Is this not what the Bible says?

Is faith a spiritual skeleton key? A metaphysical password that lets one into a secret society? Is there a handshake to go along with it? No; these are misunderstandings that must be swept away. Faith is not an abstraction that floats in a blind haze. So then—why *faith*?

Faith is trust. So what then is the relation between trust and salvation? We must see that salvation by faith is not an arbitrary assignment. God has His reasons, for we live in an ordered universe of His design. We must do away with the devilish idea that faith is disconnected from reason; that it is some absurd leap into the arms of a dark god who hasn't revealed himself.

Actions that often seem absurd can still be done for a reason. The action of faith, the "leap" itself, though seemingly absurd, can be ultra-rational—and therefore not absurd. It seems absurd to give an inoculation or to break a broken leg in order to heal—but both are seen to be reasonable if one has knowledge of the body. "Now faith is the *assurance* of what we hope for, and *being certain* of what we do not see" (Hebrews 11:1). We are assured by the precedent of existence, and certain because of the workings of reality. Faith is reasonable if one has acknowledged reality.

Faith is tied reasonably to the greater reality that exists beyond religious platitudes and human traditions. What then is the connection of faith in regard to salvation and reality?

Genesis answers this question and posits meaning to both *faith* and *salvation*.

If it is as Genesis reveals—that unbelief tears the universe into pieces—then there is truly something to this hot-button word of "faith." The original state of creation was of man trusting God—acknowledging reality of the created order; we were, and still are, called to live in entrustment to our Creator.

Stripped bare of all religious syntax and liturgically loaded language, this is what must be communicated: We are called to acknowledge reality—this is faith. And what do we need to be saved from—the deception of self-origin (misplaced trust in man as god) that spirals guilt into our souls and breaks relations with God, neighbor, self, and all creation.

We need to be saved from ourselves. It is the truth that will set us free.

To deny reality, to slight your origin that is your very life source, is to sign a contract with death. We are dead *and* in the throes of death. Now, in this context of honesty, there is a certain freedom to explore what needs to be known…

03. *To the Lion*—there is tension in the phrase; the tone of it selfless and daring in its love. These three simple words speak to us of one of the beautiful tensions that true Christianity holds—confidence *and* humility. Confidence/humility: these two must always be held together; they are facets of the same sweet diamond. If you divide them you crush the diamond. Who can hold these together? Can you?

Humility is the rightful assessment of who we are. In the brokenness of humility lives the one unbreakable confidence! *Con/fide*: this literally means *with/faith*. We are to live with *confide*nce in The Lion—with faith.

Humility is like the brightness of a lake broken by wind—each wave fracture catching and spiking great sunlight—and for being broken it is the brighter. Where there was only one sun reflection, now there is a multitude.

Why must we talk of being broken? Because somehow, deeply, we know it will tell us something of who we are and what has happened.

04. What am I? An enemy of myself; a creature caught between a finite constitution and an infinite love. Man is *in love* with and terrified of himself—but is unwilling to admit this, for to *love* what is terribly wrong is not to truly love, and our most authentic ache is for authentic love.

Have you never feared yourself at the edge of a cliff or after you woke from a certain dream? Have your own eyes never startled you when you didn't expect to be looking into them? Have you never feared that we are at fault for our fractured hearts; our worst fears?

The state of man: fragmentation. We are drawn to harmony *and* haunted by beauty, and we dwell upon the distorted and deformed. We strain after the things of heaven and of hell. From some inner fault line, we run hard and fast in opposing directions. We run against ourselves and against truth in its very name. Is this not bizarre?

We are fragmented because we are disunited with our origin; because we have fallen from our source like a wayward bough from a living oak tree. We have separated ourselves from our origin, yet we are amidst our origin's creation. How do we resolve such a conflict—the conflict of looking at reality through rebellious, deceived eyes? *We* cannot resolve such an existential conflict, though we feel its ravages in subtle and sharp ways.

An irony: when man tried to be as God he became less like God, for his *imago Dei* (his God-likeness) was shattered like a fist-hit mirror. We are most like God when we live in obedience to Him.

05. What does existential (of our existence) origin matter?—it gives us our meaning, sets out purpose. We are all questing for meaning; some reveal this secret in their lush sleeves of tattoos, some in their musical prowess, some in their drive for fame, some in their pursuit for perfect body fat content, and some in the fattening of their portfolios. There is a universal soul-hunger for identity and purpose.

Purpose comes from our origin as a fruit is determined by its seed. It is as T.S. Eliot wrote: "In our beginning is our end."

Our significance is determined by our purpose; our end is determined by our origin. That is, are we or are we not God's—and will we be in His presence for eternity? Our identity is in such things.

An admonition for the mirror gazer: Focusing on ourselves divorced of the context of the Creator we will only find that which worsens our condition; we will only amplify our nerve-stabbing anxiety. We can only find humility by looking into *The Great Beauty*.

God's beauty breaks our heart and sets our mind on fire—and then we can see. His beauty rescues us from our shame. Shame: the shadow of our pride. One can only find humility with faith, and right faith is not to be found by gazing at ourselves as we do.

Now, it would do us great good to realize that the Scriptures are more akin to a window than a silver-backed mirror. We love to call the Bible a mirror; but this is because we rather enjoy gazing at ourselves and calling it *worshipping God*. Rather than a mirror that is meant to have us look only upon ourselves and find intimations of God, the Scriptures are a window into reality that reveals the streaming light of the Creator—and when the light is just right, we, no doubt, will see our reflection in the glass—but this is secondary. We are to find our humanity in God, not God in our humanity. God is primary; man is creature.

We are in need of a mind on fire; of a heart like a mirror full of light. Yet the fire and light must come from another. By our own devices our minds remain abandoned hearths; our hearts, mirrors locked away in lightless rooms of our own concrete design.

06. Sometime between the years 155 and 230 A.D. a man named Tertullian with a satirical tongue must have grinned when he wrote the following words:

> *"If the Tiber reaches the walls, if the Nile does not rise to the fields, if the sky doesn't move or if the earth does, if there is a famine, if there is a plague, the cry is at once, 'The Christians to the lion! Christians to the lion!' ...What,* [he remarked sarcastically] *all those Christians to one lion?!"*

Tertullian was raising a reasoned shout of truth. He was exposing the absurdity of the world blaming the *People of the Way—the followers of Jesus Christ—Christians—the little Christs*, for all the disasters of life; that is, the floods, plagues, raids, crop failures, etc. He was raising a reasonable defense for the Christians who were being murdered on the grounds of the Coliseum. But wait—listen closely. You can almost hear a faint whisper in his fervent and sardonic words: "Come now, and let us reason together" (Isaiah 1:18).

Christians were blamed for turning the world upside down. It seems that Christians caused quite a commotion. A commotion of gentleness, a mutiny of mercy, an uproar of joy, faith, hope and love; these things are an awful commotion to the world. These things are very disruptive when one wants to go about living selfishly. These things are sedition to a person who wants to be the captain of a drifting and broken world.

In this world, real love causes a commotion. In this world, real love is a wild-eyed stranger with hair too long and skin too dissimilar: we are initially intrigued by the exotic vision, but ultimately reject the alien. We do not often recognize real love—we have become accustomed to its anemic, self-seeking counterfeit.

We prefer theoretical love to actual love. An ocean of impossibility lies between the two—and we are too phantom to swim the dense waters; too laden with guilt to walk the thin surface. *Theoretical love* is *safe* for it lives in our minds and imaginations; *actual love* is feral and otherworldly; it has no handles and it is dangerous—though, in it, lives our peace.

The Gospel has a way of inverting things—turning the world upside down and revealing the ceiling for the floor. It reveals feet kicking at the heavens when they were thought to be dancing firmly on the earth. It reveals arms to be swimming in the soil as roots when they were thought to be the sky-reaching limbs of a tree. True Christianity disturbs things. It is a fire that eats illusions like straw and dry paper, and proves what is silver, what is gold.

This is a good place to start the Good News—with a world upside down; with people tossing other people to lions; with death; with the everyday poison of pointing our fingers at others; and with religion's attempt to kill God. Yes, this is a great place to start! We will start with the current condition of humanity—while acknowledging it hasn't always been this way.

It hasn't always been this way…

07. We know ourselves only shallowly. There is a dissonance and distance within us. Man does not know himself.

We must be honest to the degree that we can: We both hate and *love* ourselves. The voice we most like to hear is our own; we parade ourselves loudly, yet we hide from others so they cannot know us deeply. Isn't this strange?

What is this in-between creature we are? What are we between? Why such high aspirations? Why such dirty deeds? It is as though we are not ourselves…

If we cannot see ourselves, if we cannot see that we now peer through a shattered and stained lens, then all we view will be off-color, skewed, twisted, and we will not know that we have a distorted view of reality.

Because we do not see or compensate for our biased perspectives, we naturally have de-formed concepts of God and all His creation. So we will start with humanity; not because man is the center or the measure of all things (far from it), but the exact opposite: because God is the center and ought to be seen rightly; He is worthy.

We will start with man because he is distorted and blurred. As much as we can we should compensate for, and calibrate our view. We must learn to see the rose haze and the cloudy shadows of our lenses. We must learn to see our blindness. We cannot do this on our own. We need divine sight. God help us; Help the blind man see the only one who can restore his sight.

Even by starting with man one must start with God! Man needs light to see anything, including Himself; and this means he must rely upon another even to know himself.

"In the beginning God created…" (Genesis 1:1). Here, we have the core of our identity exposed: creature. Yet not merely one among the creatures; but the only creature made in the image of God—the lofty position of man! This is the foundation for all rationality, for all identity—for trust.

How could one know of their own origin if not told to them? I would know nothing of the day or circumstances of my birth if it was not told to me. Our identity is tied to our origin—and for that, learned by revelation.

The one true *faith* must be one of divine revelation (God coming to us, Jesus coming to us), not mere human discovery or intellectual or spiritual ascent—it must come from outside of us, change the inside of us, and correct our crooked views. It must stand above us and judge us. We are too bent to see straightly the reality of life.

This is why the true *faith* must also be historical, must be embedded within the energy of history and not a mere philosophy; for the long view of history will open our perspective and help judge our hearts because it inherently testifies to the reality of existence. Also, humanity has been given this barbed gift of a conscience as well as the wide wonder of the universe to marvel at. Each one of these is a looking glass into the reality of who we are and what life is about; they are given to us to help see ourselves, in order that we may rightly see God. We will peer into these looking glasses—not to worship man, but to worship God alone.

In a god-less universe, one can know nothing; especially who one is. It is absurd and fruitless to argue that humanity can *know nothing*. This book assumes that there are things we can know—just as every other book in the world (even those written by elite professors who are sure that we can know nothing). This being the case, Christianity is a diamond-hard fact, and can be known; it is historical, etched in space and time. But, if you are worried that we can know nothing, that there is no overarching truth, that there is only chance, then read along anyway, and chew on the tin foil of your contradictions as you do—for there is a chance something meaningful might happen.

We can only know ourselves through knowing God—until then we are as amnesiacs.

08. Before our uber-violent films there was the Coliseum. Before the Coliseum there was the Olympic and the Isthmian Games (these games went far beyond healthy competition; they were life and gory death; these were not *games* of congratulatory handshakes—but of jeers and deathblows). It seems people have always liked to watch other people beat on each other; to watch someone victor over a crumpled loser. Something within us likes to watch other people fall. It seems that we like to watch other people fall more than we do win.

We claim we like to see someone victorious, but we also like to see the trail of blood and raw-knuckle power along the way. Be honest about this—for it is easy to dismiss with unexamined denial and sentimental notions. Now before you judge this and say, "I hate violence," take account of the violence that you do enjoy when it comes to the relentless arena of gossip. Some prefer fists and flashing swords; some prefer slander and silver tongues. There is also a violence of the thoughts; take account of the violence of your *secret* thoughts.

Think of the appeal of chaotic lights and whirling sirens, and danger, and our attraction to what we call "excitement." For example, we look at an accident on the highway "to see if everyone is ok" yet we really (hiddenly) hope to see something gruesome, something newsworthy. We rubberneck; our spines spring like a rubber band to the traumatic and the brutal. Just look at what we choose to view for entertainment—really look at it. Are our television tastes so different than watching a roadside wreckage with hungry eyes?

We have a penchant for action movies in which body burning explosions and piercing bullets are the climax; we watch horror movies with our hands over our eyes, yet peering through our split fingers. We eat up the twisted tales of homicidal torturers; we are magnets drawn to the steel of serial killers. Exaggerations? Just look at the ratings. We are drawn towards violence against man. Even in romantic movies we are excited by the incendiary fights, the heartbreaks, harsh words and the violence done to the soul by selfish sex.

So why do we rubberneck? Why do we peer through protecting fingers? What, really, do we want to see? Why do we enjoy what we enjoy? Why do we gravitate towards the dark corners and the dirty shadows? We should ask ourselves these questions; they are telling—but are we listening?

Let us not only look into the contents of our thoughts, but also into the very way in which we think. Even if the contents of our thoughts are obviously ill, we will still think the best of ourselves if the way in which we think, the way in which we cognate, is ill itself. An obscure lens will obscure beauty and deformity—even confuse one for the other.

The eye is directed by the heart; ultimately, we see through the optic of the heart.

We should ask ourselves questions about the automatic impulses that spring within us, without thought and without volition. As Christians we should ask ourselves many questions. But I fear as *Christians* we often fear to ask questions. To have questions is not to doubt God; but to not trust God with your questions is to doubt God.

Let us question question-less Christianity.

One cannot have adamant faith without having questions; it is a false faith that is question-less.

If one is a creature with the ability to reason, there will always be questions.

The question mark is not by necessity a sign of faithlessness—often it is the sign of wonder; wonder birthed by faith. The question mark is often the sign of trust. "*I don't understand, but I trust in you.*" Yet man's bold exclamations of an answer are often the sign of doubt, of self-sufficiency, of denying the God who is above all. When man removes the ultimate question mark he becomes the judge and chops at the world with his saber-like exclamation mark. *I say this! That! This is how! No! Yes! No! No!*

Those who followed Jesus Christ in the first centuries after His Resurrection were often taken to the Coliseum for their adamant faith and unbending wonder. They were sent to the lion because they had met *The Lion* and would not leave His side. They would not leave His side because they were given/had caught a glimpse of the Glory: the shattering beauty of God. They could not deny Christ, for He had changed their very desires; and to deny Him was a death worse than death. Their lives could never again be ordinary—they had become the living.

09. Blessed are those who go to The Lion. There is something redeeming and beautiful in the irony of Christ's followers being sacrificed to the lion of the Roman Coliseum and the reference of Jesus being the Lion of Judah. God is the master of perfect irony. As Christians we should understand irony better. We must learn to see the irony in the Scriptures. This will help us see the truth.

Irony is the difference between *the real* and *the ideal*; the difference between the expected and the actual. It's the difference between the "is" and the supposed "ought to be."

As Christians who live in this world, yet as strangers and wayfarers not yet home, we ought to live in the tension between the *is* and the *ought to be*.

The existence of what we call irony presumes a standard, a meaning—it presupposes God. If there is no God, then there is no *ought*, and as Dostoevsky said, "Then all things are permissible." No one lives as though *all* things were permissible.

The Bible tells the story of the glory of God, and it does so in two main ways: one way says *"you are the man"* in reference to the prophet Nathan exposing David's sins with Bathsheba; and the other way says *"behold The Man"* in reference to Pilate's words about Christ (that are perfectly ironic for Christ was the perfect man—the Second Adam). How interesting—one, a prophet of God calling a *man after God's own heart* badly broken, and the other, a cruel man of the world unwittingly speaking the truth of Christ's perfection.

The Bible is realistic (*you are the man*—the heart experiences this darkness—sin) and it is restorative (*behold the man*—the heart yearns for this restoration—it aches for perfection). So the Bible points its fiery finger in accurate judgment at all humanity, *and* it beckons with a velvet hand of restoration for us to trust in Christ.

Throughout the whole counsel of Scripture this tension bears friction and light, and the glory of God glows over and over again. It is the cross of Christ, the sacrificial love of God that holds this tension true. See these passages: 2 Samuel chapter 12 and John Chapter 19.

One cannot escape the pricking fact that there is a certain reflex of the soul that shouts *"it ought to be different—it should not be like this!"* It is as natural and automatic to us as an impulsive yelp from the crushing of a finger or the stubbing of a bare toe. There is an anxiety that rattles within us because of the current situation and the desired supposed-to-be situation.

We deal with this anxiety usually in two ways: One way denies the reality of *what is*, and the other denies the reality of *what ought to be*—that is, it denies a universal standard. Both are flights from reality; both are lives of denial and compounding illusion. God offers a third way: redemption. The Bible, the Word of God, is the tenacious bridge that clings uncompromisingly to both sides of this divide.

You are the man—this is *the is*. *Behold, the man*—this is *the ought*. There is a standard and the world is fallen from it. God's revelation upholds both realities and calls us to acknowledge the same and to trust Him.

Irony stands by two legs—the *is* and the *ought*. History runs by these two legs. Their movement points towards God's existence; their trajectory aims at Jesus Christ. History is like a child learning to walk, and heading wobbly into the open arms of its beckoning father—Jesus Christ.

There is life in losing one's life. This is essential. If we are to see the world right-side up we must first learn that the world is upside-down. This means, too, that the church is often upside down; its steeple often a deep squeezing ravine in the earth rather than a resolute pointer towards heavenly freedom. God forgive us. This book has been written because of this very point: For I have looked and I have found the world in the church, and the church in the world.

Steeples are often erected not to point to God's glory, but to give God a collective and giant middle finger, and to stab His sky. "Forget you! We'll do this our own way!"

Don't be deceived by religious trappings, they often move in diametric opposition to the Gospel of God. White is just as much the color of a crypt as it is the color of a church building. White is just as much the color of leprosy as it is *religious purity*.

Steeples are often anorexic towers of Babel.

There is a strange phenomenon in history that begs for some attention. It is strange yet extraordinarily ordinary; it is like smooth velvet thread weaved through abrasive burlap. There is this hilarious tendency of light to stream out of darkness, of freedom to flow from iron fetters, and of diamonds to burst from chalky coal. What is meant for bad is turned for good. It has been said that the blood of the martyrs is the seed of the church. This is true.

No one can get an upper hand on God. God can invent a forest from ashes; the Baltic sea from a baby's tear. What one man destroys in the name of vanity God redeems creatively in infinite wisdom to bless many. God is sovereign. He works everything beautifully into His plan—so the reality of Christianity cannot escape irony. It is sadly ironic that few Christians see the irony. See—it is inescapable!

When we miss the irony we miss the force and splendor of redemption. Much theological error has warped belief, fueled hate, and birthed wars simply because it lacks the near *and* far-sightedness of God's irony.

The whole history of Israel is ironic; or to put it another way, God's plan is not what we expect. When we try to force the Gospel into what we expect it to be we should expect problems.

When we force truth into *our* "ought to be" molds we distort reality. God uses the underdog over and over again, yet we bet on the Übermensch (the overman), the superman. Like beating our heads against a wall, we try to muscle grace and to white-knuckle humility. But God has a different plan...

Christianity has bi-focal sight; stereo vision. It sees distantly *and* closely. Separate these two and depth perception, perception of reality is distorted.

Here is an irony: unredeemed humanity is like a man who hates dandelions, so he blows them all to pieces to destroy them—only to the effect that God has used this man's angry breath to spread millions of seeds of sun-yellow flowers.

One scowl of anger becomes an exponential curve of smiles. The more evil struggles to breathe, the more it is suffocated by itself. As a lie multiplies to survive, it exposes and destroys itself. This happy justice will someday be revealed in full, and for now is only revealed in part. What great hope!

There is great joy in a joy not fully known.

We expect might and miracle. God comes as a poor boy born in a cave, a servant and backwater laborer. Then, when the glitterati chase Him, He refuses to wonder them with sensationalism He is quite capable of. And then comes the great wonder (or great anti-wonder to the worldly man)—the grace of the cross.

We would not expect the cross; it is offensive to the sensibilities. It is too violent for our easy days. The cross is too odd and obtuse of a shape to fit into our paradigms of circular success and *rationalism*. The cross is too firm to fit into flabby notions of love. It is not gilded like our desires; it is not hollow like our promises. It is too angular to fit our soft compromises. Our selfish paradigms are prisons that make the obvious invisible.

Irony helps us see that the upside-down world is not right-side up. Things are not as we expect.

10. There is an intriguing story about a man named Telemachus, a Turkish monk who was disturbed by the brutality of Rome. He intervened in a fight between some brawny gladiators to protest the madness of man carving up man for sport, and he died in the fray (or was stoned by the crowd for interrupting the entertainment). Somehow touched by this Christian's strange conviction and martyrdom, an emperor named Honorius banned the gory gladiatorial games. Some contest the exact historicity of this. Whether the truth be by stones or swords, it is true that God's irony shines. For centuries the Christians were stolen away to be fed to the beasts of Rome's arena—but with a twist in history and a grin on God's face, a Christian willing to put himself between the raging testosterone and flashing metal of dueling men put an end to the death games with his own life. A Christian *to The Lion!*

God smiles not at human death but at love that conquers death; at sacrifice that trumps sin. In God there is no pleasure in the dark things, but in the redemption that will rain out of them. In God there is no darkness—only the fire and fragrance of perfect light.

11. If we do not go to The Lion then we are not Christians. If we do not deny ourselves then we are not following Christ. Many people attempt Christianity without Christ—they are not Christians, they are spectators in the Coliseum; they wear masks and eat expensive religious sweets. They are voyeurs rather than voyagers. This is an epidemic in our world—voyeurism. And like amusement, *Christianity* has become voyeuristic.

A true Christian lives in the arena *and* the armchair! True *theology* does not happen in an ivory tower alone; it is not secluded thought. Theology happens in the fray. By trying to keep our hands clean in avoiding that grisly business of Christian living, our hands only become a deeper and darker red.

To the surprise of many, there are two fangs to the serpent of sin; there are two chambers to the dark heart: commission *and* omission—and for this there were two beams to the cross! Often, what we do wrong is what we don't do. This is a wake-up prod to all the *"good"* people who *don't do* wrong things. When was the last time you asked forgiveness for what you didn't do? This is a hard truth. Ask forgiveness for what you have not done.

We cannot follow Jesus if He has not changed us, if God has not called us; it is not within us to simply make ourselves desire that which is the ultimate good. (This sentence just seized you; it just set you in fight-mode if you read it correctly—for you must wrestle with this truth. You must wrestle with the gravity of its implications until you find its sharp blessing. The human heart rebels against this truth.) How can we make ourselves desire that which we not only don't desire, but that we fundamentally despise?

Yet, we must go to The Lion for everything; for there is nothing that is not claimed by Him. Jesus is the Lion who devours our rag-heart and clothes us in the innocence of the sacrificed Lamb. He is that Lamb; in Him we are white as summer bleached wool. Jesus is the Lion *and* the Lamb, not the Lion *or* the Lamb. A tender, bleating, wooly lamb; a muscular, good, and majestic lion; a suffering servant *and* just judge; these are tensions to hold within the expanse of the heart and mind—in trust.

Jesus is the incarnate Servant *and* the exalted King! The Bible is a pale shadow of itself, a moaning zombie, if we believe that Christ is only a sacrificial lamb, or only a roaring lion. When the two are divided we see an anemic caricature of Christ. Truth shows us He is both—and both at their top level of energy!

~Paradox/Tension~

12. Christianity is full of paradox as the oceans are full of water. A paradox is a statement of reality that appears contradictory, yet is not. That is to say, it is panoramic truth seen through a limited lens. It is that which is true, but seems as if it couldn't be true from the angle we are at, or through the optic with which we perceive.

A paradox is how we perceive an intended tension; how we acknowledge truths that are beyond our current insight.

The great paradox is this: God is just *and* merciful. If mankind is in rebellion as the Bible says, and deserves wrath (due punishment), how then can God be merciful yet remain just? It is this paradox that has been lifted high for all to see—for it was a worldwide explosion with a healing fallout. Distant echoes of it are seen in thoughtless gold jewelry, cobalt blue tattoos, chrome car adornments, and carved Italian marble. It is the cross of Christ.

Without the cross, justice and mercy are irreconcilable opposites—a contradiction.

How can we be a Christian and do away with tension? The cross is tension—the heart of God the Creator lay over crossing beams of wood; an infinite God on finite lumber! To be a Christian and throw away tension is to be a Christian who throws away Christ and His Gospel—and for that, they throw out Christianity; then all that is left is a dismal idol with a nice-looking Jesus mask.

Christianity is not meant to banish tension, but reestablish it; to reweave Shalom and tie again the bonds of man to God.

Shalom is *original* peace—that which is more than the absence of war and pain; but that which is *active peace*. It is well being, nothing missing, or broken; it is all as it should be—complete, whole.

13. Christianity is not an easy road, but it is *the* good road. It is no smooth drive in the A/C of a decked out Lexus. It is the beautiful but muscle burning path to paradise. When we look for the easy road we will not hear the cross because it is a *foolish* moan of love; a cry of agonizing victory. That torture device, that odd symbol of ultimate love in action—the cross—is essential; that is, it is of the essence of the Christian.

As fallen humanity, we start at the crossroads of life in a certain tension of anxiety, and as a Christian, we find the road has brought us to the cross, another kind of tension; not a tension of unraveling as before, but a tension of weaving together. The cross is the loom upon which *Shalom* is weaved. What a wonder!—a metaphysical cohesion, a spiritual construction—a perfect and productive tension like that of a bridge binding together opposite and longing shores.

14. There is balance in tension. There is rest in tension just as one can rest upon a bridge with taut cables. Yet humanity hates tension; so we attempt to do away with it. This breeds wild extremes and imbalance; and imbalance bears chaos and violence, unraveling and unwinding.

We like to do away with tension because it asks too much of us—our working mind, our whole living heart, two laboring hands—it asks for more strength than we have. Tension asks us to be less than the truth; to bow down to it and to not box it within our heads. It asks for us to leave some mysteries unknown and other mysteries laboriously explored. It asks us to trust. Is not faith trust? Tension asks us to be dependent. Is not being a Christian being dependent upon God for all?

When we embrace the *Christian tension* we live beyond the *typical*—of the *type* of our race—of Adam, who cracked apart the cosmos. It is typical to be imbalanced; typical to be drunk and dizzied by one's selfishness, and in the falling down, grab and tear at what is around. One can only embrace the Christian tension by strength of the second Adam.

An irony: When we fight divine tension (original tension), we thrust ourselves into a tension that destroys rather than heals.

One can find no rest on a bridge with lessening tension—where the tautness of the cables is becoming less and less—unwinding, fraying, unraveling and snapping. Rest always occurs where there is a tension that is balanced and centered—that is, where tension is anchored by the infinite. There is no rest in the unanchored heart.

It is not enough to say "original (in regard to our origin) tension asks too much of us." Rather, it should be said, "it asks the impossible of us; the bar has been raised too high; the shores are too far for us to bridge! All is lost!" It asks for only what God can be. This impossibility is, in fact, why we must embrace it.

The universe was to be held in the hands of the Creator, not in the hands of a creature. Even Atlas couldn't hold the world in his hands; it bent even his muscle-clad back. The rarely understood fact is this: When we try to hold up the world we are crushed by its existence—and we do our best to crush it back! When we try to hold the world together it tears us apart—and yes, we tear back at it.

15. *Original tension* reveals that the secular and the sacred are intimately twined; this reveals how the *epic* is fashioned in the *ordinary*. This speaks not only of how God walked the Garden in the cool of day, but of how God could have dust on his feet or nails in his wrists, how heroes can have normal careers, and how evil can look so banal.

Saecular: sacred/secular. We must not carve up reality into *secular* or *sacred*. If we do this absurd thing then we divide life into *what is God's* and *what is not God's*—this is paramount to the murder of God. If all is not His, then He does not exist at all! All is God's; every spinning atom and every long mile between stars; therefore, we should acknowledge all as under His hand.

To draw a line in thought that says "This is under God's rule and this is not," is akin to drawing a knife down one's body and saying, "This side is more important than this side." When the knife is drawn, when the thought is traced, one can know only a shell of life; a dead semblance, something gross, and nothing more.

16. Tension and paradox are immovable reminders, divine thorns in the pink skin of our pride, given to us to show that we view God far too often maliciously and condescendingly—that we scale God down like a chessboard miniature to be shuffled about at our whim. Our view of God needs to constantly be amplified. We need to see Him as His revelation reveals Him to be—and this means *trust*!

We are created to be rational, but we are not to try to cage God by rationalization; this is only reasonable. We can know God truly, but we cannot know Him exhaustively. How do you comprehend He who gives you your comprehension? The question itself is absurd—so the practice even more senseless.

If God does not grow more unfathomable, more mind boggling infinite, then we are not in right relationship with Him. Relationship with God moves in a double movement: it humbles us and it expands us; it ignites confidence *and* births meekness.

What is paradox? Paradox literally means "beyond opinion" or "beyond belief." *Para* meaning *beyond* or *against*, and *doxa* meaning *opinion* or *belief*. A paradox is what seems impossible, yet is found to be possible. It is beyond our ordinary opinions, yet it is extraordinary and true. It is truth beyond our scope; it is a sky so blue we can't see the stars; a sea so deep we can't see its treasures.

A paradox is not beyond reason, but it is beyond *rationalism*. We live in a rational universe, but *rationalism* is thoroughly unchristian. *Rational* means: relating to man's ability to reason consistently and coherently. *Rationalism* is: an ideology that believes we can know all that can be known by starting with *only* ourselves and looking out into the world—that is, it thinks so highly of the self that it needs only itself to conquer the world. *Rationalism* rejects revelation and rejects the Creator.

For reason to exist so too must paradox. Why? Is it reasonable to agree that we only know in part? Who would be so arrogant to say otherwise? There is that which we can know, and that which we cannot; for clearly, we are not omniscient. So, the ideology of rationalism is not rational because it does away with paradox by supposing we can manhandle all truth into submission to our minds. The Christian is rational, but does not put his trust in his own mind to conquer the cosmos. He does not put his trust in a mere drinking glass to hold the oceans.

17. Some are wise to define paradox as *contrary to expectation*—this sounds a lot like irony doesn't it? Yet, irony is not the same as paradox, though they are related. What we call irony and paradox are different pointers to the greater-than-us-reality that God has revealed in a myriad of ways. Because our views are smaller than these things called irony and paradox, we see them as tensions; we either embrace such tension in trust or we cut it apart and judge the amputations.

We cannot be an orthodox Christian unless our beliefs are paradoxical. This means that we cannot be orthodox in our beliefs unless we are reasonable about the mysteries of God—unless we believe God to be God, and man to be creature.

Orthodox does not mean *lemon-faced* or *thick, musty books* or *grey wiry beards* or *embalmed by tradition*. Orthodox means *right opinion* or *correct belief*. It means dynamic reality—in this there is energy and life! The right opinion or correct belief is that we cannot fully fathom God; that we cannot put Him under our greasy thumbs; that we are lower than His high ways, and therefore, we must have faith and trust in Him amidst mystery and unanswered questions.

Those who follow Christ obey because they trust and love, not because they understand. If we are waiting to understand God then we will never obey. The most important thing to understand is that we stand under Him, and that we should trust and obey.

Orthodoxy is, so to speak, the movements of ultimate reality—there is a call of original purpose in all that is orthodox. Orthodoxy is not a brittle papyrus text, an antique creed—it is the firm and beating muscle of heart that beats for and by God.

18. A faith that does not hold mystery and reason in tension does not entrust itself to reality. One cannot hold these two together on their own strength: we need a helper, a counselor, a point of intersection between our frailty and adamant reality. We need a God that is mysterious, whose depths are unsearchable, and yet, who had dust on His feet.

If we had waited to understand the laws of light before we enjoyed its grace in our lives, then we would live in the dark, hiding from sun and fire like silly monsters. If we had waited to understand the process of thought before it guided us, then we would be waiting with empty brains forever, like staved scarecrows in empty cornfields.

The mystery that should really trouble the *rational man* is how one can have a faith that has no mystery.

Now, we must understand this word tension that I use. There exist two antithetical tensions: the tension of Shalom's weave that is *rest*; and the tension of self-origin that is *disquiet*.

The Christian who ought to live in the tension of a world held by God is often merely in the tension of self-origin—living in the throes of a religion that, if followed through logically, will lead them further from reality, and increase the buzz of anxiety and true guilt. It is a tragedy that much of what is considered *Christianity* has given up orthodoxy, and traded one tension for the other—having traded a unified existence, one that holds reason and faith together, for an existence of self-origin that divorces faith and reason. It is the unbeliever that can find no correlation between trust and truth, faith, and fact, reason and the sacrifice of Christ.

These antithetical tensions are differentiated by their centers: the tension of Shalom's weave is centered on Jesus Christ, on trust in the Creator; the tension of self-origin is centered on fallen man, on the creature.

Do not confuse the holding of tensions with *compromise* or *mediocrity*. Is there not a more horrible word than *mediocre* to one who seeks to be in the presence of perfection? Christianity most certainly cannot be a halfway sort of thing. It is no chimera, no hybrid or amalgam something—it is full unison, it is that which *wills one thing*. It is the full motion of passion, the full arc of the swing, the total shunning of lethargy.

We must not confuse *holding two good things in tension* with *chopping two things in half and stitching them together*—this only makes for monsters and messes. But trust, faith in Christ, makes beautiful souls out of the stitched and the torn.

Mediocrity is our malady; what has the church to do with mediocrity but to expose it as the curse it is? Let us be aware.

~What Is Wrong With the World/Exposing My Heart~

19. Mankind is the divine-born *and* self-distorted. He is both beautiful and broken—both fallen and redeemed. We are the dignified and the disturbed. Yes, we are broken, but our origin began in perfection. We are made *imago Dei*—made in the image of God. We ache for beauty and we tear it down—hence the anxiety within us; we loathe what we love.

We are deeply broken, *and* we are infinitely loved. We have an infinite abyss that only an infinite and unfathomable God can satisfy. This is why no mere rationalism or pragmatism will ever do—because the abyss that is within us is not rational or pragmatic. Yet it is infinitely yearning and only God is infinitely satisfying. We are in need of an unfathomable yet real love.

What I mean is this: evil, rebellion from the Creator is never rational—it is absurdity. We can talk about it within the framework of reason, but reason alone cannot overcome the senseless. One is never argued out of evil; one is never convinced out of insanity.

Our abyss is an abyss of affection, of self-desire. This means that we long for and hound after the great impossibility—that we can be God. This chase is the twin birth of absurdity and tragedy.

We are: Broken/Beautiful.

Though man is broken, he is no demon; nor is he an angel, or was he ever meant to be. He is a human being, and that is why he can feel as both—bat-winged and cruel or radiant and winged-white as flying snow. He can feel as both because he was meant to rule over both; and now, he feels as though he were meant to rule even over God. Hah!

Benjamin Disraeli once asked and then answered himself, "Is man an ape or an angel? I am on the side of the angels." But this is a false dilemma—for to be an ape or an angel is less than to be man.

We are not to choose to be either. We love false dilemmas; they give the illusion that we can call an evil a good. It is not fit for a man to be an angel—he is to be a man.

Contrary to a very popular idea, man was not meant to be a chubby cherub reposing eternity away on a miniature nimbus cloud. Man was meant to stand tall, to work, to make culture and to care for creation, all the while in praise to the God above. Man's devilish tradition to make himself a lazy angel is a denial of God in gilded religious wrapping—like a birthday present all silver and gold-foiled, but nothing inside.

Hah! For man to make himself an angel is an attempt to make himself God who metes out the roles of all things. Man is above the earth, above the animals, but below God. We must stop twisting these roles all around.

It is interesting to note that in the order of creation man was to stand above the animal and be the steward, but in the fall it was an animal, a serpent, that was leading and guiding man—*stewarding* him into absurdity.

Creation: God →Man→Animal
Fall: Animal→Man→God

In the ancient temptation was a sick attempt to invert what God had ordered; a subtle attempt to separate what He united, and to unite what He had set apart. It was a reversal of all original tensions.

The current condition of humanity is not the original condition. We are not mint condition. We admit this every time we vote for human rights, every time we wince at raw cruelty, every time a jury sentences someone guilty, every time we read the news and are haunted by a world that seems off-center—a world that seems more like wavering autumn than it does spring.

We are like a coin placed on a railroad track and deformed by the steel wheels of a heavy train we could not control. We are warped and now incapable of our original design. We need to be recast. We cannot recast ourselves. We cannot re-forge ourselves. We must give to God what is God's. God must remake us. How can we give ourselves to God if we are at odds with God—why would we give ourselves?

Though we are bent and broken, we may still shine at many and varied points. We must remember that though we are broken, we are the broken image of God, and we are of inestimable worth. We are still copper, just twisted copper. But a penny is cheap and human life is precious—so I like this analogy better: we are like a costly wedding ring placed on a railroad track. We are still platinum and diamond, but we are twisted and torqued, crushed and cracked through. Still, the analogy fails for nothing in creation was considered as good by God as man.

There is no greater joy, nor deeper sorrow to be known, than being a man.

We are made in the image of God. We are not worthless—we are wounded artistry of God; we are a traumatized bride. Wounded, our heart has turned from trusting the very one that can heal us even though He was not who wounded us. We are like a fox in a self-sprung trap; the one that can help us free, we snap at and back peddle from, only to further open the wound that we caused.

Though we are clutched by our fractures, a greater embrace ultimately rules our lives. We must remember a fracture is secondary and derivative; it is never something of its own. Sin can never exceed grace.

20. We are neither god nor animal; we are human. Yet, the world is perennially trying to convince us that we are either a beast or a god. Here is a strange truth: we become our own gods if we believe we are beasts, and we act most like beasts when we believe we are gods.

An irony: the lauding of man as the architect of a coming utopia will always disintegrate into the deepest of cruelty and collapse into tyranny. Failing to acknowledge our nature unleashes unspeakable horrors. The greatest capacity of human reason is to see our limits and our lesions; it is to measure the height from which we have fallen, and to acknowledge the wound run clear to the bone.

Our greatest depths are plunged into when spurning our greatest capacities.

The 20th Century, once myopically named the "Wonderful Century," showed itself to be the deadliest, most craven, most murderous age humanity has known. Ironically, it was a lofty and golden view of humanity that belched the grey ashen rings of the Auschwitz crematorium smoke stacks to the sky. It was not one monster that murdered millions—it was many ordinary men and women who believed in their inherent goodness (ideas proudly promoted by the still-applauded philosophers Rousseau and Nietzsche—both who entrusted in humanity's basic goodness).

It was ordinary people who believed in the benevolence of man, in the progress of education, and the possibility of utopia by man's will at the wheel of science. It was ordinary people that believed man was not between God and animal, but that he was the apex of nature's progressive ladder—just a wonderfully thinking beast. Others, consumed by the power of the human will, thought themselves as gods, and judged others to die like slaughter house animals. Both *human-beast* and *human-god* worldviews are the bearers of genocide and all that is inhuman. Do not confine this to one nation or one demonic man—this speaks of all humanity.

What a sad and sick irony—man wanted to take God's heavenly throne: yet when the sky was thought godless it was filled with the smoke and ashen remains of man. When man was thought only to be the latest link on the evolutionary chain, he was soon herded and branded like cattle.

If there is one pressing lesson from the 20th Century it is that all of a man's nature is affected by the fall—this includes his intellect. Thinking the intellect is untainted will inevitably lead to worship of the intellect, and a re-ordering of the world from the throne of the mind, from the throne of the *intelligent designer:* our gray brain. Could anything be more foolish than to worship the human mind?

We must not be blind to the portrait of humanity the 20th Century has revealed. It is no wonder that many have denied the actuality of the Holocaust—for it is too revealing of our condition to look honestly into its recesses. The 20th Century greatly excavated our chests as we placed the human mind upon a pedestal. But what has been unearthed? A treasure or a curse? You know, there are tales of cursed treasures among the myths and stories of men…

We are made in the image of God; we come from God. He is our true origin. He is our source. We have intrinsic worth and dignity just for being created by and in the image of God. Born handicapped, born unwanted, born of strong body, born of sound mind, we have intrinsic worth just for being born human. Male and female, we are purposed, valued, and born to bear the glory of God. We came from perfection and we are haunted by perfection. The human race carries great glory, yet…

21. There is something wrong with the human condition. There is something wrong with our be-ing. I believe this because the Scriptures declare it. I believe it because it is unreasonable not to. I believe it because history tells of it in twist after turn of century after age. I believe it because I have access to the locked chambers in the dark wing of my soul.

I believe it because I have seen the movie *Gone with the Wind.* I believe it because of the infamous character of Scarlett O'Hara; because I could not stomach Scarlett; because I saw a world of red sprawling within me; because the author, with a human heart, created her; because the movie was about a so-called *civil* war; because the war in the movie was a historic war—and it was infinitely worse than the PG movie portrayed.

All of history, from time immemorial, has been marred by war. There is war as you read this very sentence. Right now we are loading our guns.

I believe there is something wrong with human nature for a million interrelated reasons—millions of thin and thick reasons zigzagging together into a web that is often unseen, until wind, water, or light expose its near-invisible and inescapable net.

History, *mystery*, and *histrionics* are three reasons I give for the hope I have within me in the Lord Jesus Christ. Do not forget that we are to give account of why we believe; see 1 Peter 3:15.

I believe there is something wrong with human nature because I know there is a dividing line that runs like concrete and razor-wire through my own heart—a dark cardiac axis; and in my mind—a Siberian gulag of facts and ideas. Experientially I know this, though the reflex is to deny this—the denial itself is damning.

I believe there is something wrong with human nature because I met Scarlett O'Hara before I watched *Gone with the Wind*—I met nearly every villain and cruel confused soul before I read or watched their exploits. I was them before I met them. I invented them in my heart and mind before I was introduced to them with my eyes and ears. In my soul they dined, and drank tea and mocked God's beauty.

Hold dearly to this: We have incredible dignity; we have an inestimable destiny. Our hearts are shaped for heaven, yet this is the very reason why they can bind us to hell.

22. I know there is something wrong with the human condition. I have a television. I have seen school shootings replayed a thousand and one times, interplayed with poppy commercials for facial soap and glossy-violent movie trailers. I listen to the radio. I have heard the song lyrics of sickness and dejection that connect with the masses—and therefore win Grammy Awards. I watch movies. I drive through city streets. I see the cardboard signs for

help; I see the cardboard signs that have lazy lies written on them and those that have scrawled honest pleas. I hear people screaming at each other through celluloid-thin apartment walls; I see lovers ignore each other. I hear tele-evangelists rape Scripture for riches far beyond job security. I read history. I hear Americans crack *jokes* about hardworking immigrants. I see immigrants drag the American flag under car and over American city streets in stark ingratitude. I hear Iranians and the president of Guatemala scapegoat America. I have witnessed American presidential elections and mud campaigns—mud slingers in designer suits. I have seen many *infallible* leaders fall at terminal velocity. I read books. I have read *The Great Gatsby, Crime and Punishment, Heart of Darkness, Lord of the Flies, Wuthering Heights, and Moby Dick*—each coming from the human heart and bearing its troubling mark. I read newspapers. I have been to college, high school, elementary school. I have been to preschool and have deep seated memories of tauntings and teasings. I have taunted; I have teased. *I* have broken dreams. I *have broken* dreams. I have scars across my hands and my heart. I have read the Bible; I have studied world religions. I have felt boredom and sloth pace about and recline within my heart. I have watched my friends divorce and then lie about the hurt. I have seen dead bodies. I feel entropy. I say "I" too much (and it is less then I think it). I had an easy time writing this polluted stream of a paragraph; and if restraint did not hold me it would be as long as the Nile. It is a dreadful and honest list.

23. What is wrong with the world is what is inside me. If I see there is a splinter in my neighbor's eye then there is a Redwood forest in mine; if there is a hand grenade within my neighbor, there is an A-bomb in my soul. If I am honest, I will admit to being an armory and an open tinderbox inside. I feel the tension of wanting to be like a dove, but I know that the unredeemed human soul is more like the Enola Gay over Hiroshima.

If I cannot acknowledge this then I cannot acknowledge Jesus Christ, for He is the truth, and this is the truth about the splintered human heart: it is in need of reformation. Here is a harder truth: we cannot reform it. If I claim that I am free from such broken and dark things, then I must claim that I am *free* from Christ—that I do not follow Him and that I do not know Him. If I claim there is no darkness in me, then I have not seen the light.

If I deny human sin, sin by nature and therefore by choice, then I call Jesus Christ a liar. If I claim that humanity is *good*, then Jesus cannot be.

The heart is darker than the actions as a source is deeper than its stream.

The word *Gospel* means good news; we must remember why it is good news. It is good news because we were first in a bad way. It is good news because God loved us when we were on the rebel line, tearing at and deconstructing the world He sweetly ordered. God loved us and moved to restore us when we wanted Him dead and cast into the sea, cast outside of *our city gates*. This is not good news—it is *The Good News*. There is nothing more existentially important than this!

When we play down the existence of sin, of true guilt, we neutralize grace rather than emphasize it. We castrate the King and wonder why there is no royal lineage born of the eunuch. We need to understand that the Good News rises like a fertile mountain out of a murky deep—out of the tar-like condition of rebellious humanity.

Can you imagine someone saying, *"Doctor So-and-So constantly debases me! He keeps bringing up my cancer whenever I go to him—he is so negative. Why can't he just say I'm doing fine? I really must find another more congenial doctor!"* This would be a bizarre and idiotic thing to say, yet it is said everyday with a straight face in regard to God.

The reason the doctor is talking to you about cancer and about disease is not because he thinks you are worthless and a sickly nothing, but because he values your life and is trying to help save it by diagnosing the disease and applying the cure. It is because you are a creation of worth and that there is hope that the doctor is speaking to you of this cancer inside. This is why Christians speak of sin; this is why Christ spoke of it. A diagnosis has a double edge *because* it is a good thing.

Christ spoke of sin because He was the radiance of love. Light reveals all it falls upon: hidden bruises, dusty crawl spaces, skeletal closets, greasy motives. Light must tell the tale of sin. It reveals truth with disregard to whether we like what is exposed or not. Light is not meant to tickle the ears, but to spike our eyes awake, and light the way out of our self-enclosed cave of stone—the ears are to be tickled by the sweet wind that meets our face; that traces our ears and hair as we step from the cave of self to the open atmosphere of love.

Christianity is not about smirking at a corpse; it is about applying love-crafted defibrillators to a seized heart. It finds no joy in bearing the message that *man is dead*—but it sings over the message of life that follows the autopsy! It is restorative; regenerative!

Christianity is not about throwing brimstone; it is about telling others that Mount Vesuvius is going to blow, so they would be wise to run from its volcanic slopes, and to grab a rescuing hand.

The Gospel of God is good news because we are sinners and because we are wildly lost—this is the starting point of the Gospel and it must be communicated. If this point is mute, then grace is a hoarse whisper, and Christ just a wise teacher. No! Not even that! He would not be a wise teacher; He would be a great fool because it is He who so often speaks of the sinful heart of man in need of grace!

Why does the idea of sin offend? Because its existence is a universal indictment. It does not appear in isolated spots like polluted springs with limited reach, but it is a gray and steady drizzle over all human hearts. And this is no heroic rain, no romantic fall—but an infernal rain; a bone-soaking anxiety; an annoyance like a constant tap on the forehead, first causing a giggle, then an agitation, then anger-bearing pain at the continual tap-tap-tapping.

One cannot acknowledge sin without acknowledging its universality. One cannot acknowledge sin without being indicted.

If we are offended by an assertion of truth does this mean that it is not true and not good? Or does it mean that there is something within our desires that is obstinate and contrary to reality, and is then not good in itself? Could we be the offense?

Can offense at an assertion of truth ever be an acid test for its veracity? Because you are inclined to not like it, does this mean it is wrong, or bad? Who then can be taught anything?

It is a horrible murmur—the broken soul saying "You'll never break me" or "I can stand alone." Like an orator with a broken jaw trying to recite beautiful poetry, it is an absurd and painful thing to hear. It is a sad and broken state to not know we are sad and broken; to be these things and not know it is what we experience in the buzz of anxiety and the terrifying silence of boredom.

It is when our despair is exposed that we can then hope—and only then. Sin is not something we sometimes do—it is something of our mis-aligned essence, it is the pervasive agitation of dissonant origins chaffing the soul. We all suffer from despair in the soul, the restlessness of existence—but like a hidden cancer, we are unaware of it until the crisis, until the physician diagnoses us with it.

If one cannot speak plainly and boldly about sin, then neither can one speak plainly and boldly about grace. I can already hear the jumble of complaints seething in my inbox…*sin…so negative…I don't like this…not my God…God of love? God of love!...killjoy…but we are basically good…but my children…are you telling me….but what about love, love, love?*

Interesting the impulse to justify ourselves—why so reflexive and aggressive?

Interesting that it is one's own finger that is tap-tap-tapping one's own forehead. Tap. Tap. Tap. Tap.

~On Being *Good?*~

24. There is a worldwide myth that taps every human heart, if at least for a brief moment. This golden myth is the source of all gilded sentimentality that derails one from honest exploration. The myth goes like this: "Once upon today, in a land not far away, there was a man and he was basically good…" This is the myth of blood, of the slaughter of men and the rape of women.

If we are basically good, then why do we burn when our brother becomes famous, or when our sister becomes an heiress? Who cannot claim at least one scar from the tenacious green heat of envy? Who is fireproof to this? Each one of us has a tendency to start fires and then to stand in them. This green heat has licked and singed every one of our hearts.

What is envy but the questioning of the goodness of God's sovereignty? What is envy but un-trust in providence?

If you have not envied, then you are a liar. That too reveals our nature.

If we are basically good then why is revenge more automatic than forgiveness? Why is lust more sudden than love? Shouldn't these be the aberrations rather than the status quo?

Why do we have locks on our doors? Why do we walk around with a ring of keys in our pockets? Why do we have armies ready on go and budgets for foreign defense policies? Why police? Why do we have terms such as *incarceration*, and *solitary confinement*? Why does the news anchor recount such horrible dealings? Why are we not more troubled by them than we are? Why do we so easily gloss over the news of "*thousands dead*" in some other country? Why are your secret thoughts so, shall we say, *uncharitable*?

25. The mantra of the world says *humanity is basically good*; but it cannot find a resolution to the terrors in the world. Its jury-rigged solutions are twice the problems; its drug-induced cures are twice

the cancer. The voice of God says that *we are fundamentally broken,* yet knows and renders the perfect cure for the sad diagnosis. This is good news; this brings great hope! See the book of Romans, chapter five.

What does it mean to be essentially good? Scripturally, it means that our natural inclination would be to reflect the goodness of God, to run towards God's benevolent ways, to count Him worthy, to acknowledge Him as the center of our lives—our central relation. Since God is good, then to be in right relation would mean that He be our mediator for everything, so in everything we are right and good. Yet our heart's inclination is to dodge God and place ourselves at the center of the universe.

Our heart is disengaged from God, though He has written Himself into its auricles and chambers. This is why we are spiritually dead and existentially discontent—because we are separate from the vine, the tree of life. Spiritually, we are a detached branch, a disconnected network, an amputated limb. We are alienated, unplugged, uprooted. Like an arm or branch, we carry within us the DNA, the makeup of the body we are separated from, but we are dead and wasted apart from the life source.

Because we do not live from our true source, we can claim no existential goodness even though we do pious and nominally good things. This is not merely because of wrong motivation (for many people do good things because they honestly judge them to be good); it is because of wrong origin. All the DNA of an amputated branch calls out for it to grow and function—yet it cannot in its separation from its source.

26. Before we are born again (John chapter 3), before our heart is transmuted by the love of God, rebellion is our defining nature. As rebels, it does not mean that we don't do what we commonly refer to as "good things." And as saints, it does not mean that we don't sin, but rather our defining nature is a love towards God, a right relationship, an alignment of heart that enjoys and desires ultimately in Him. I stress this because many claim that Christians

are those who do good things and non-Christians don't. This is idiocy, an obvious fallacy, and will only be disproved when one experiences a wider world outside of their Christian subculture.

Though we are rebels, it does not mean we don't do what we commonly call *"good things."* What is does mean is that we do not give God the credit or ultimately ascribe the good that abounds to Him, its rightful author. Rather, we take the credit for good like a brazen plagiarizer, calling ourselves the source, stealing someone else's due; or we transfer His goodness and place it onto something less fitting (like a lover or a career or a religion or a biomechanical process or a…).

We live in another's house, stroll through their halls pocketing what we want, and knocking over what we will. We mock the paintings and mysterious portraits on the walls; we ignore the great sculptures upon the pedestals in the great hall; we disregard the hand written notes left on desks and end tables. We don't ask for permission; we give no gratitude. We are brazen in our razing and usurping of another's provision.

We can host a party in this house, feed the poor in its dining room and let the homeless sleep in its bedrooms—but ultimately the glory is to be the home owner's.

27. We believe we are basically good partly because we misunderstand *sin* for *sins*, and *being* for *doing*—we mistake our *defining nature* for our *nature's ramifications and extensions;* we mistake the *root* for the *fruit.*

But what is sin? Let's acknowledge what *sin* is before we use it mindlessly, mechanistically in tradition. Sin is: *contradicting that which is the ultimate good.* It is that which makes us less than who we are meant to be. Sin is a distortion of *being*, not merely *doing*.

Sin is not the breaking of an arbitrary rule. Sin is denying reality. Sin is re-ordering the universe to our specifications; it is disuniting intended unions and uniting what was divided. Ultimately, it is the judging of God by disbelieving Him—it is un-trust. It is missing the mark of our purpose: to trust and obey our good Creator.

Sören Kierkegaard, a great Christian thinker, spoke of sin as "building your identity upon anything other than Christ." This is revelatory—thinking of sin and identity as correlated! This is biblical! Sin is not a mere external motion, but the very atmosphere of our core, the ambience of our will. Sin is an identity that bears actions.

It has been accurately said that, "we are not sinners because we sin; we sin because we are sinners." This is a hard saying, but like diamond it is cutting, illuminating, and incredibly valuable to behold.

Moralism/religion diagnoses *sins* as the problem; The Gospel diagnosis *sin* as the problem. *Moralism/religion* will exhaust itself into despair by cutting down fruit that will always come back; The Gospel finds rest in the death of the root, struck down by the life of Christ!

28. There is no good act that lives apart from God.

Doing *good things* is different than having righteousness. We must not confuse *doing good things* with righteousness. Righteousness is living in accordance with reality; it is being conformed to God's perfection.

One can do what we call good things yet be a brutal criminal. One can do good things yet deserve a death sentence. One can buy a bouquet of flowers for his mother on Mother's Day and still rob banks by knife-point and club other old ladies for pocket change. A criminal can honor an oath to a partner in a heist, yet break every oath he as a citizen has made to the law of the land. A rapist can donate money to a charity. Need I go on about the obvious? Those who "do good things" are still "the guilty" who have ravaged the truth of the universe.

We must not consider ourselves good simply because we compare ourselves to those with more blatant and extravagant crimes. Man is always considered above average when he picks the reference point, for he always chooses to compare himself with those more *observably debased*. But the standard is perfection, not the life of a faulty neighbor. The standard is perfection—and all fail.

Is this absurd to you? – *The man stood in front of the judge and said, "Yes, I did it. How can I deny it? I stole the cash and repeatedly beat the man and his wife. But I didn't lie, and I won't lie about it! I didn't kick the dog they were walking, even though it barked obnoxiously at me. I didn't kill anyone else, and I didn't run the red light as I drove away to the red light district—I didn't even speed. Now that I think about it, I have never even had a parking ticket. Oh yes, and that very day I gave a dollar to an old man panhandling on the corner of Main and 3rd!" The judge, now thoroughly impressed by the man's good actions, smiled and said, "Oh, well then, you are not guilty if you did not break all the rules of society; clearly you have done good, there is no penalty, you're free—off you go and enjoy your day."*

Is this no different than the way we view ourselves in light of God's good commandments? We feel that if we do not *heroically* break every law then we are not guilty. This is polluted thinking. If partial transgression counted as innocence then no one would be sent to prison—for many rules appeal to our selfish desires and therefore we live by them, not wanting to break them because of our own selfish inclinations. Some rules we don't break merely because we are breaking others.

We are often guided into what is commonly called *good* action by the steely tracks of our own selfishness. Often, self-sacrifice is merely other-manipulation; that is, we do what is right not because it is right, but because it will get us something.

If we break one rule, we break them all—is this unreasonable? The First Commandment of the ten—think about it—it is not merely chronologically first, but it is primary, foundational so the others can stand upon it. I will discuss this later in the chapter called "The Beautiful Standard." We must come back to this.

A righteous heart is not a heart that does not fail and fail again. It is a heart that knows only God can redeem it from its many failings; this is why it is righteous—for it relies upon Jesus to cover its shame. The success comes in knowing that God alone covers your failings; that God alone unfreezes the arctic heart to release a green mantle of spring.

Ultimate failure is attempting success without God. Ultimate success is recognizing our inevitable failing, and acknowledging the redemptive love of Jesus.

A heart at rest with God is a heart in tension with the world. A heart at rest with the world is a heart in tension with the Creator; we can see the opposite tensions slam fists here.

To be *righteous* means to be approved, accepted, to conform to a standard.

It is not for us to approve what is or what is not *ultimate reality*; but it is *Ultimate Reality*, the Truth, God, who is to approve of us. As creatures, we are called to acknowledge truth, not to approve it. The greater approves the lesser. Whenever we approve of God we are setting ourselves as a higher god—and in doing this, we cannot trust or praise Him. To approve of God is actually to disapprove of Him and to disavow Him!

How idiotic is it to define perfection with ourselves as the standard? All would then be perfect—and if all are perfect, then no one is perfect.

We are approved in our acknowledgement of the truth. It is in this way that life and death hangs upon trust.

How can He who is the source of perfection approve of what is broken? How can infinite love accept selfishness that caves-in upon itself?

The man who acknowledges the beauty of a clear winter night is reasonable. The man who says he disapproves of the arrangement of stars and of the way one glows brighter than another is proud and therefore foolish. He only wants to move the stars because he can't; and this essential inability is an offense to the offensive soul.

Some people believe they are at rest or have found peace apart from Jesus—but death is different than peace; numbness is different than salvation, than sweet relief. The frost bite we incur from standing naked in the deep winter of rebellion does not count as peace. Sentimentality does not count as innocence.

29. Let's speak of innocence—for we are guilty of misusing it!

There is true innocence and there is a sentimental notion of innocence we use to hide behind. This maudlin notion of innocence means to say that we are above reproach—what a great weapon for the guilty soul to brandish!

We often confuse being a child with being innocent. The true sense of innocence means that we have done no evil, are not responsible for harm—that we are untouched by sin or guilt. Literally, in Latin, innocent means *no-harm*. But who is above sin, above hurting just one other? There is no existential innocence before God who sees what plays upon the screen of the heart.

There is a popular misunderstanding about innocence. It is not that we experience an *end of innocence* or *dissolution of innocence* that converts us from a child into an adult; but rather, what we do experience is the *dis-illusion of innocence*, or the potential *beginning of innocence*. Let me explain, for this is volatile, and mis-handled it will bear damage rather than joy.

There are many movies, great stories, and personal memories that imply we are intrinsically innocent before the court of the universe, but then through some heart stuttering tragedy or twisted sexualization or war or death or criminal act, the golden youth of innocence turns dark, fades to shadows, or shatters like thin glass. This *end of innocence* is a misnomer.

What we commonly call the *end of innocence* is really the *disillusion of innocence*. The disillusion of innocence is the revelation that we are part of a race that is deeply flawed, fundamentally crazed, and that we have long been deceived by a thin gilding, that when poked through, reveals a dangerous shadow beneath.

What is revealed to us is that we too have the villain, the bully, the monster within us. We too are capable of what our enemy does to us. There is a frail paper veil between the victim and the victimizer. The truth is that we have never been what we call *intrinsically innocent;* only misguided and deceived; only hurt and unjustly traumatized by other human beings of the same entropic lineage. Our nature was never blameless when it comes to divine justice and offending God who is the Ultimate Good.

There is a thin veil between the horror story and the coming of age story. Is it any wonder that certain authors known for terrifying their readers with monsters have also written golden tales that speak of childhood innocence and the trauma of growing up? Is it unreasonable for childhood to be the canvas that many authors explore the realm of monsters and the macabre?

The *end of innocence* is a great theme in the arts and we have seen it over and again in movies telling the haunting *coming of age* story. If we understand that it is a telling of the *disillusion of innocence* rather than the *end of innocence*, then we can see why this knowledge is so painful to us, yet so engaging and magnetic—it is because it is not a mere losing of what was good, but it is a revealing of never having been wholly good! It is a revealing of having been born in a world off-center and cracked through. This, no doubt, is a trauma to us. But like other traumas, we look through split fingers—both drawn and repulsed.

When a child faces an abusive parent in a *coming of age* tale, then he also faces what is within himself. When a young woman faces death in a film about innocence violently stolen, she faces herself and the pale-fruits of her own soul. The tragedy comes not solely in these individual stories, but in the universality of the trauma, and in the facing of our very own soul.

For these reasons, these films and stories of *innocence dis-illusioned* are powerful, troubling, and alluring. All this seems to make the world much darker—yet strangely, ironically, it gives it much more hope. In contrast, the light grows brighter and the hope greater.

Do not misunderstand. For there is an innocence of childhood that is sacred; but there is not a total innocence that runs clean and clear through our entire being that can be used as leverage against God. No one has *leverage* against God—not even a child. Really, when we lay claim to this mythical total innocence, we are claiming that God owes us something. God—*owe us something?*!

But what of the children who suffer; what of the nice people who perish? "Far be it from (God) to do such a thing—to kill the righteous with the wicked treating the righteous and the wicked alike. Far be it from you! Will not the judge of all the earth do what is right (Genesis 18:25)? Abraham trusted that God would do what was right; so too must we trust God.

Do not grieve. There is great news that follows in the wake of the *disillusion of innocence*. There is redemption; there is deliverance! We can experience the *beginning of innocence*. The *beginning of innocence* is the humility of repentance, the reception of God's saving grace, and the innocence of Jesus Christ covering us and claiming us from the fractures of the fall. In Him the guilty are innocent.

The popular myth of the *end of innocence* tells of a universe that knows innocence for only a short time, and then the lasting victory of entropy and guilt. This is a cruel tomb of a universe. Yet the *beginning of innocence* reveals a world where we live eternally in a perfecting presence; where stains are washed clean, and where violence and ash are traded-out for beauty and restoration.

The *end of innocence* worldview is tightly held to by the world, though it is ultimately deterministic and bleak; the *beginning of innocence* worldview is thought reprehensible by an unbelieving world, even though it tells of freedom and joyful redemption. Isn't this strange?

Though we were never innocent in heart, we have always been loved. It is better to be born loved than born self-innocent; for the love of our Creator is the only thing that can make us *the innocent*. This is the wonder of God's love. The Gospel is love; our guilt and sin is the darkness against which it shines, like a diamond-star on the black velvet cloth of night.

The truth of the Gospel gives us both love and innocence; the popular worldview that denies our sin gives us neither *bona fide* love nor innocence. The world says we are born innocent and die guilty; the Gospel says that we are born guilty and can die innocent—which would you rather? Would you rather a golden memory or a platinum eternity? And for that matter, if we choose the platinum eternity, won't it make even the past glorious?

The truth of our nature is certainly traumatic. We must face this wound in order to know the healer. The possible discovery of this trauma is why we run from ourselves, why we rather remain an amnesiac. It is violence that brings upon amnesia—and we are amnesiacs because of the violence man has brought upon himself by beating against reality.

Again, I quote Eliot from his poem Four Quartets:
"The wounded surgeon plies the steel
 That questions the distempered part
 Beneath the bleeding hands we feel
 The sharp compassion of the healer's art
 Resolving the enigma of the fever chart."

We turn to monster tales in order to cope with ourselves while we remain hidden from ourselves. Reading tales of stark evil is an upward thrust of the soul, an exposing of itself though it was told to stay hidden. We are intrigued by vampires, by psychotics, by phantoms and shadows because we are intrigued with who *we* are. We look at ourselves through split fingers—shielding, yet seeking.

Does all this sound shrilly in our ears? Why do we flinch at these explorations? Why are we so adamant in claiming our innocence despite the overwhelming evidence of the basic human condition? Maybe it is because we have an aversion to real love.

30. Do not mistake any of what I write as calling humanity worthless. We are precious for we are created *imago Dei*—made in the image of God. We are not worthless, but we are unworthy of the cost of our salvation.

Do not mistake any of what I say as justifying harm or disrespect towards any human being. Quite the opposite is true—only when we accept our accountability and condition of sin do we gain the dignity of being a moral agent. **This is the restoration of dignity, not its disintegration.**

This traumatic reality is spoken of as a cancer, a parasite to be done away with because there is inherent dignity in the human condition. The cancer is called out because the person is loved, not hated. Surgery is done because of the value of human life; not because the patient is worthless and so cut haphazardly upon.

We are unworthy of salvation—yet our Creator's love has saved us from ourselves. What kind of love lives and dies for that which is unworthy? This love is not of man.

We have worth but we are unworthy of the cost of redemption. The difference is staggering. We are loved more than we can fathom, and in ways that our reason cannot conquer or absorb.

Acknowledging our finite nature reveals the wonderful infinitudes of God's love.

One may claim that God cannot be love because His Word says that humanity is not intrinsically innocent; this is because they know not of love—only power plays and camouflaged coercion.

One can only claim that God is unloving if they do not know who they themselves are—and humanity's dark responsibility. To call God unloving is the confusion of the amnesiac.

We are far more wonderfully made than we can conceive; yet, "No one is good but God alone." What could Jesus have meant by such surgical words? Surely He could not have meant anything other than *God alone is good.* Then why does the common Christian posture seek so relentlessly in grasping at some degree of goodness for mankind? Because we must ascribe goodness to where our faith and our salvation ultimately lies…

Again, I ask: Then why does the common Christian posture seek so relentlessly in grasping at some degree of goodness for mankind?

Attempting to be good is like attempting to tear a star out from its socket in the ordered sky and hold it in one's pocket.

We can only worship God when we give up the absurdity of being good on our own. Attempting to be good is moralism, and moralism is only the manifestation of envying God.

And religion?—it is the hand of moralism. It is the action and institutions of man's attempts at self-salvation. The Gospel saves us from such absurdities.

~The Pride~

31. Envy is one of the bastard-sons of pride. We are prideful beings. Pride, or *hubris*, is wanton violence towards God; it is motive-less outrage against reality. In this violence, envy is born like an imploding star.

Envy has a twin—Apathy. Apathy is sterile envy; it is so desirous of what is greater than itself that it tries to destroy not by directed rage, but by whole-sale disregard. Envy hates the world and tries to burn it; Apathy hates the world and so it won't look upon it—it burns it all in the darkness of self-blinding.

Envy lunges and lacerates; Apathy shrivels and shuns—but both are an unjustifiable attack, both the children of violence against reality.

To be *fallen* means to be less than what we were intended to be; to not fulfill one's existential meaning. To be fallen means to not only have fallen from a height, but to have collapsed inward.

Pride, in seeking to advance its position, only finds further regression.

We were intended to be in right relationship with God just as a fish is in right relationship with the sea, or an eagle the air—yet our current state is one of separation; separation that twists like a receding spiral whose center is the self. But this spiral is like that of an onion: peeling and spiraling inward until nothing is left but a sour odor.

32. People laugh when you say that humanity is fallen; they say it is a mythic and a storyboard-like concept. We should note that people do not laugh only at jokes—but also when they are nervous, as when truth suddenly cuts to the soul. Might their laugh be the laugh of the fallen?

To what can we compare the effect of the fall? It is as when one stands upon some great height, and then dropping an object, notices that as it falls, the object appears to be diminishing in size, becoming less and less than what it was when it was held in the hand. With the fall of humanity, not only did we fall from the height of reality, but we caved-in, collapsing further inward, and becoming substantially less and less as we refused to live in harmony with truth.

The prideful heart is the heart that caves-in upon itself even as it believes it is ascending.

Here is an irony: in a world without God, love is more mythic and more storyboard-like than being *fallen*—yet it is an assumed reality; it is universally longed for and not scoffed at. As fallen humans, double standards are a forte. Truly, the evidence of all history and psychology lean heavily in the court of us being a fallen rather than an innocent race.

In a God-less world love could only be self-preservation and the random knocking about of chemicals. So it is foolish, naively mythic, to speak about this thing called love in a world created by naturalistic means only. Love is destroyed by the ideology of naturalism. The possibility of love is destroyed in the death of God.

Hah!—Naturalism is not natural!

The refrain has often been proudly sung: "Hey, I'm not perfect?" The trouble is in the very thinking that it is okay to *not be perfect*. Yet we must be perfect! Could this be true!? Must we be perfect? This is a hard thing to say! Yes! We are to be perfect (after all, it is something we do truly long for)—yet we can only be perfect, if by grace, the righteousness of Christ covers us. Now then, what does it mean to be perfect?

This is our purpose—to be perfect through Christ. We are speaking here of *being perfect* in regard to our existential condition (our relationship with reality); not a cultural perfection defined by image driven media, but a perfection of existence the Creator calls us to.

An irony: we often think we are perfect and/or we desperately long to be perfect; yet we despise God's command that we be perfect. Also, surely we strive for perfection, yet we despise that God says we are not perfect. Interesting, isn't it?

In the Scriptures (Matthew 5:43-48) Jesus tells us that we are to be perfect as our Father is perfect. The Greek word for perfect is *teleios*. *Teleios* is an adjective form of the noun *telos* which means *end*, or *purpose*.

Simply stated, *teleios* means *that which achieves its purpose for which it is planned*. So we are to be conformed to our purpose, conformed to our end and ultimate meaning—to live for your ultimate end—the end of everything is the glory of God. Christ is telling us that we are to fulfill this meaning and purpose for which we are created by loving others—this includes our enemies. Yet we can only do this through Christ; only through His grace that changes us. Please, read for yourself this passage in Matthew 5.

"Be perfect, therefore, as your Father is perfect" (Matthew 5:48). Man is to be man as God is to be God. God is Creator, but man tries desperately to be more than a creature. By trying to be God, man dismantles his purpose.

This is what it means to be conformed to the image of Christ: to be conformed to reality! "What other creature that God has created has been given the Spirit of God and is being conformed to His image" (1 John 3:2)?

It is impossible to be *perfect* in our love for others unless Christ Has changed our hearts and now mediates all our relationships. When we are *perfect* in our love for others because of Jesus' perfect love, then we glorify God for what He has done and for who He is! When we love others to the glory of God we realize our purpose for living—for to truly love others one must love God.

To be perfect in our current lives means not that we have *arrived*, but that we are arriving, and it is being done by Christ's strength.

No one is sinless unless they look into God's face amidst the ambience of eternity. Now, we are to be striving, straining for that goal of the gaze of God by resting in Christ. Simply stated, it is our purpose to seek God's face in trust; yet now we only see in part.

To be perfect means that we acknowledge our sin! That we acknowledge our need for Jesus! Our eternal need for Christ!

To live according to your ultimate end is *to love like God*. This love is an unconquerable goodwill that seeks the best for all mankind. The best for mankind is to reflect God's glory. Pride hisses at each of these like a snake of steam from a boiler.

33. If anyone is in love they are in debt. True love never believes itself worthy; it always believes that it received the better end of the deal. If we are in love with God, then we understand this *debt*—but if we feel worthy, or feel that we are treated unfairly and haven't gotten our due, then we do not love God. If we love God we will live a life of gratitude expressed in praise, for we know who and what we are, and His beauty that lit our lives while we were yet seething in darkness.

Love understands that grace can ask anything from us and be justified in doing so. This is why grace is judged foolish by the selfish heart: because self-surrender is intrinsically tied to authentic love.

If we are creatures, then what can we claim being worthy of in relation to the Creator?

34. Man in his fallen state is a reductionist—a deconstructionist tempting to isolate and sever, judging what is what, in order to control and manipulate. We want easy answers, and to be told which way to go. We don't want to have to work it out for

ourselves. We love and hate laws. We want to work it out ourselves. A list of rules is what we abjectly long for—then push away. We require boundaries in order to put our minds at ease—yet we redefine them at will, and justify each selfish movement. We justify ourselves. We love lists: *Do this, not this.* We crave boundaries—we push for them as adolescents, we identify ourselves by them as teenagers and adults. We desire to transgress—we push more envelopes than an urban postal worker. We are a blind bundle of contradictions, bumping into ourselves. The great keystone to our fallen nature is pride. It is what holds all our other stony sins in jumbled place. It is what crushes us. We revel in it; we revile it in others. It is why we cut ourselves, pierce ourselves, wear Italian suits, sculpt thick muscled bodies, school our minds, seek political office, and chase the lime-light of the stage, etc. etc.

Pride—the one word in itself is a contradiction!

35. We are either slaves to sin or slaves to God. One cannot be both dead and living. One cannot be pregnant with love *and* sterile with the selfishness of self-reliance.

The heart cannot have neutrality—for it always desires something. That which desires is not neutral.

Many do not like the Apostle Paul; they struggle with Him, and they feel him arrogant. This is because he knew and expressed this truth of heart-slavery that we repress. Paul called himself a *doulos*, a slave for Christ; his understanding and his living-out of this reality forces others to crisis and to see their own half-heartedness.

It is our human nature to bind ourselves to something or to someone. We can bind ourselves to our narrowing selves and call the suffocation *freedom*—or we can bind ourselves to an infinite God and know increasing liberty.

To be a slave, a bondservant, is to give oneself over entirely to the will of the master—that is, we no longer reserve trust in our self, but in the will of the one we serve. Yet, you may say, "this is dangerous to give yourself over to another, isn't this ignorant and perilous—isn't this what makes an Eichmann or the other *tools of tyrants?*" Yes; but Paul did not entrust himself to a man; he placed all his trust in the will of the Father, in the God/man Jesus Christ—who in Him there is no tyranny, only beauty and goodness.

It is exactly this danger of becoming "a tool of a tyrant" that God calls us to abandon by abandoning ourselves entirely to His will. When we abandon the tyrant we serve—ourselves—then we can be free. And, recognize too, that Paul in becoming a slave to Christ did not abandon thinking—but His thinking was a gift now used for the service of His good master; a gift given to higher and greater potentialities now that it was aligned with its source.

"No one can serve two masters. Either he will hate the one and love the other, or he will be devoted to one and despise the other. You cannot serve both God and money" (Matthew 6:24). Jesus speaks here of money not as a tool, but as a surrogate for God, an idol one entrusts themselves to, an alternate origin to live from and for. Notice he refers to man as *serving* the money—not man using money as a tool.

One will either serve the self or serve God.

This means that one cannot eat of the tree of life *and* of the tree of the knowledge of good and evil. One either trusts or distrusts God; one either entrusts themselves to provide for themselves, or they entrust themselves to God for provision. In a universe founded upon trust, there is no neutrality.

36. The tree of the knowledge of good and evil, the ancient temptation of autonomy, the ever present desire to live from ourselves will always lead to tyranny because it always moves in distrust of the *only* source of life and of love; each successive movement will then only be a curving away from reality, a debasing of human dignity because of an abandonment of the Creator.

God's sovereignty does not allow for boasting or man's pride. Sovereignty means that God is self-sufficient, He is the supreme authority. Pride is an attack upon God's very nature; if He is sovereign, which He is, then all good comes from God.

Therefore, any boasting is a direct assault on God's divine nature, robbing Him of His due, His glory (the highest opinion, ultimate reality), and taking credit for His nature ourselves. Pride and self-boasting are fundamentally wrong because they cut against the very nature of God.

Pride is the anti-God state of being. Pride is the anti-reality state of being.

Pride is spitting at the sun and cheering oneself on. Pride is spitting at the very sun that grows the food that feeds the livestock that is eaten which gives you the energy and life to spit at the sun. You cannot sizzle it out! The very thing you try to sizzle out is the very thing that sustains and energizes you.

Pride seeks to conquer, but is self-defeating, and therefore foolish. It is senseless, incongruent; unreasonable—that which is in direct opposition to the *Logos* (the reason of existence—Jesus).

Logos is the Greek word for *reason, wisdom* and *word*.

"In the beginning was the Word (*Logos*), and the Word (*Logos*) was with God, and the Word (*Logos*) was God" (John 1:1).

The only boast that is not a lie is this: "*See what God in His glory has done!*" This sounds overtly religious and empty, a rote thing to say, but it is not; it is the densest reality—the weightiest truth. It is the order behind the constellated stars in space, underneath the skin of the oak tree, and within the drop of sea water.

When Jesus told the people of His day that they were *not free*, they were instantly indignant. "*Us! What! You are a madman; we are not slaves to any nation and we make the choices we want!"* But what they could not understand was that they were slaves to sin—their very *nature* made them "not free" for they were bound by a self-serving heart.

Yet Christ came and said "the truth will set you free"—*I will set you free*. And still, these words sound like foolishness to us. "I am free to choose," we say—"I am no slave. Sin does not control me. I am free to break beyond the restraints of sin!" But the words of Christ still stand; if we are not free in Christ then we are bound by sin. Bound by ways that bring destruction; ways that bring self loathing, self-absorption, contempt for humanity, mental disorder, physical disease, caging envy, a black hole of ego, and green pyres of envy.

Are we the truth? If not, then how can we set ourselves free?

37. There is no spiritual fence. The idea of spiritual neutrality is a crafty and desirable lie. It is a justification for playing in the shadows and metaphysical manipulation. If you are serving neither God nor the deceiver, you are serving yourself—and if you are serving yourself you are serving the deceiver.

One cannot be a blank slate, a so-called *tabula rasa*. A blank slate makes no choices because it has no desires from which to choose from. We make choices, we have affections, we have desires—we have a bent, therefore we are not neutral.

An irony: we desire to be neutral, therefore we cannot be neutral. Desire cannot be neutral.

Only that without a will can be neutral. Are you neutral? Yes, *I bring this up again and again*; but I do so because it is brought up again and again to justify man's attempts at scaling heaven. It is a deep soul-splinter.

38. The opposite of love is not hate; it is selfishness. Selfish-love is pride. (I am not here speaking about *selflessness*, for we are to "have

a self," to love ourselves and take care of the life and body God has given us.)

But do we have to teach ourselves to "love ourselves" like the therapeutic culture says? Jesus takes it that we already do love ourselves. "Love your neighbor as yourself, " He says; He apparently did not believe we needed to be taught to love ourselves. Could He be right?

Pride is absurd, for selfish-love cannot be love. It is a *wooden-iron*, a contradiction of itself, an expedition into meaninglessness.

Man's self-origin is an inorganic origin. God is man's organic origin. One is mechanistic and rusts itself shut—the other blooms for all eternity.

I once read about an ancient symbol called the *ouroboros*. It is an ancient symbol of a snake with its tail in its mouth; it is in the shape of a circle—it is eating itself. I think it must be adopted as the symbol for pride! It is ever diminishing, shrinking into itself, unsatisfied, self-reliant, destructive, narrow-sighted, eternally trapped, less and less substantial, and inward bound.

I believe the symbol for love should not be an iconic heart, but a cross: two beams that have a holy center, radiating forever outward, growing, full of sacrifice and service; they are four radiating rays of obedience—obedience which is love; and on the center, divine grace from which the rays are born. It is the symbol of ultimate freedom.

We must stop trying to define love—Jesus defined love for us: "If you love me, you will obey what I command" (John 14:15). Obedience? Could this be love?

Love is to obey Jesus. But what did He command? Did He give a list of *moralisms*? No. What He commanded right before He spoke those piercing words about obedience was this: "Believe me when I say that I am in the Father and the Father is in me; or at least believe on the evidence of the miracles themselves. I tell you the truth, anyone who has faith in me will do what I have been doing" (14:11-12). Love is trusting Jesus; it is acknowledging the reality of God— that the Creator and Savior are one.

Despite the reality of our total dependence on God, we try to subsist by ourselves. We consume ourselves; we become less substantial, less significant, more phantom. Hell is a vast and isolate wasteland on the tip of a needle.

Pride tastes of dust, though it looks like nectar.

39. God is love. God can hate. This is not a contradiction. God can hate and love. God can hate *because* He is love. Because He is love He hates pride and the self-swallowing coil that is sin. He hates it when we eat ourselves and do not live by His bread alone. God hates all that is ungodly because all that is ungodly is not good. Always remember—good only comes from God.

Any human who claims to love, by necessity, must also hate. Many hated the war and the government that sent young people to Vietnam or to Iraq; yet their dominant reason for the hate was *because of their love* for an ideal of peace or for family members in fatigues.

If imperfect humans can hate because of a measure of love, how much more can a perfect God hate because of perfect love—and do so righteously and in right proportion?

Christians should hate sin. This is not a contradiction; it is just a disliked concept because sin and selfishness are liked, and are buried in our pulse and our marrow. Like an alcoholic's blood is unwilling to let the addiction go, so is the unrepentant heart unwilling to let the desirous life of sin go.

God, by being the ultimate good, by necessity of who He has revealed Himself to be, must have anger towards the wicked.

Wicked? This sounds like such an antiquated word—what does it really mean? This only means that there is a reality and it has been twisted and warped. Wicked, like *wicker* and *wick*, means to twist—and most assuredly there is a twisting of what is real.

Righteous wrath: This is not intolerance…unless you want to classify the condemnation of rape, murder, thieving, and destruction as intolerance. It is right to hate what is wrong. It is evil to be tolerant of what is evil. Do rape and murder make you angry?

If one does not believe in absolutes, in right and wrong, then one cannot even argue "tolerance!" as universally right. This is one of those straws in the bundle of contradictions; it is one of those straws we pull out when we want to justify ourselves—and then we put it away when we want to condemn another.

Tolerance is an empty term. If the tolerant were so tolerant they would not be trying to change those who they thought were intolerant. They undermine themselves. They chainsaw the very branch they sit on.

Tolerance is an empty buzz word wielded to justify selfish actions. The buzzing is loud, but we have become used to it and concede to its noisy rhetoric. This false thrust for tolerance is a product of pride—likes its source, it destroys itself.

Tolerance is a misunderstood word. Tolerance means *a fair, objective, and permissive attitude toward those whose opinions, practices, race, religion, nationality, etc., differ from one's own; freedom from bigotry.* Here comes the irony again. The only one truly objective is God. He cannot be intolerant; He is only just. There is no bigotry in God—but there is grace and truth.

When we call God a bigot, we are only slandering a god of self-design—a god made in our image.

Justice is not intolerant. It is a categorical error to call what is just *intolerant*.

God hates sin. This is tremendously unpopular. If this were the first sentence read by a passer-by in a bookstore, this book would be swiftly shut, the reader hoping that no killjoy-Christian-brimstone had been inhaled or had burnt a sulfurous hole in their hip shoes, and they might walk away muttering bitterly something about tolerance and love. This is to be expected.

"Ah—but Jesus was ever-gentle—we should just be nice like Jesus was!"

Jesus snorted like a wild horse—this is what it means when it says that Jesus was angry over the death of Lazarus (read John chapter 11). Jesus was angered by death—death is the penalty for sin. Death is unnatural. When we are enraged or found weeping because of death, it speaks to us that we are made in the image of God, and that there is now a fatal disconnect from our great origin, from our divine taproot.

Does it not make great sense that if we are sinful by nature, thrusting inward by the corroding engine of pride, we would balk at the idea of being sinful? A drunken person will argue he is not drunk despite their bottle-breath and spinning room. A dead person is the last to say that he is dead. A prideful person will heroically proclaim his humility.

40. When I was younger I held a golden view of human nature. I grew up in the blessings and hexes of the church. I had a very dear friend who was troubled by the world; he had a rusty view of humanity. He didn't believe in God, or a god, any more than he believed that the gifts on Christmas day were from Santa Claus and not his divorced parents. My good friend believed that there was something nasty about human nature—he instinctively felt that there was something wrong, some arsenic in the water of life, like we were born with twisty thorns curled in our hearts or acid rushing through our veins. He had no silver spoon blocking his view; his childhood was a cold war. I miss seeing him.

My friend was partly right; I was mostly wrong. Though I grew up in the church, I had a false view of the basic goodness of humanity. Naively, I believed we were essentially unselfish, that something more like sweet ambrosia filled our veins, that benevolent thoughts populated our minds, and that monsters were somewhere out there—that they were in some shaded alley, or in some desert-like country wearing odd outfits and speaking strange tongues. My friend had a view into the heart of reality that I did not.

Sometimes I think the world has a better grasp on our messy souls than the modern church does. Watch the movies, listen to the poetry of the musicians, or read a classic novel—you will hear all about the dark corners and oily curves of the human heart. Christendom often lacks the acknowledgement of our twisted essence—the world lacks the reality of hope, joy, and salvation by grace. The Bible speaks loudly of both.

The Biblical view is that we have neither acid nor ambrosia in our veins; rather, we are filled full with…human blood. It is not a toxin or nectar that poses the problem; it is a heart that is prejudiced against God. We have a heart that wants to do things its own way, to rush into its own desires; a xenophobic heart that considers God a stranger—a dangerous stranger and a threat to our fragile kingdoms.

41. The heart—what do I mean by the heart? This is important, for the Scriptures speak much of the human heart, but so do Valentine's Day cards, sentimental songs, and our rote greetings and goodbyes. Just throw in the word *heart* and suddenly you are speaking with conviction, or the deepest of love. The word *heart* is amorphous; it means nearly anything, and for that, it has come to mean nothing.

The heart is the seat of our desires; it is the seat of our affections. We make choices from our desires, and our will moves in accordance to the object of our affections. When our heart's desires are set on anything other than God, when the object of our ultimate affection is less than God, then we live a life in struggle against the truth—the heart is restless. It is restless for it denies its deepest knowing.

We all have an ultimate affection. There is an ultimate *something* that we live for or cannot live without; this *something* is what drives our hope and despair. The human heart is a mandatory throne; it is where we set what we "glorify" (what we will sacrifice for; what we live for). The throne is never empty; it is never without an object of affection.

It is a popular and poetic misconception that the heart can be empty. The atrocity is not that the heart is a vacuum, but a throne with a horrible king. The heart is never a blank space—but often a tyrant.

When we feel empty it is because a puny idol sits on the great throne of a great king. The heart is a great throne; it has eternity inscribed into. How pathetic looking is a finite something that sits on the throne of the infinite one!

Pride is the defiant rejection of reality. Pride is misplaced trust. Pride is the violent motion of unbelief.

The postures of the proud soul are *the sulk* and *the clench*.

The clenched soul: the eyes, fingers, mind, all squeezed tight—all clutching and pulling the universe into a pinpoint of self under the illusion of expansion. Pride is a chain reaction of implosions, each more violent, yet each clinching tighter and more regressive, becoming less and squeezing itself out of reality with a near inaudible whimper—though attempting to send a scream across the universe.

The irony of pride is that the more it strives for importance it achieves more and more impotence.

42. Can heaven be seen in a handful of dust? Even in the lowest of all creation there is symmetry, evidences of the order of God.

There is divine wonder seen even in the uniformity of all our woes; seen even in the skyward trajectory of our curses. In all, there is a deep order that cries, "Heaven, the very throne of God the Creator does exist—for the creation exists. God is there!"

The humble will see God in a bit of dust; the proud will reject the clear voice that comes flying from the sky, stands before them blazing in a miracle-fire and says, "I Am the Creator; all the treasuries of hail and lightning are mine!"

~Mystery of Technology~

43. Being embraced by truth is like being thrown overboard: much that was is now not; breath is invested sharply with meaning; water is more than an idea or image; all is action and there is very little theory. Vertigo has flipped you all about, you mistake the deep well of sky for the deep of water, you flail, and then suddenly you are on dry land regaining your still swimming senses (though you will have a headache for a good while). The greatness of this trauma is that when the headache subsides enough to see clearly, you recognize it was no yacht you were tossed from, but a garbage barge or some sad slave ship.

There is no Christian without crisis. Salvation comes in a crisis of life and death, of all or nothing, of "Nothing will ever be the same again! How now do I live?!" There is no true conversion without baptism of the heart—without death and the overwhelming inhale of new life. The synapse, the pulse of conversion is a mystery. Who can explain it? Sometimes the crisis is loud and in the bright light, and sometimes it is a whispering, a quiet moving in the soul—but whether soft or violent, it is a crisis of death or life nonetheless.

Is one born into the world a Christian? No. Then one must undergo a crisis.

When I speak of conversion I do not speak of the irreligious converting to the religious; I speak of the dead quickened to the living. For the irreligious to convert to the religious is like an alcoholic trading gin for whiskey—it is merely another taste of the same poison.

The irreligious and religious—two sides of the same counterfeit coin.

Is it not a crisis if you are to choose between yourself to live or for another to live instead? To trust God is to kill the autonomous man. This is why salvation is a crisis; for crisis means to judge, to separate, to divide—*a turning point.* It is the death of and separation from the self as judge, and the newly born entrustment to God as judge over all. This is why we are to first judge ourselves— to first pull the beam from our own eye—for until we judge that we are not the judge of all, that we are eye-beamed and broken, then we are still judging God, and by that, acting as god—and heaven knows, we cannot save ourselves; for even beams and splinters ruin us!

A paradox: man's best judgment is to acknowledge he is not the judge.

Man can only rightly judge man when he recognizes that God is the judge of *all*.

44. *The dead quickened to life, the judges judging themselves*—it all sounds quite like magic! There are reasons why the human imagination has filled its works with the enchantments of magic woods, chosen heroes, age-old curses, runes of power, and monsters of lore. Magic is the substitution for miracle just as monsters are the substitution for our suppressed nature; reality will, and does, express itself—even in our dreams and fantasies. We dream of Merlin because God has moved among men.

Salvation is a miracle. Birth is a miracle. But remember! We are never born fully grown; we do not spring to life fully mature like Athena from Zeus in the Greek myth. We must not judge or treat a newborn as an adult. Would we slide a pacifier into the mouth of a crying teenager? This would belittle and anger, but never pacify. Would we have a rational talk over coffee with the newborn who consistently messes his diapers? I tell you, it would ruin the coffee and the child!

What does it mean that "we are not born fully grown?" It means that we as Christians will be conforming to reality in a continual process of growth, not a mere snapping of the fingers.

This also means that Christians are necessarily in various levels of growth, though they are in Christ. Understanding this helps us to reconcile the great diversity within Christianity. This diversity exists because Christianity is not moralism—it is entrustment. To demand that every Christian act externally the same is to demand that every human being on the earth be the same age—and if they are not, then there is no such thing as true humanity. Absurd! But the notion is common.

We must not think of the Christian life as one moment; it is infinitely more—it is every moment. As for a baby, there is a moment of birth, but a moment of birth leads to a life of growth. Birth is not the whole of living—the whole dynamic chain of countless moments is the living.

The Christian life can never be *a moment*, because *a moment* is finite and Christ is infinite, both Alpha and Omega. Christ is the Christian life—the life that is eternal and is in each moment, that transcends each moment, for it lives through the ever present I AM.

Man always tries to make Christianity a moment, an event, rather than the ever-present. In doing so, he tries to rename God—but it is God that renames man.

45. There came a one-eyed prophet. He walked down Main St. and gathered a crowd at the center of town. He stood and spoke with an authoritative tone: "You must repent! You have bad eyes! You have sin in them, I know! We are to fix this! The Word of the Lord has come to me—it says that we are to put out an eye, for we will have less evil to fight, and we will have won half the battle by silencing its wicked gaze! Yet, we will still have one eye to see and fight the evil! And so I say 'put out an eye!'" And the church became half blind. How passionate they were who looked through one eye! How zealous and driven! But how bad their depth perception! How often they angrily bumped into each other! How often they fell off cliffs and misjudged curbs! How deceptively flat is their world! Such is the church of the one-eyed prophet, the church that does not have stereo vision!

When one tastes with the heart and mind that we are fallen, that a hero is truly needed, and the sweetness of knowing that hero, the world shifts fundamentally, as if it were a sketch becoming a sculpture. It is as if one were born into a parallel and more dramatic world—one that is both darker and more radiant at the very same time; a world with greater gravity, and more buoyant possibilities; one more cruel, yet more beautiful and benevolent.

In this newly acknowledged world of deep relief, what was foolish now makes the greatest rational sense, for in the transformation, the lock and key have met to match. Here, a tree might bear heavy fruit that can send humanity spiraling from paradise (because there is a God to assign right and wrong, and it is insanity to deny His good authority); water might turn to blood (because both streams are at the mercy of the Creator's hand); blood might turn to victory (because life and sacrifice are invested with meaning); and selfless love between a woman and man might rise to exist (because the cold, selfish heart can be reborn like the dawn).

Oh to have two eyes and see the gravity *and* the grace! To see the midnight of sin and the bloom of day breaking open green and gold! To feel the despair of self-service, and the joy of costly love! To love the world, and for that, despise its gross coil and soul-collapse!

Proximity to God increases our awareness of our sin—proximity to God reveals that Christ is our righteousness and has freed us from our sin. The closer one is to a streetlamp, the longer their shadow, though the better they can see. We are not free until we are seized by our enslavement. Good news comes to the fallen by way of a break and a healing.

We need not a new vision, but eyes remade, eyes to see the truth of our deep-rooted bondage.

46. Technology is often an artificial salvation—it is that which makes for greater gravity *and* grander graces, higher hopes *and*

deeply mined lows. It often redeems what is thought lost; it often destroys its inventor and murders its master.

What is odd, is it not, is that we often believe we can be saved by what our own hands have crafted. Hah! There we stand, over what we have made, and then we bow to it! What is odd, is it not, is that what we have drawn out from ourselves, ideas from our mind, from our hearts, can then be used to try and fulfill the soul from which they came! Is it not like pulling up a bucket of water and then dumping it back into the well—and then over and over again to fill the well up!

Can water rise higher than its source? "Aha!" some will say, "Yes, with technology! For there are pumps and water wheels and other devices!" Very well then, what is the technology that allows technology to rise higher than *its source*? What is the pump, what is the water wheel that lifts technology beyond man to savior? A source higher than man? God? And if so, than salvation is no matter of technology.

It seems the fairy tales of youth and our fascination with technology both speak to something within us about reality; they are something akin to looking through split fingers at horror movies. They are substitutions for necessary explorations, and we are drawn to them in various degrees. Glowing buttons, blue and amber LED's, the green angular landscapes of microchips, and high-definition flat screens all display our desire for mystery—a mystery that is somehow controllable.

Magic was not the invention of the superstitious medieval serf! It is of every man in every age. We deeply desire magic—we just buy it at the media store rather than quest for it in a misty mountain deep, or lost forest, or in the scrawl of an ancient text.

We like controllable magic and mystery; we like that we can turn it on and off at will. We especially like magic when it is remote controlled, and we don't have to take even a step to watch a hero trace the miles of his journey. We like fantasy novels and films—

we enjoy their epic struggles, and then press pause when we are uncomfortable or want a snack.

Worlds and realms that we can control—such is the signature desire of the human condition. Yes, we like to get lost in these fictions as well, but at best it is a surrogate lost-ness, or a vanishing by voyeurism—nothing that really threatens our ill sense of self-reliance. We long for the wilds of mystery, for the half-shaded woods of magic, but we are reluctant to lose control, unwilling to let our lives rest in the hands of an untamable God.

47. There is nothing new under the sun. We live under the *illusion of progress*. It is an illusion we desperately keep that we may live the way we desire to. The honest person must admit that the world is not getting better and better, but is being driven more and more by entropy. This past century surely should have cured us of the myopic Utopian dream (but it seems that we are still sleeping and twitching).

With greater technologies there have been advances and good gifts—yes, this is true. But with greater technologies we have amplified apathy, made brutality easier, streamlined murder, and have glamorized the dark things of the world. To argue against this is to disregard every newscast everyday everywhere—it is to argue against the blunt force of reality. To argue against this is the suicide of reason.

Technology is an extension of the human heart—it is creativity, longing, beauty, ache, hate, hope, lust, and strutting pride. These are nothing new. Today we have digital lyres, faster chariots, and atomic slingshots. Do not be fooled, Cain would pull a trigger in the very same way that we do today; Ahab's iron heart would roll iron tanks like those that scar modern sands. Let technology roll on, but let us acknowledge that progress is only progressive if somehow, amidst its hum and gyrations, we turn to God and He gives us a heart of love in place of our hearts of darkness.

To say that civilizations have advanced and to believe that this means the modern human heart is somehow more advanced than a man of a thousand, two thousand, three thousand years ago is sheer folly. It is akin to someone saying, "Nowadays we are an advanced race. It used to be that our children were born as infants, but now our wives bear them right away as adolescents—and tomorrow, teens!"

The human heart has not progressed *en masse*, for we cannot start from where another heart has left off. Obviously, progress has given us greater means of mass destruction; yet, man's heart always starts nascent—so now, infant hearts are given progressively bigger machines and larger-scale weaponry to wail and tantrum with. The union of the heart with the reach and muscle of technology has troubled this world—and will trouble us at increasing speeds, at wider berths.

An irony: if there is no truth, no standard, then there is no progress. One cannot progress through the ages if the standard changes with the winds. Progress without a God means only change, neither better nor worse, just shifting about chaotically. A culture that is relativistic *and* progressive is caught in the seizure of blatant contradiction—they must disavow one or the other, for the two claims are mutually exclusive.

48. The God of the Bible is the God of the *wide fiery blue*—the God of the untamed sky that expands and expands. From inside the church, we often view God as that which we can define more and more until He comes to a point like the converging angles of a vaulted sanctuary ceiling. If we want a metaphor for God, let us look to the unbound sky that is the backdrop to our fancy buildings, but not the finite buildings themselves that man has made with his frail hands.

God is not a small point, but an increasing mystery! The church should know God to be more and more of a mystery as they come to know Him more; it is the one who doesn't know God who thinks they have God figured out and chased into a tight corner of definition. So what does this tell us about much of the church who thinks they have God figured out—cornered?

When we look into the infinite, we are convicted of how little we know.

Pride cannot bear the gaze of the infinite. It must hide, turn away, or be transformed. Pride's desire is competitive, its essence is the desire to be greater—and it cannot be greater than the infinite. This is why Adam and Eve who had the knowledge of good and evil tried to cover themselves—the infinite was looking at them; they could not bear His gaze that showed them disconnected and finite. God's beautiful gaze caused them shame because they could not bear to be less than He.

Reason reveals our ignorance; it is the telescope that can't see far enough; it is the word that speaks of our inability to communicate fully. Is all this not reasonable?

49. The Gospel is not without mystery—real mystery though—not some dark shade of the imagination, but some unfathomable light of God.

Beyond the sun are a million new wonders, bounded only by the wonder of God's glory—infinite and unbounded. "Holy, holy, holy" the angels sing at each new wonder revealed.

The Cross of Christ is taller than it is long. Christianity is not a revealing of all mystery, it is the revelation of mysteries. And for this, it is reasonable.

~A Message of Fools~

50. Three men sat in arm chairs. One man spoke to the other, "I don't quite agree with you! Your points don't seem to have that razor edge I need to judge something as *truth*!" The other retorted, "But what you call razor proofs are only your preferences!"

The first man said, "But my preference is truth!" The second man: "But if preference is your truth, you mean to tell me that it is truer than my preference! Surely there is a standard?! Now that standard is history, and I can prove to you He exists, for I have letters from Him, I have heard Him speak, He underwrote the cost of my home!"

First man: "But how do you know the letters weren't forged? How do you know you weren't dreaming when He spoke to you? How do you know someone else didn't just use His name and wear a mask at the signing of the contracts? How do you know?"

The Second man: "Because I believe the data, and the irrefutable science that proves it!" Meanwhile, in the third armchair, the man whose very existence was being debated sat tapping his toe, drinking his tea, looking at the other two men in quiet, but very real dismay. As they continued to argue, He got up, and he left the room.

51. God's essence is His existence. He is. I Am that I Am.

To try to prove the existence of God is to try to prove existence. As if one could prove the most obvious and all-enveloping essence if it is already called into question! If you, dear reader stood in front of me and yet I said, prove to me your existence—what could you do? What could you say that did not speak more rationally and clearly than your presence? If what is obvious "needs more proof" to be trusted, then one is already operating under the force of the absurd, and no reason, no data, no blatant miracle, no God-in-flesh saying, "I Am," will reason the absurd rational.

Existence is such that it is to be trusted; its pervasive obviousness, its blatancy, its just-is-ness makes the motions of proving it sheer folly. It is like proving water is wet or necessary for the thirsty! What can one say to the deluded man who says, "But maybe this is all a dream; all is a dream!" Pinch them (but in love of course)—this is the common sense way to see if anyone is awake or dreaming. It is scholars in ivory towers (who need to come up with some new theory to secure another degree) that come up with such obvious absurdity as "Well who then can prove or not prove that they are an apparition in a dream, for all is part of the dream?" Such philosophical games are just that—games to distract and games to feel elite.

There is a *law of obviousness* that all observation and science is based upon. If we doubt that we can understand anything, what is the point in understanding such doubt? These games are like *Ring Around the Rosey*—they go in circles, and then fall down.

52. For humanity, there are three great books to read from that can light our way: these are the Scriptures, conscience, and the wonder-laden tome of creation—but light from these presuppose us "seeing" them. So here is the rub: blindness is never in the failure of the things to be seen, but it is in the seer; the fault lies not in the object, but the optic. Where we are blind, we cannot *will* these blind spots to suddenly see. We cannot *will* the cataract optic clear.

The moon cannot spin itself fast enough to make its own light; it can only glow when the sun falls brilliantly upon it; neither can we rewire our own eyes to see. Yet part of the foolishness that is volleyed about here on earth is the desire to be the light bearing sun and not a moon; not a reflector but an originator of light!

So, can we heal ourselves? Obviously not (or is it?). A blind man cannot make a pair of bifocals, let alone recreate his own intricate eyes. This quandary of how a blind man can see that he may see the truth is so odd of a mystery, that the mystery itself reveals something: that we are not God, therefore we need God. We need God to see, we need His Spirit to transmute our hearts so they are not blind marble, but seeing flesh.

"Even if our Gospel is veiled, it is veiled only to those who are perishing. The God of this age has blinded the minds of unbelievers, so that they cannot see the light of the Gospel of the glory of Christ, who is the image of God. For we do not preach ourselves, but Jesus Christ as Lord...For God who said "Let light shine out of darkness," made His light shine in our hearts to give us the light of the knowledge of the glory of God in the face of Christ" (2 Corinthians 4:3-6).

To see has more to do with the posture of the heart than the parts of the eye.

53. The Gospel is foolishness; it is a stumbling block! These are not the fighting words of an atheist—these are the words of an apostle! Paul spoke these words.

We make a mistake when we present the Good News as perfectly rational to the unbelieving world. The good news of God is foolishness to the world that lives by presuppositions born of a selfish origin. This is one of the many dumb things Christians believe: *the Gospel makes sense to anyone with any sense*. The Gospel doesn't make sense to an upside-down world because the Gospel is right-side up. A conversion, an inversion, is necessary.

If it were true that *the Gospel makes sense to anyone with sense,* then there would be no need to bow, only the need to process data. This thought that is meant to empower man for apologetics and evangelism only steals from man; it makes man no more than a data crunching android—and for that, devoid of choice and moral responsibility. It is an unchristian thing to believe and propagate.

The Gospel is rational, yet it is not the heady philosophy of the self-proclaimed intellectual, not the self-addicted musings of the scholarly elite. The Gospel is powerful, though it does not come through brute force, but by service and humility. To the muscled and to the minded, the Gospel is foolish.

When we present what is *foolishness to the world* (the Gospel) as that which is reasonable to the popular paradigm, the world sees us as unintelligent, our conversations become stifled, and we are unable to speak wisely about the truth. Is one wise about the Gospel if they believe they can argue another into the wonders of grace?

We must be aware that this message of Good News is foolish to the world. But this does not mean we don't speak with reason about the Gospel of Christ. This does not mean we bypass our intellect. Yet, when we play by the world's rules of what can and cannot be done, when we play by the rules of "under the sun" we compromise the heavenly truths.

An example of this is the issue of miracles. We must talk about miracles logically, but we must not capitulate to the thought that to be logical we must do away with miracles. We must not play by the rules of secularized thought; to do this is like playing tennis with our hands shackled behind our backs—and then told that if we do not play well we are a bad player. We must not speak of Christian things in compromised ways. Let the truth flow in what are called "secular channels," but let this be only because it flows over and through all, not merely guided by the ruts cut by man.

The Gospel is for the heart *and* the mind because the heart and mind are for God and the reflection of His Glory. Logic and mystery are fast friends. It is unreasonable to think otherwise.

We must reason in accordance with reality, but we must not let popular opinion dictate what is reasonable and what is not. When we play by the rules of popular philosophy we end up trying to sell a watered down wine to a world that only knows water and despises this lukewarm and dull pink liquid, this mediocre pollutant. We would be better off giving away freely the foolish, rich, red wine of heaven.

At Pentecost, when the world received a rich taste of the Holy Spirit, everyone thought the Christians were drunk. How foolish.

It seems that nowadays Christians are rarely accused of being drunk. How foolish.

54. If the church is not passionate, it is not the church. Passion is necessary for the church—but not sufficient. Passion is a dime a dozen; it zealously sparks in a million ways and places; but it is not enough. Passion must be in accordance with knowledge; the energy of the zealous must be in accordance with reality. Our faith must correlate with truth. Read Romans chapter 10.

The busy church not in accord with the knowledge of God is like the man who tried to rearrange the beach with a pair of tweezers. He carried this grain of sand here to replace it with that one there—all the time running back and forth, sweating and exerting ferociously, but never doing anything. Are we merely rearranging the beach?

More often than not, our zealous movements are only a distraction, a frenetic diversion away from communion with the one who is never fooled—the one never distracted.

55. If humanity is in a *state of rebellion*, then it is understandable why the Gospel is foolishness. We must not forget this basic fact. If we wonder why the message isn't accepted, then can we be preaching the message of God?

When someone speaks against Christianity with a caustic "that is foolish!" then I sadly smile. The drunken man has protested too much; he has given himself away with his sudden flailing arms, crass speech and volatile reflex. It is interesting that Jesus Christ and His cross are so volatile to so many. Yet, begin a speech on Buddha and the Bodhi tree, or start a discussion on karma or an impersonal god of ambient energy, and hardly a soul will raise a flag of defiance, nor a finger in protest.

Has anyone else noted that there is far too much protestation of the Gospel in a world with many faiths—is this not a bizarre thing? Is this not inordinate? Why does the name of Jesus meet with such reflexive violence? It is not because we are ambivalent towards Him—it is because we hate Him, because He is the radiance of God that makes for envy. He makes our low-lit souls squint and dilate. His name meets with reflexive violence because His truth is like a bullet to the rogue soul—instinctively we attempt to dodge. Yet we only try to evade the love that will heal us; the death in us does not want to die by the hand of life.

We often attempt to dodge this "bullet" by proclaiming Christ was just a wise teacher, a genius of ethics. Yet this is profound absurdity! Christ taught that He was God, that He was the Messiah, the way, the truth, and the life. When one understands what Christ really taught, what all the Scriptures affirm, then one cannot call Him a mere teacher. If Christ were a mere teacher He was a horrible teacher...for He taught the Gospel—and the Gospel is a cigarette pack of lies if He was not God!

Here is the irony: one can only call Jesus *"just a teacher"* if they do not know what He taught. This is the blind teaching the blind how to paint a sunset. "Swipe some gold over here!"
 "What color is gold, and where is it?"
 "...I don't know! Here let's try this one!"
 "Is this even paint?"

Has anyone else noticed the wide respect for Jesus even among the staunchest enemies of Christianity? Take Nietzsche for example. Isn't this strange that Jesus also has a high reputation among many who wished God to be dead, and who signed His so-called autopsy report? These are strange dealings, the reflexive violence and odd respect that arise in the wake of Jesus' name. Who can explain this?

We are born into this world with a deep hunger for God—yet hating Him. We are born with a strange pull to set ourselves within His needed hand; yet we clench ourselves like a fist and set ourselves against Him. Why do we hate and hunger for God? We hate God because He limits us; we hunger for Him because He frees us and He is authentic love. We hate and hunger for God because we need Him. It is a scary and beautiful thing to need something—to need someone.

Revelation of dependence is traumatic to the proud heart.

To *need* means to not be God.

The Good News is foolish because man hates God. I know—it is politically incorrect to refer to human beings as "man," but it is also politically incorrect to talk of Jesus as He is revealed in the Scriptures. Throughout this book I will use *man, mankind,* and *humanity* to refer to us (Homo sapiens), both female and male, and all the wonderful versions of melanin; and as I do, so will I respect women and men the same—both fallen and both deeply loved by their Creator. (I would have lost any PC police a long mile ago—I believe this is a good thing. One simply cannot follow Jesus and hold favorable opinion with those concerned about political correctness. Jesus often steps on toes as He crushes the head of the deceiver. Better a bruised toe than a broken soul!)

56. I had once nearly driven myself mad, a grass-eating basket case in need of Prozac and crayons and plenty of time sitting quietly in the sun's lithium light. The voice that roused this insanity was the one that whispered "Christianity is an intellectual problem." I ran myself in circles (making deep ruts indeed) looking for that one synapse, that one perfect idea that would make the celestial-intellectual connection, that would save someone if it popped into their understanding—a synaptic salvation, if you will.

I was also exasperated by the evidence I saw around me. I knew men and women who were the avant-garde of smart, who were brilliant, who could deftly maneuver through courses in quantum physics, nonlinear equations, master's courses in philosophy and cryptic literature like that of James Joyce, Milton, or Blake. Some of them devout followers of Christ—others staunch atheists.

Then I looked to the artists, the authors, the world leaders themselves—brilliant—but some atheists, some Christians. Also, I have known people who never finished high school, or even secondary school; people who are self-proclaimed *simple*. Yet many of them have found the idea of God a horrible idea (because that is all He was to them, *an idea*) while others gladly give their lives in Christ's service.

There is no IQ divide. Christianity isn't for the weak in mind, and atheism isn't for the brilliant and rational—or vice versa. How easy it would be if the list of verified geniuses and polymaths were only atheists and all the Christians idiots; then, *maybe* we could say that belief in God was a naïve thought of the simple and dull. But this is not the case. The list of absolutely brilliant Christians runs as long as the arm of history. The list of mighty-minded atheists runs just as long. Test this by examining the records of history. What are we to make of such things?

Salvation is dependent upon I AM—not IQ.

57. The enlightened mind does not overcome the darkened heart.

It takes more than the mind turning over facts to overcome our God denying tendencies. Yet we must remember Jesus called us to change our minds. The first words of His divine ministry were "Repent, for the Kingdom of Heaven is at hand." Repent means to change the mind's orientation. If we are to change the mind's orientation, we must know more than the content, we must know its trajectory. Religion focuses narrowly on *content*; the Gospel of Jesus transforms *trajectory*, and in the momentum, it recharges the shape of all the content.

Though the enlightened mind does not overcome the darkened heart, knowledge is of divine import: "Brother's my heart's desire and prayer to God for the Israelites is that they may be saved. For I can testify about them that they are zealous for God, but their zeal is not in accordance with knowledge. Since they did not know the righteousness that comes from God and sought to establish their own, they did not submit to Christ's righteousness. Christ is the end of the law so that there may be righteousness for everyone who believes" (Romans 10:2).

What right does Paul have to speak of the zealous Jews thrashing about in discord with the truth? He, too, was of the same zealous nature that pushed and strove in self-righteousness, for he also had not known the truth of Christ, His true origin. What right, too, do I have to speak of many within the modern church as *zealous but not in accordance with knowledge*? I was of that sickly Christian brood that confesses Christ easily upon the sleeve, wears a wide smile, but within, a scowling and mortal man sat upon the throne of the heart—a humanist god!

My god—a humanist! No more! *Scali paradisi*—by my means I attempted to ascend to the divine; I my own ladder to paradise! But I am only so tall—how foolish! Jesus alone is the reality of Jacob's dream; the lone and perfect ladder from heaven to earth; the one mediator between God and man.

I was a nominal *Christian* thrashing about out of a zeal that was void of the revealed righteousness of Christ; a light without heat, a message without the Word! God forgive me!

I have been forgiven of mocking Christ, for having used His name on my own strength. But, now look upon your selves. Is there agreement between your *Christian* fervor and the Gospel of Christ? I see a hundred thousand points of cold light, but the heat so rare, so wanting. I hear multitudes making a statement, opining, but truly saying nothing because the words are not mediated by the Word that births, that quickens with reality and substance.

The steps of Jacob's ladder were not made of ascending textbooks or university degrees, or any energetic thrust of man—no! They were made of wounds and perfect motions of obedience; Christ alone is our mediator. He is the ladder upon which angels come and go. Much of Christianity forgets this and forges new stairways—but these stair cases of rickety moralism only run smack into a ceiling. Hopefully we hit our heads hard enough to help us wake up! The grace of a bruise!

Man can only inform; only God can transform.

58. (Wait—hasn't all this been done before? The salvation of humanity with the mind, the manifest of utopian dreams with the shining intellect, the powerful will, and strength of man—oh yes, that's right—the enlightenment, naturalism, humanism, Nazism, Communism, etc. Now I recall. How unoriginal. It seems I was treading the oldest of dead-ended paths.)

Historically, what were the fruits of the governments who divorced themselves from God to become wholly atheistic? Those who pinned their future hopes on man alone became the most murderous and criminal nations the cosmos has seen. Think of Mao's China, of Stalin's Russia. Both slaughtered millions more than Hitler. Also, recall Pol Pot's killing fields; in a country of approximately seven million, the God-less Khmer Rouge murdered near two million. What hope has humanity if humanity is our only hope? The answer is found among the scattered bones.

59. It is not that there is insufficient evidence for the existence of God and the truth of the Gospel; it is not that there aren't any prompters to quicken belief; it is simply that we do not want to believe in God, so we suppress the prompters, and we stifle the response to grandeur that we experience in our soul.

We do not want God to exist. He is not our desire. Like a long-ago acquaintance we don't want to talk to, we turn away sharply and make believe we don't see them, all the while hoping we are not spotted or called out. This dark hope of not being "called out" is the anxiety of man.

Our heart will ever betray us until it no longer betrays its maker.

The problem of our existence is not intellectual; it is moral. It is not a math problem; it is a problem with the heart, with the soul—and making equations with these is dehumanizing.

There is a peculiar rock band called Mute Math; it is a wise name because it reminds us that there are many things that math does not speak to, and that existence extends far beyond finite formulas. Love is not formulaic. History is not formulaic. Man cannot plug facts into a grid and discover tomorrow. There is a history of mathematics, but there is no mathematics of history. There is a love of mathematics, but there is no mathematics of love. There are no equations for the heart.

Though, and we must admit, math does speak to and sing about more, much more than we know. It is a beautiful hallmark of design! Beauty reveals math; math is exposed in beauty. It seems to me that mathematics is God's scale of music from which He has made the wonderful and ordered things of the world.

I am thankful for scientists and engineers who seek to understand the notes and musical theory of God's varied songs; but to try to disprove God with mathematics and reason is like trying to disprove the songwriter by analyzing his song.

To try and disprove the existence of Pythagoras by appealing to the Pythagorean Theorem is simply called madness. God cannot be disproved by anything within the cosmos; the Creator cannot be dismissed by anything within the creation. If one wants to disprove God, then he must first disprove the universe, himself, and his very theory that God doesn't exist. It is a rather poor proposition.

60. When we think of God as a puzzle He becomes something to leap over rather than someone to bow down to. How can we solve a person? People are not equations and they were made in the image of God—God is not a divine equation. He is a divine relationship (the perfect union of Father, Son, and Holy Ghost).

Christianity is not a puzzle, but a relationship. A puzzle is mastered, taken apart, and put back together. A relationship is marveled at, takes us apart, and puts us back together. A relationship with God may be puzzling, no doubt, but we are not to relate to a puzzle, but to a living being, an infinite and loving God. He is always puzzling, but never a puzzle.

The problem has never been with sufficient evidence for God's existence. The problem is we are spiritually dead. Door nails. Corpses. It is hard to see evidence when your eyes are milky with death, or slammed tight in temper tantrum, or overlaid with coins.

We must understand this: if the deceiver can get us to believe that God is an intellectual problem then he has blinded us from grace and the love of God. If salvation is *only* a matter of electrical impulses, of synapses, of wrinkles in the brain, then we are only mistaken in our thinking rather than natural haters of God. This nullifies the concept of sin and turns it into ignorance.

If the problem of existence is simply with education, then we as human beings are basically good—just blank or dirty slates that need to be written studiously upon. If we are basically good, then the need for God disappears. Poof! God disappears in the rising shadow of mankind. Poof! Man is not dead, just dumb. And know this: we will quickly argue ourselves "dumb" as long as it squeezes God out of the universe. After we have argued ourselves dumb then we will write self-help books to help ourselves! It is lunacy…but lunacy that sells so well! Madness is an apt synonym for sin.

Man believes that if he can call sin *ignorance* then he will be successful in vanquishing God. This is the madness of pride. It is a spoke that denies the reality of the hub that turns it. Sin is no mere lack of information; it is a madness of the heart, it is the violence of volition that spurns its Creator.

61. Our pride is so hulking, so obtuse, that we would rather become *the insane* than to admit there was one saner than we!

Sanitariums are for those who claim to be Jesus Christ, not for those who claim to follow Jesus Christ. Those who slight Christ and believe they can get along just fine without Him are those who place their salvation upon themselves, and by doing so, consciously or unconsciously, claim to be the Christ themselves—self anointed to save themselves. The sanitarium is for the man that believes he needs no savior to save him from himself. This is indeed what we need, someone to save us from ourselves!

62. *Disclaimer*. I know the human propensity for imbalance—I feel its frenzied pendulum within myself. Because of this, let me explicitly say that education is important and must not be abandoned. It must be honed and given back to God. It must be honed sharper now that it is given back to God. Education under God gains even more significance than under an empty sky. This section is not a critique of reason; it is a critique of *reason as God*.

This was merely a smashing of the idol of intelligence. If intelligence could save us then Frederic Nietzsche would not have died insane with syphilis and in the belly of depression. But he did. This is but one tragic example; countless more abound.

63. The Christian worldview can be said to stand upon two pillars: *Forgive me* and *thank You*. In these simple four words we find the beautiful tensions of true Christianity.

Forgive me tells of a standard broken and guilt incurred; it tells us that there is *an ought, a should be* to the warp and woof of existence.

Thank You speaks of grace, of mercy, of the goodness of the Creator and Savior, of redemption from the guilt incurred.

The *You* and the *I* speak of a relationship, the existence of love, the lover and the beloved.

The *forgive* and Y*ou* speak of the personal and infinite nature of God—the Sovereign Father. The *I* and *thank* speak of personal moral responsibility and do away with determinism.

Forgive me acknowledges humility of being a creature; *Thank You* acknowledges the glory of the Creator and Savior. In these two phrases we find humanity, the triune nature of God, the fall, and the redemption by God as Savior. The world calls these two pillars of strength *weakness*. To the world they are foolishness.

64. The Gospel is the wisdom of the one God (*Hear, O Israel! The Lord is our God. The Lord is One!*), and for that it is the most foolish thing to disunited man.

Man hides from the truth that hunts him; he runs from the healer who comes for him. Why? The Gospel seems foolish to the man who hides—for man hides from himself in madness. Man will try to hide his guilt and existential madness not by slipping under a rock or into a thin shadow (he is too *smart* for that), but by throwing stones at all the world and making all the world a shadow. He tries to make all the world crazy and dark so that his own guilt might be buried in the bedlam. He tears at the brains of all existence, for then he feels that he could not be held accountable for the madness of his own soul.

He attempts to make all the world a shadow by erecting a religion—and then he hides in the shadow of the erected god. Religion is not a chasing after light—no, it is the kicking up of dust and clouds to confuse, to darken.

He attempts to hide behind the stones he throws—throwing them at all the world to distract himself from himself. Religion casts stones externally because it cannot throw away the heavy stone heart within.

65. To what can we compare the foolish message of the Gospel? A stubborn man with a crooked leg—a femur shaped like a V— reluctantly went to see the doctor because his pain had grown worse, and his gait more warped. The Doctor said to him, "Good news! I can fix it right now—I must break it!" Grumbling, the stubborn and crooked man hobbled out of the office, cursing the uncivilized ways of the doctor who had obviously gone mad. He

grumbled with each step, walking in awkward circles until he was paralyzed with pain—ever despising the *crazy* doctor who supposed he could heal by breaking. The madman!

~Why There is Religion~

66. We hate God. That is why there is religion. That is why there is atheism.

Atheism doesn't proceed from the facts of science; it didn't come nonchalantly out of Darwinism like many moderns and postmoderns naively like to think. Rather, Darwinism sprung from atheism like an odor from rot. Darwinism sprung from the human heart that doesn't want God to exist. Atheism is merely a justification for self-interests; the justification to be the judge of the universe.

Evolution is the crutch of the self-wounded man.

Many think atheism is the conclusion to a set of verifiable facts. This is not so. It rests not on truth, but on assumption. It is the start to the process of looking for a set of verifiable facts to prove there is no Creator God.

It is not that there was no Creator to be found; it is that there was no desire found in the heart to find the Creator. The desire found in the human heart was to kill the Creator, and macro-evolution is that man-made mechanism, the handgun that attempts the murder of the Divine.

Atheism is a desire that is assumed to be true. Atheism is a *belief*; it is trust in man to discern what is what. It is a religion.

We would be wise to remember that proof does not create faith, but faith seeks out evidences and builds its correlating institutions. Every worldview is a faith through which we seek supports and rationalizations.

Laying supine beneath the scientific method is a body of assumptions, a hidden faith, an entrustment of one's self to the order of physics and the naturalistic realm. The Gospel of God rests and runs upon the risen body of Christ—upon entrustment of ourselves to the One who established and sustains the created order in which science functions. What is the point? Everyone has a faith, a worldview, a set of assumptions by which they live by. The materialist, the naturalist, the atheist—they are not without a faith.

67. We must learn that the conflict of worldviews is not religion against reason, not faith against science. Such false dichotomies come straight from the bias and desires of the heart—they come from the heart of man in rage against the truth. The true naming of this conflict is faith vs. faith, belief against belief.

The fundamental clash of existence is a clash of trust. It is between the reasonableness of one faith vs. the reasonableness of another faith. There are two options: faith in God or faith in man. One is the Gospel; the other the fountainhead of all idolatry. And from idolatry (the trust in man) spring two polluted streams that have baptized all history in bad waters: overt religion and covert religion. The *overt religious* are obviously the religious—the *covert religious* are the irreligious such as the atheist, agnostic, etc. They are both the flailing motions of idolatry, both self deceived, and both unwilling to recognize that they are both founded upon ill assumptions and the pride of man.

68. There is either the Gospel of God, or humanism. Humanism (the idolatry of man) constructs all the various attempts at usurping God's throne. The two trees of paradise presented the only fundamental worldviews—to worship man, or to worship God. The Tree of Life is the worship of the creature to the Creator; the tree of the knowledge of good and evil is the arbor of humanism—the creature becoming the measure of all things—the creature taking on the role of the Creator and worshipping himself.

Did Jesus come to show the atheist that there was indeed a God? No—He came to show religious man who the true God was. He came to save man from the tyrant-god of man. He came to dismantle idolatry, and clothe them in the true God—Himself.

69. *We, the Prophets*

We, the prophets without gods, have found the way
To speak from the dirt, biting our tongues in two,
Divorcing all that we feel straps us to dust;
We prophesy a line, a divide, to break
You, a hard God who would bind our pulse to you,
And a heart to the mind to form a trust
Amidst the synapse of a ne'r ending word,
That before history's spiral home was heard.

We, the forms of logic, who tear at our chests
Because you would have them hold us in one piece;
We, the angry, bound to reason our reason
Into illusions of order-less tests
To rend good from good to find our own need
To be the makers of unfruitful seasons—
Though we still must set in form our hate of you—
Your love of order, though rebuked, runs us through.

And by dry rivers we dream of ways to say,
"These banks of our design are dry, but some day,

Some day we will taste nectar to brag and prove
That we could be more than this dust without you;

We can devour ourselves with divine lust
Rather than be spent like a seed in your trust."

And by dry rivers we dream of ways to rest
On banks dried by our fashioned treasons called tests

To show the sky empty—look, no rains release
To fill our streams—*We* must be the water Kings!

We must be the ones who move on, who trod on,
And divide the heart from the mind that needs—God!"

70. The world generally thinks religion is a searching after God—the Bible reveals that religion is a search for life apart from God. But this sounds upside down!—yes it does.

Many believe that throughout history religion was thinned out and watered down; that somewhere in humanity's long and distant past there were originally many tribal and primitive gods, and eventually they eroded away and melded into one hodge-podge god. Therefore, they believe that monotheism is a weak great-great-bastard-grandchild of strong and rich ancient religions. This is wrong. The truth is the exact opposite.

The truth is that polytheism and the various gods of world religions are a deforming and partitioning of the one true God. Humanity did not reduce the truth down to one God; rather, we tried to chop the one God into tiny controllable pieces, like building blocks we could manipulate; like toy blocks we could assemble and disassemble at will.

Pride could not deal with the God who was over both wave and flame, so we had to fashion smaller separate gods for each element. Soon the gods were small enough to fit into our pockets and set upon our dashboards.

Devolution didn't create Judeo-Christianity. Entropy and human sin created *religions* by attempting to tear the unifying truth apart.

We—humanity—created religions because we have found it offending to worship the true God. We found it offending that we were not God. This is frustrating to us; we want to be God. We want to speak oceans and animals into existence. We want to set the horizon on fire with the snap of our fingers and enjoy the day we have made. We want to bend light with our words; we want the ocean tides to be dependent upon our moods. So we justified and substituted. We did this because we were fallen. This is why every people group across the earth has religion; we are *homo-religioso*! We all have within us the same impulse of Adam and Eve—the impulse to justify ourselves.

What was the ancient temptation? What was the garden deception? That they too could be as gods—they could be their own origin. All religion is a dressing of this temptation; the Gospel the only remedy. All religions live and breathe out of the knowledge of good and evil. All who hang upon this tree are cursed.

71. Many people have argued that Christianity is some kind of wish fulfillment, like a perfect invisible friend for a lonely child, a mere coping device. They argue that believers simply invented a God that they wanted. It is all fancy hope, an opiate for the masses, magical thinking, a happy delusion, etc. This is a foolish argument against the reality of God. This argument itself is magical thinking that abandons reason!

Here is why it is foolish: Because the God of the Bible is someone that we would not invent. He is too difficult to understand; too holy; too strange and noncompliant to our own desires. He is not a cosmic, stalking butler. He is too wholly different than us. He is too cryptic, too revealing, too graceful, and too bold. He is too much of a servant, too much of a bleeding heart, too much of a lover, and He is far too just. He is deserving of all worship, and He doesn't worship us. The fact is that He just doesn't look like us—or what we want.

God is no opiate, but a consuming fire that awakens our humanity! He is what sends nerves sparking and arcing light; He breaks the ice-shelf of the mind, exposing fertile fields of reason.

If we invented the God of the Bible, then why are we always trying to reinvent the God of the Bible into something more acceptable. Would we devise what doesn't please us?

What then would we invent? A world where we (in all our great glory) are the culmination of all natural processes, the very apex of time and matter. A world where we are gods and goddesses with no divine being above us to arbiter our disputes—no authority above us to rule or call out our faults. A world where we are not eternally held accountable for the things we do in our brief mortal life. A world in which right and wrong are merely reflections of the latest poll—where morality is dependent upon popularity and *zeitgeist*. A world in which pleasure is king and tolerance is the beloved court jester constantly tripping over himself. A world in which our power to will is sovereign—where power and brute force rule. A world where survival of the fittest is the *greatest commandment*. A world in which good news is foolishness because we are backwards and don't recognize wisdom. A world in which there is a rampant insanity that says, *"There is no God, but there is love. We are the products of blind evolution, yet human life has more worth than a pond amoeba."* A world blind to its contradictions. A world where reason collapses in upon itself because there is no heart of truth.

Let it be strongly noted that many people often do invent versions of Jesus, variations of God to be used as a happy delusion, a smiling shield from the truth. I do not deny this; the Bible in fact teaches this and it is common. The real Jesus of the Bible is not wanted, and so He is not invented. The real Jesus is constantly re-written, edited, and replaced by a lackluster god that chuckles, smiles vacantly like an idiot, and then looks away from our perversions and selfishness. Jesus is no Pillsbury-Dough-Christ who giggles at our indulgences.

I have learned a very important term: *practical atheist*. A practical atheist is someone who says they believe in God, but in all action, in practicality, they live as if there is no God. How this term has not become a buzzword, I do not know. Maybe it cuts too close to the bone…

Many professed *Christians* are merely practical atheists.

72. The God of the Bible is no man-made God. Rather than being ran to, we have run from this true sovereign God and made many easy gods instead. We have substituted some other *god* in God's

place. We have traded the ultimate affection for a lesser one. This is what the Bible calls idolatry.

We should learn that idolatry is more than a proverbial *pagan* kneeling or chanting to a carved piece of stone or wood. That is an easy out and quick dismissal. It is some *uncivilized chap* in some technologically malnourished country, we think. And surely, that is not us (because we are *civilized* right?)—so we like that definition for it has a distancing, a buffering effect to it. The truth is that most likely the *uncivilized chap* has more of an authentic communion with God than those of us who believe we are not religious, who lean on our technology, and haven't learned divine dependence. Could this be?

We hate God; that is why there are idols.

Rather than a few sacred stones or a village totem, our idols are manifold, many, multitudinous, and multiplying. Idolatry is a poison that can be poured into any straight or curved shaker, glass, or fancy flask. I looked, and I found idolatry in the shape of paper money, pointy white picket fences and bloated houses with unused rooms, super-juggernaut-mega-churches and small parishes, numbers (big and small), asceticism, hedonism, scholarships, careers, titles, music, muscled bodies. I looked again and found idolatry in the contour of television, the blur of the light field, tradition, politics, friends, lovers, and versions of Jesus—versions of Jesus probably being the most toxic. Where did I look—in my heart.

Idolatry is reality upside down, thinking it is right-side up. It is deception deciding what is true.

73. No one can claim ignorance of the knowledge of the Creator God. The problem is not in knowing, it is in inclination. The problem lies in the calibration of our moral compass. We believe we are walking north when we are really walking southeast into the wasteland of ourselves.

We are born with a dark magnet that stutters and disorients our moral compass. This heavy magnet is our sinful essence. (Yes, even newborns have this crooked compass; they just haven't started to walk yet. But it is a short time before they start to pronounce their judgment upon the world.)

We enjoy darkness. We enjoy when others join us in darkness. In the darkness we believe that we are basically good, that there is nothing wrong; we believe that when someone speaks of sin or repentance they are just an ugly person who is jealous of the beautiful party goers. In the darkness it is easy to pretend to be anything we like; in the light we are unable to pretend—we are exposed.

74. A very religious person once asked me if I had ever seen a newborn. I said yes. He said he believed we were good by nature because "newborns glow." If I could have that conversation back I would remind him that before he arrived at the hospital the serene and glowing newborn had been slathered in blood and placenta, and was crying with a high pitch. I would remind him that soon the baby would be a toddler, beautiful and full of worth, but selfish to boot and lying about who had colored the walls with crayons or who broke mommy's porcelain vase. I would remind him that we call them the terrible two's, not terrific two's. I would remind him that no one has to teach a child to lie, cheat, and blame. These things just bubble up from somewhere within. It is not because the child is demonic or something ridiculous like this—no, it is simply because the human heart is rebellious from the start. Please read Psalm 51 in its entirety; then read the book of Romans.

I do not deny that newborns glow—I have seen them glow, they have filled me with wonder and I have cried. I am amazed by their fresh eyes and delicate toes. I am sure God smiles and a chorus of angels sings when a woman gives birth to a baby created in the image of God; a child that God has made with a purpose. I am all for babies. I am all for marriage and raising families.

What I do have a concern with is the judging of internals by externals. "Newborns glow" are just pretty words that allow us to keep tight our pride and hide the raw necessity of the Savior. It is a loaded appeal to emotion. We couple *goodness* with *babies* in hopes that no jerk would call a sweet baby bad, and then we could declare that we are good. What misdirection!

A baby's *glow* does not mean that the human heart they have is not inclined towards rebellion. Their *glow* does not mean we are good people on our own right. Cigarette butts glow, but I would not call them intrinsically good. We must look deeper than glowing surfaces. And no, babies are not like cigarette butts; they are image bearers of God full of worth and dignity, loved and cared for—but they are not innocent. Let me explain.

This may sound as though I believe children to be nothing more the tiny-bodied monsters until they recite some churchy incantation—this is wrong, very wrong. Children are born innocent in that they have not volitionally sinned. But children are born with an inclination in the will to sin. We all have a natural bent to choose selfishly and un-lovingly; it is the genome we have been passed, it is the race we have been born into—and so, inevitably we do wrong, and in short order! Inevitably, by our will's nature, we desire to sin and we do so, and fall short of what we were purposed to be.

Every person is not a born murderer of mankind; but every person is a born murderer of God—for everyone will attempt to dethrone God. Our worship is askew even from the womb. We have *all* sinned and fallen short of the glory of God. If this sounds offensive to you then grace cannot be good news. But, and you must remember, we are loved by God. Don't divorce our guilt from God's love and leave man hopeless, meandering in the dark—for it is love that metes out justice and freely offers mercy.

Ah, but wait—if one is a murderer of God, then are they not a murderer of true humanity?

75. Though we have this natural prejudice, it does not mean that we don't do *good things* as I mentioned before. This is a good place to speak again of such things. We all know children, teenagers, and adults do *good* things. But for the most part these *good* things are done without any thought of God, without any reverence to His goodness. When this is the case, a good is done, but reality is not served because the glory is not given to God—and more so, it is directly averted from Him unto man. Man no longer is the steward of good, but the supposed source.

In reality, we eviscerate any good that we believe comes from our own self—because it then is an act of *good* that comes from idolatry rather than the true God, and in man's misdirection and misappropriation, what makes the good intrinsically good is stripped away. So the momentary act of "the good" is externally good if others benefit (or it leads us closer to the revelation of Christ), yet the internal motivation of "the good" is judged by its relation of dependence upon reality.

We must refrain from proclaiming that Christians alone are those who do what we call good acts and that those who aren't Christians don't do good acts. This is a false delineation; this is sheer religious folly, and the everyday evidence exposes it as a lie.

Christianity is not about "making bad men good and making good men better"—such is the ideology of all other religions, for their seed and core is that man is basically good and capable of such improvements. Christianity is of the peculiar movement of bringing dead men to life. This is why all other religions are faulty—you cannot make a dead man better; he must be made alive. What does a better dead man look like—more masterful in laying supine, maybe smiling coldly but with no warmth of heart?

Only God, by Jesus Christ, through the Holy Spirit makes the dead the living. How is one made alive—by being united to its life source, its true origin. Religion is fuddling around with man's self-origin—dressing up a corpse and posing cold limbs; the Gospel is bowing to the true Creator in the warmth of living.

76. Recently, I was speaking with a man wearing a tie and neatly combed hair. He looked at me very piously, very intensely. He was, no doubt, zealous. He said that he believed there was a flaw in Christianity—he called it the Pacific Islander Syndrome. He said that if God really loved people, how could He let the poor Pacific Islanders die without knowing Him (without missionaries taking the Bible to them)? This man claimed the religion he was representing wisely corrected this oversight in the Bible by allowing the living to perform a saving rite for the dead. He was very happy with his observation (an observation that made him decide to leave his unpleasantly strict protestant upbringing). He smiled at me with his hands folded, feeling very pleased that he had just debunked all of Christianity in my apartment living room. I sat thoughtful for a second, read a portion from the first chapter of the Letter of Romans to him. He *hmmm'ed* and said "I never thought about that. I don't remember reading that." He smiled and changed the subject without blinking his smile.

Many people think that humanity cannot be held accountable to God because they have never been introduced to Him in a formulaic religious manner. *Cue choir music; enter appropriately dressed clergy; now*—*So-and-so, meet God. Hello God; nice to meet you. I guess I'm accountable now.* This is silly. We believe all sorts of stupid things and this is one of them. People meet God everyday—they just snub Him because they don't like Him. Snubbing often means overlooking unconsciously because of a hard heart, a dark heart that covers the mind's eye.

When our worldview is on the line, we will do whatever it takes to not lose all that we know; even if what we believe is internally incoherent and doesn't correlate to reality. And so, in the face of truth, pride will multiply and double-coat its lies, packing on its heavy, crushing armor. There is nothing more devastating to the human being than realizing your world view is wrong.
To those upside-down, pride has a stronger gravity than truth—it is like a black hole that won't let truth beyond its event horizon—and it takes a miracle to turn its black vacuum into a light-bearing star.

The Gospel is the ultimate threat to the self-addicted man.

Repentance is when your whole world no longer stands on its head, but upon its feet, and you realize those feet were made for walking the earth, not kicking the stars out of their sockets in space.

77. One should read the first three chapters of Romans. They are more *realistic* than the ten o' clock news and are filled with more tragedy and epic romance than any violent and popular movie. They will stand the test of time and outlast *Beowulf* and *The Odyssey*. One should try reading Romans 1:18 over and over again until the density of the words sink in. They are thick like black molasses. In fact, they are too rich to eat alone, so read the entire chapter. Read the whole nourishing book. Replay these words like your favorite scene in a movie or chorus in a song that haunts you for some unknown reason. It should haunt us. It is us. These chapters are a divine exposé of human nature, and for that, they are an exposé of religion.

~Heart Reasonings~

78. Human reason will only be rescued by the God trusting Heart; the heart of man is rescued only by the God who authored reason.

We have been given the gift of reason. Humanity can reason *and* reason correctly. Yet prejudice must be removed in order to reason in accordance with truth. Good reason on a twisted premise will result in a greater twisting of the truth. Think of the progression of prejudiced reason as a shadow added to a shadow—they layer each other for a deeper darkness, though each shadow comes from a light source.

Next time you are on a tennis or basketball court at night, look at your shadow(s). The four (or many) lights above the court cast shadows in different directions. Where the shadows meet, they grow darker.

Is light what makes a shadow—no, it is a disturbance, an *obstinance* that makes for the blocking of light. We have made our selves opaque in pride, and the casters of shadows.

Correct reasoning on a faulty premise is like construction on a leaning foundation; the taller the building becomes the more obvious and more dangerous the slant. The foundation's flaw will serve to topple the top. The higher the faulty tower reaches for heaven, the more obvious that it is a silly structure that will topple, and end up buried in the ground.

This means that logic built on the premise *there is no God* will inevitably be found twisted and faulty; it will expose itself in incoherency. Logic built on the premise *there is a God and He is the God of the Bible* will be sound and consistent the further it is taken.

We can argue logically from faulty footing. But though we argue logically, the end will be widely warped because the beginning was warped. My Father has been in construction all his life. He knows that you must start a building project with a strong and level foundation. This is obvious wisdom—it needs to be said though. It seems an enjoyable hobby for most people is to build a wild mansion on uneven sand, and then wonder why it soon becomes a mobile home.

Jesus was a carpenter; He knew about building foundations. He recommended stone over sand, but we prefer the beach life to a life of sacrifice. Jesus is the bedrock that one is to build upon; the cornerstone and the keystone.

Man is dust—no high-rise was ever built on a foundation of dust—no lean-to would stand staked to dust! Yet we build churches upon the foundation of men! No wonder the fracture!

79. The Bible says *"the fool says there is no God."* I believe this. I believe there is a God. Not because I have been guilted into it so I don't feel the fool, but because there is a powerful web of reasons that lead me to believe there is such a thing as sin and there is a wide wonderful universe that the wicked web is spun in. If there was a myriad of reasons to believe that we are fallen, there are a million myriads of reasons to believe there is a beautiful God we have fallen from. For every inch of dark shadow there is an acre of white light. To the shadows' chagrin, the shadows *and* the light both bear witness of God.

There is a good and personal God. There are many reasons why I believe this. One of the reasons I believe this is that I live in Colorado. I live on a fertile and golden plain at the foot of the Rocky Mountains. Every day I am confronted by impressive stone monoliths; they make me feel both painfully small and yet strangely significant. The weather here is moody but beautiful. On most summer nights I see the constellation Orion and his hunting companion (Sirius, the Dog Star) vaulting over the mountain range in the mysterious playfulness of the cosmos. There is a brilliant and spiraling order in nature. There are patterns in aspen leaves and sticky heads of wheat. There is an inescapable symmetry that laughs at chaos. I find new colors in my bride's eyes—like emeralds in the sun, they show me the magic and science of light.

I believe science and reason can show us truth—so I believe there is *a* truth, an authoritative truth. I see dignity in human life. I believe two plus two makes four, not five, no matter who you ask, when or where. It is said that order shows intelligence, and intelligence and order show design. I believe this—for it is far more reasonable than saying that information and its complex order means nothing. Yet, I also believe there is a benevolent and personal Creator for reasons that are much more mystical.

There is something haunting in the fall of cold Colorado rain that stings the fingers, but raises the soul within to fight an epic fight. Something in the rain and in the autumn speaks of lost perfection, of beauty rusted and pierced through by time. There is something supernal in the buzzing blue sky of summer that often frustrates into thick thunderheads. There is something miraculous in the taste of sweet corn after a bite of sharply acidic red tomato; something wonderful in the way August bleeds to September with a subtle chill—the leaves becoming more passionate as they give up the ghost in a falling flame. These are romantic thoughts, I know—and that brings me to another reason. The fact that there is true, epic love—not shallow silicon movie romance—is another reason I believe in God. There are perfections, ideals, and hungers that remain unfulfilled in our current human state—these un-sated longings point me to God. The infinite abyss in my heart points me to an infinite and personal God.

Then there are the cinematic islands of the Caribbean; the choppy waves on the California coast; the untamed miles of Florida everglades; the earth like a checkerboard of wheat, barley, and alfalfa fields when seen from a small airplane window; the black sands of the Mediterranean; the genius of humanity sprawling across the floors, walls, and ceilings of the Sistine Chapel, and across the Louvre; the sheer existence of melody and song. There is the way my human body could malfunction in a trillion different ways—nerves misfiring, runaway cells duplicating, enzymes missing, blood clots horribly forming, RNA failing—yet my body holds together day to day. The existence of hope, faith, and love. Love. Love could not exist if I were random atoms, if you were haphazard bio material. If there is no meaning, then there is no love.

All these things add up within me; a very distinct portrait is painted. And if I were to walk along a hallway and see a portrait on canvas and say, "what a random mix of oil markings!" then I would not be a person guided by reason, but only by a biased heart.

A God-disavowing cynic was even prompted to ask, "Why is there something rather than nothing?" Not only is there something—but something wonderful.

80. One can speculate how the heart is changed. We can talk ourselves every shade of blue in trying to pinpoint just when and how a heart is turned towards God and can now see the wonderful. Some will wake up one ordinary morning not believing Jesus is the Son of God, and that evening fall asleep as a redeemed disciple of Christ, believing in the incarnation, crucifixion, resurrection, and ascension of Jesus. Someone will go to the store to buy a bag of carrots as an atheist, and come home a follower of Jesus. Just how the heart is changed is a mystery; *who* changes the heart is not.

When and how the wind blows, how it seems to annoy one person and how it seems to comfort another is never fully known. But who moves the wind—that is no mystery ever since the breath of Jesus altered the air of this world.

And so, I can give a long list or wide web of reasons why I suppose I have faith in Jesus as my Lord and Savior, but I cannot ever really know just what turned me from a pseudo-follower into an enamored follower of Jesus Christ. Some can pinpoint the exact moment, some cannot—but the definite *why* is elusive. It is elusive, save that God did it; save that it was appointed before the foundations of the earth were laid.

Why do some people get rocked off donkeys and supernaturally blinded? Why do some come to faith while traveling to the zoo in a side-car? Why do some go to the sea side to catch a fish only to find out they have landed the calling to feed the Shepherd's sheep? Why do some people go to work humanists and come home humbled by the God of the universe? Why do some hearts remain as marble? I don't know. But I do know this: salvation is a good thing.

Do all good things come from God? Yes, all good things come from God. Salvation is surely a good thing, the best of things. Salvation, then, is of the Lord.

I would not say that I have found God, but that I have been found. Like an unconscious castaway, too weak to move or yell, I have woken up to find that I have been found.

81. It is said that many *fall away* from the church because they are disillusioned. This seems sadly ironic to me. It is the church that should spread the news of dis-illusionment; it is the Gospel's holy aim to shatter illusions (to dis-illusion) and reveal the truth of our origin and purpose.

The reason for such pervasive disillusionment is not God's failure to meet His promises, but our failure to understand what He has promised us. We have traded true treasure for inferior versions; we have swapped waterfalls for gutter puddles, jewels for children's plastic-glass jewelry.

God promises joy—we seek the lowest common denominator of happiness. God promises peace—we chase ease and comfort. God promises His presence—we call for cheap presents. We are like children offered a first-class feast, and we only want our familiar fast food. We desire a party with a room full of kids we barely know rather than an intimate room with our true lover. We desire neon over natural light—but the hum and buzz will eventually drive us crazy.

We are so upside down that when we think we are looking high at the noon sun, we are only staring at a second rate glare on the ground.

82. Often people ask for *a* single reason to believe in God. This seems narrow (and is only meant to divide, not unite). It is like asking for proof of your own existence. It is many things: my arms, my legs, my eyes, my thoughts, my relations, my history, my presence, my actions, etc. Evidence is in the multiplicity—not the one simple item. This is another diversion of the deceiver: *give me one proof*. By asking for one proof he pits all the proofs in a battle against each other. Instead of adding up to one great volley of evidence, they subtract to a small reductive claim that can be easily tossed aside with an ill twist of logic or verbal gymnastics. You can hide a small pebble away, but you cannot ignore the grandeur of the mountains running north to south and piercing the western sky. The deceiver knows this, so he tries to grind mountains of truth into small disposable pebbles—and we are more than willing to pull out our sledge hammers.

Collapsed man does what his father does. Satan divides and tears, so too does man who has listened to the words of the deceiver: "you will be like God."

Give me one side of a diamond—and I will give you no diamond.

If asked for proof of the existence of this book, which *one* word would you use? Or would you use the whole text? Could one word be used for proof?

Why do we desire to dissect the Creator? Our want to reduce God into a simple statement, an easy definition, a verbal box, is not because we want to discover Him—no! But because we rather that He die; that He be put under pins and scalpels and then thrown away.

We must understand that if we can understand God, then we have put Him beneath our gaze. If we cannot understand Him, He is beyond our control. We want to control God, so we seek to understand Him. The higher always dissects the lower; no cat or frog has ever dissected a man. Never has a cadaver dissected a living man.

Trying to prove God with *one simple thing* is like dissecting the frog to find its small, defined center of life. The deeper you go, the *deader* the frog gets and the life is lost, not to be found.

The creation all around us is great, overwhelming, beautiful and powerful. The Creator need be greater.

If a Pacific Islander does not believe there is a Creator God, it is not because another person didn't tell them that there was one; it is because the islander refused to acknowledge the power, abundance, and beauty of the ocean, or the brilliance of the stars hung over the island canopies. It is because he refuses the testimony of nature and he shuns the light of his conscious. It is because he prefers to be alone in the universe rather than be under a Creator God; because he prefers to be alone under an uncaring sky on a beautiful beach—a meaningless beautiful beach. It is because the desires of his heart do not desire God.

83. We so easily forget the world is a miracle. We sigh in awe over cheap illusions—at white tigers disappearing, incantations over mirrors, and the crimson sweep of a loaded cape. We must learn that a miracle is not a parlor trick.

Miracles are not for amusement. They are signs—or as the Book of John calls them: semeia. This is an important distinction. A sign is for direction—not distraction as we so often hope and think!

A sign is for aiding one in travel—not for camping under, and then building a home in its shade.

We think of water turning to wine and wish we had just a small sample of that wine left in a vial—then we would have proof of a bona fide miracle! Then, yes, we could believe! But we forget that there is a greater vial to be seen—call it the ocean. We swim in the ocean yet we forget God! What wet fools we are! We forget that God created the earth by His word. We forget that we wander through a miracle daily—earth speeding through space at 66,000 miles per hour (much faster than a speeding bullet), all the while oak leaves move lazily on nervy branches, we walk and run about expertly on soft sod and red dirt, and the river waters pour themselves patiently into the Atlantic as libations to God. We clap over a card trick yet we tromp about ignoring the blatant miracle of our existence in the world!

84. It is strange—we have a tendency to either be completely blind to the artistry of nature, or we see it as a god and worship it. We suffer from the *amnesia of the steward*. We are under the delusion that we either own it all, or have no responsibility at all—but we can't recall the truth.

How often have we cast aside our stewardship of nature in fear of finding ourselves in bed with Mother Earth and her New Age patrons? Is it not possible to see natural creation as a *sister* who needs our care, and not as a seducing goddess? Nature is not a cunning devil, but a wounded sibling. The deepest of forests is not a great snare waiting to devour the traveler, but a garden of God weeping to be redeemed. The dark winter sea is not a fiend—rather, a friend lost within its own bewildered waves. The desert is no dry demon—it is our dehydrated *sister*. Nature is wounded, and with each natural disaster the groan grows louder, wilder with each storm, like a woman's last cries before the release of birth.

If we are reluctant to hear the incessant cries of nature and continue to deny our responsibility of stewardship, not only will God's creation suffer, but so will we. Nature is pregnant with wisdom and God's glory—the wise men and women of God have always found lessons in its mannerisms and movements.

There is much we should learn from nature: Nature teaches us to mourn when the leaves are drained of burgundy and begin to wither; nature teaches us to celebrate amidst the bursting white plumes of spring; nature teaches us to dance by the brilliance of sun-glimmers on water; nature shows us faithfulness in the cycles of the moon; nature tutors us in mirth when a riot of gold breaks through a heavy black sky; nature offers us humility in the labors of the vegetable garden; nature reminds us of our helplessness as we stand in a January wind.

Yet, nature has never taught us to worship *itself*—nature, with every daffodil and wise blade of grass has always pointed towards its Creator, and has always despised the idols made from its rich storehouse. Its fire has always consumed the golden icons, always turned ashes from the wooden goddesses. Its wind and sand have always defaced the monuments of tyrants, always beaten against wicked temples. Its great waters have always swallowed the sordid silver and corroded the egoist's coins. Its strength has always shaken pagan shrines to pieces and ruined proud city gates. Nature abhors idolatry—for its very rocks cry out for the worship of the King.

85. I use to hate the wind; it reminded me I was not in control. I would fight it only to lose to its infinite unseen hands. It battered me sweetly with the reality of being a creation of God; I could not control the wind.

When one embraces the wind, what was once annoying becomes heroic; the frustrating bluster now becomes the wise wind that carries the seeds of life. The wind that chapped your skin, messed your hair, or blew dust in your eye is also the wind that carried the germ of the garden flower and the iron redwood tree. The wind has brought fragrance and shade, fruit and beauty. The lesson of the wind is freeing: We are the created.

We are not in control—though religion would have us believe otherwise. For this reason, the Gospel is set against religion. The wind of the Spirit blows against man for the love of man.

~And Trembling...~

86. There is joy in trembling. Like the shimmering burn of sunlight on a moving lake, true joy lives only amidst trembling. Joy can only exist if there is a standard that we are to be in unison with—but since there is a standard, there is also trembling.

Joy is the radiance born in being who we were meant to be. Joy is the harmony that resounds from trust corresponding to reality.

To say there is a standard is to say there is a reality. Trembling is for those who do not live in a fantasy realm, but who live in the world that is real and metes out joys and justice.

The reality of God should make us tremble in the bones *and* burst out with peals of silvery laughter. There is a tension in Christianity of trembling *and* confidence. These two must be held together...but again, we are incapable.

87. Holiness and happiness are not opposite poles as commonly portrayed; they are not an argument. This is another either/or lie of judgment that is used to divide the Kingdom of God.

True happiness only lives within the bounds of holiness. Happiness is a fragrance of holiness; it arises from a life of Godly obedience. Holiness is not a rigid face that has mastered the scowl; holiness is a grateful countenance that is ever learning how to smile genuinely and how to cry in trust.

The world spins and changes definitions. Changing definitions is a subtle attempt to undermine truth; it is a tactic of confusion and creeping compromise. It is a normalization of a deception. The word goblins have rewritten the dictionary entry for *holy*. In crooked handwriting it reads: **holy** – 1. constrictive; joy killing; waste of time. 2. self-righteous; oppressive; a church-clone. 3. a droning noise of un-creativity; stifling; the opposite of *cool* or *hip*; the death of cool.

88. The reason such *definition distortions* are adopted so easily is that we often do not think for ourselves because we fear freedom—and we have this overwhelming tendency to avoid annihilation. The first reason speaks largely for itself (though I will still comment). The second reason seems odd (and obvious) at first, and may need some backing, so I will speak to it as well.

Does humanity fear freedom? Many philosophers have believed man to fear his freedom of choice; isn't this odd? Why would one fear freedom? We fear only because there are real consequences—and there are only consequences if there is an *ought to* about the universe. One fears only because there is a right and a wrong. One trembles because there exists a *great good*.

To have freedom we must also have a standard.

The first thing man does when he understands that he is free is to hurriedly seek out a surrogate self, and to then hand over his freedom. Man cannot bear the weight of his own freedom because he is fractured, his soul is not sound. Man fears true volition, true moral responsibility, because he deeply knows he will abuse it.

We often do not *think* for ourselves simply because if someone chooses for us, somewhere in our labyrinthine psyche we hope *they* will be held responsible, and we can pass the buck if something goes wrong. (Yet we would most assuredly take the credit if all goes well.) We fear freedom so we let others choose for us. But this is a choice in itself. We will be held responsible.

Jesus makes us aware of our responsibility to choose, and our inability to not choose. There is no passing the buck when we face the loving and just God. We resent Jesus for making us aware of our inescapable choice between the trembling of joy and the gnashing of teeth.

Trusting is volitional, and choice is where heart and mind kiss.

89. We fear the Holy Spirit because He is the wind that melts our therapeutic ice and blows the seeds of truth that will break stubborn ground. With the human soul, it is as Eliot said in the poem *The Wasteland*: "April is the cruelest month, breeding lilacs out of the dead land, mixing memory and desire, stirring dull roots with spring rain." Spring is beautiful, but bears a painful thawing and plowing

We fear annihilation. We run from *the holy* because *the holy* makes us see ourselves as "the created." In the light we are cracked creatures; in the dark we can imagine ourselves as golden gods.

Being created makes us less than the Creator—remember, the Creator need be greater. In the presence of the holy we are found wanting, unworthy. This, no doubt, is threatening to us, and in a sense it is annihilating. It is a shattering of the ego; it is a dismantling of self-righteousness. Yet God does not leave us annihilated—He creates us anew. God does not melt our ice to evaporate us, but to release a pure-water spring. And so, in the light, we are also found to be loved and redeemed as well as undone.

Who is the man who loves a seed? One who hides it away in a locked box, or one who sacrifices it to the soil?

Could a gold-plated seed grow and produce fruit? To gild what is living shows not sacrificial love, but a murderous heart. Religion gilds, but the Gospel breaks open the heart's shell to live.

It is not our *self* that is annihilated, but rather, it is our sense of self-reliance, our moralism, our sense of being judge, and our synthetic spirituality that is devastated. Holiness is what redeems us, not what destroys us. God does not smother or destroy our personhood or unique humanity—He unshackles it from its self-destruction so it can expand.

When our self-esteem is blasted and then restored in the glow of holiness, only then we are released to be our authentic personality;

and that is a unique bearer of God's image. Insane is the man who thinks light will make all look the same. It is in darkness that all looks alike.

The seed must be buried to live. Baptism symbolically speaks of holiness: it is the double-stroke of death by perfection and rebirth by grace.

90. We must return to the true definition of *holy*. In burnished handwriting it reads: "**holy** – 1. set apart; different in a most perfect way; beautifully uncommon; the other. 2. an awesome mystery; awe-fullness; ultimate beauty; to die for. 3. right-side-up; transcendent; towards our origin; our intended state; 4. the adopted ones of God."

In the Scriptures, whenever we read of someone amidst the presence of the Holy One, they were overwhelmed, amazed, full of dread, and a heaviness of unworthiness overcame them like a thick winter coat. It overtook them like a dense coastal fog. These were people prostrate on the ground in sudden and dire humility; not people standing tall, casually smiling at God with their hands raised as if they were at a sporting event.

In the presence of God lips quiver and stomachs tremble like pudding; man is aware of his sin; man is overwhelmed by the radiance of perfection and fears annihilation of himself—as he would be if he were to stand three feet from the surface of the sun. God created the sun; His radiance would vaporize even the fiery engine of the sun if He willed it.

When we raise our hands in worship, may it be to show that we have empty hands with nothing to give to God but what He already gave, and not that we are giving Him some special gift originating from ourselves. All our positions of prayer and praise should show our dependence upon God; whether it is open hands or folded knees. Prayer is deliberately living in dependence upon God.

91. With Christ as our savior, our trembling is not the anxious fear of unraveling or being obliterated, but a tremble of mounting joy and gratitude. In Christ, fear and confidence meet—and they bear joy.

Like the adrenaline shakes from an escaped collision, joy is the tremble of the soul who has seen its death but found redemption instead.

Joy is not some gift that is suddenly unwrapped when we physically die. It is not a posthumous present, but a present portion of coming glory; a down deposit of heaven's unfathomable King. It is not held from us until our breath leaves us. Joy comes when Christ comes—at the dawn of our living.

The tremble of joy comes in our death throes—the death of our old nature, and the rising of our new humanity under the authority of Christ. There is a good reason why the Gospel is called the Gospel; it is good news! God is the God of the living! Only the living tremble.

Jesus was a man of sorrows. We must not fall prey to our own narcissism and believe that being a Christian is all about our ease, or wipes all sorrow completely from our lives. Joy and sorrow can and do live together; if they don't, than neither one is truly itself.

Joy *and* sorrow—these two are twin pillars in the Christian's heart. The temple of the human heart cannot live with only one standing. One who doesn't acknowledge reality's sorrow does not know of God's holiness and humanity's dark debt; one who doesn't acknowledge reality's joy does not know God's perfect mercy.

In the Christian's heart gratitude and sorrow burn side by side at their full capacity: Sorrow for the stubborn world that rejects *true origin*; gratitude for the love of God that loved the unlovable to make them the living.

92. Beware Christiandumb! What we often call Christendom is merely a religious instrument of the world; a *kingdom of man* defined by worldly rules of success and power; its face is set hard against the Sovereign God.

Yes, I mean *Christiandumb* not *Christendumb*—for we have already christened (accepted and inaugurated) what is dumb; and now the kingdom of Christiandumb is thriving like an infection.

Christiandumb is full of affluent ascetics—parodies. They have taken vows of silence, and for their vows will not speak truth, will not preach the Gospel. Mute witnesses? Mute martyrs! Hah!

The problem with Christiandumb is it has successfully improved upon true Christianity! *Improved* Christianity?!

Christiandumb is the kingdom of man that fears the evanescent opinions of men, rather than the eternal omniscience of God.

Christiandumb is the kingdom that shies away from offense—even at the expense of truth. It is the kingdom of moralism that converts evangelism into the process of widening Heaven's gate rather than simply pointing towards the narrow gate that must be entered one at a time.

Christiandumb lumps everything into a mass; it destroys community for the sake of the crowd. Yes, our journey is *en masse* (together), but our entrance is intimate.

Christiandumb rules with a heavy scepter; the Christian Church rules by a crushed reed. One's power is in its affluence—the other's in its impotence. God rules with the ultimate scepter, for so powerful is He that he could rule by being a crushed reed.

Christiandumb is the kingdom of men who praise God as if it were their due—and with such zealousy they stand so *worthy*! They stand and say, "love, love, love"—but how can they know love if they know not of fear?

Perfect love casts out fear—perfect love is to fear the Lord, to obey the King.

Many are casualties of casual belief. Casual belief is an opiate for the masses, this is true —yet Christianity is not laudanum! Christianity is smelling salts. It is electric shock to a flat-lined heart. And so holiness is not a religious malaise, but a blazing fire; it is lightning that charges the static atmosphere of our soul with the electricity of life.

93. My father has often said that people "do not know the fear of God." I believe he is correct. This fear is not the kind of fear that causes someone to run in anxiety (for many do this in response to God)—but a fear that causes one to suddenly bow and be silent in the presence of a magnetic fire. It is reverence. It is silence that erupts in praise. It is a hard cadence that bursts with a sweet harmony. It is a silent epiphany and then a loud and celebratory doxology.

Let us not blunt it though—the fear of the Lord is fear that we may displease Him, fear that His perfection might fall even lightly upon us, and crush us like an empty and ancient cocoon.

Holiness is overwhelming, frightening, and attractive. Holiness is the intimate kissing of fear and fascination. It is what we peek at through spread fingers. It is terribly beautiful *and* good. Holiness evokes the desire to taste eternal life, but in acknowledging such, it calls forth the understanding that we are not eternal, but that we are fading flesh and bone cradled in entropy.

In the *desire* of holiness is realized the ego-killing *need*.

God is not scary—He is holy; there is a difference. Scary denotes something that is malevolent, something bad like the boogey man whose pleasures are in twisted things. Scary speaks of corruption; holy speaks of purity. Holy speaks of that which is so good, so perfect it threatens us—because in comparison to The Holy One, it is us that now look like the boogey man—something warped and dark.

94. We think our souls as the color white—but set next to holiness we are seen to be a jaundiced yellow—no, a noxious pale green—greater still, tar black. We are terrified of *holiness* because it exposes what we truly are. There is no greater cause of anxiety, or angst, than that ever jittering fear of exposure. When we are set free by redemption we no longer have to worry about exposure, for we live in the acknowledgement of our brokenness and salvation. We can live in honesty and confidence.

To fear God is to live in confidence, in bravery. To fear God is to invoke the anger of men.

The Pharisees were considered *the best of the religious best*, title champions of the holy circuit, the holy ones of Israel—yet Jesus exposed them as pale and viperous. Jesus showed their *moralistic pastiness* to be like tombs filled with the disconnected bones of the dead. Jesus exposed the Pharisee's true colors merely by being among them, by standing next to them.

When a plumb line is set next to that which is crooked, the difference is obvious. Ultimately, they hated Christ not for what He did, but for who He was.

They hated Christ? —We hated Christ! I hated Christ! But grace…

Grace is what allows us to be in the presence of God and not burn to a haze like a stick of incense. Grace is what placed a burning coal to Isaiah's lips. Grace is what has called us into the throne room of God.

95. There is a laughter of the redeemed. Laughter is like irony—for they both show dissonance, incongruence between two things: the real and ideal; earthly and celestial; perceived and actual.

Laughter shows our darkness and dignity. Laughter speaks to redemption; its mirth reminds us that we are undeserving of the Worthy One who has given His life for us. Heaven will resound with laughter because it is paradise—unworthy man in the presence of Holy God! Hah! What is more unexpected and joyful than this?

There is laughter in grace—there is no laughter in merit. There is smugness in merit. There are plastic trophies in merit, tawdry bronze medallions. Merit smirks; redemption laughs.

Laughter is another reason that I believe in God—another reason why I believe humanity was meant for dignity and was made in the image of God, but is now fallen.

Comedians make their livings by shocking us with their acute observations of life; mainly about sex, death, and bodily functions. These things show us to be mortal—they call to mind the mortality of our body and throw it alongside the eternality of our souls. We laugh at strange and twisted things because it reminds us that we were meant for paradise and yet we feel like forgotten junkyard dogs. We laugh at flatulence—children do, men and women of all ages do. It is more than a funny noise—it is a sudden reminder that we are mortal, that are bodies are of soft flesh under entropy, yet we long to be gods.

96. In his tragicomedy style, Mark Twain said, "Man is the only animal that blushes—or needs to." This is good theology.

Is it not interesting that human beings blush? Why is it that only human beings blush? Dogs do not blush; monkeys do not blush; the finch does not blush; I don't believe there is any animal species that does blush. Has a sparrow or an elephant ever felt shame. Do they not care about all the embarrassing things they do? Blushing is useless—except to show that we have a dignity beyond the animal kingdom, a meaning beyond naturalism. I believe we blush because we are made in the image of God—we blush when we feel our finite nature. Only one called to everlasting life could feel finite. Now some will argue using Latinate medical terms explaining the detailed goings-on of blushing and attempt to explain it away through physiological mechanisms—but still, we cannot deny these bodily mechanisms' connection with shame, embarrassment, and what we call modesty.

We blush for the same reason we avert our gaze from another's eyes. There is existential shame.

97. We cry because our body knows pain, because nerves fire and sting; yet we weep because of evil, because it wounds us, and because we wield it. Animals cry, but animals do not weep. No one weeps in a godless universe. We weep—we weep often.

We weep because our hearts cannot find the reason they beat.

~Sovereign of Good~

98. Salvation is of the Lord, and it is the place of men to proclaim it!

Christiandumb has a difficult time evangelizing (literally, *bearing a good message*) because its actions do not correspond with the Christian worldview. As seen by its behavior, it believes in a God that is less than sovereign—and for that, it can never bear The Good News. What can it bear? Messages of manipulation; religious gymnastics choreographed by men.

If one has a worldview in which the secular and the sacred are divorced they simply cannot *Evangelize* because God cannot be sovereign. Yes, they can preach a message, quote scripture, and establish orphanages, but they cannot *Evangelize*. Why? Because the Good News is that salvation is of God and not man, for all is God's and not man's. All belongs to Him—the Creator and Savior.

No wonder it is often hard for us to find a bridge from the secular to the sacred shore when we are talking with our friends, our co-workers, and the world. If we have to throw in a quick, unrelated statement, a sidelight completely off topic in order to introduce *the sacred kingdom that exists outside of the office*, then the awkwardness of the conversation will be easily felt, and our lackluster, un-integrated faith sharply exposed—and no *Great Sovereign* preached in word or deed!

When we have a *less than sovereign God*, then we live in a world that is divided into the secular and the sacred—for God does not rule every atom of it. This is unbelief; in this unbelief we will play at Christianity, spending our efforts making shaky bridges from our secular lives to our sacred lives. Let us forget these toothpick bridges and tell of the one true bridge that unites the shores of man and God—Jesus Christ.

How can we *Evangelize* if we do not believe? It is the sin of unbelief that allows us to neatly set aside and compartmentalize the things of God. It is the sin of unbelief that kicks against God's sovereignty and tries to annex His world. Unbelief divorces intended unions; faith unites that which is meant to be together.

Religion is the great incubator for the sin of unbelief. It is unbelief to place anything over God—ethical action, benevolent tradition, even love, even freedom. For without God these do not exist.

God is sovereign *and* we are meant to evangelize. Many sever these two from each other—this is not biblical. God's sovereignty is the very reason for evangelism! This tension is pivotal and painful for mankind—God is Sovereign *and* man has volition.

God's sovereignty/Man's Responsibility

99. I have gone through a strange fire of faith. It came upon me suddenly as when you drive over a hill and then find yourself in a low lying fog; yet this bright white fog was illuminating; in it I knew I was lost.

For weeks I could not sleep; and when I could, they seemed as useless hours because they brought no rest. I would wake in the middle of the night trembling—it was as if the left and right side of my brain no longer wanted to be in the same housing, and in their agitated state, they were vigorously trying to separate—and I was to choose which lobe to side with. As these weeks went on, I noticed it was as if my heart was trying to do the same odd thing: the left side and right side stretching and peeling apart, dividing lots, casting arguments—and me having to choose which side to give my allegiance. It was a rather awkward and agonizing time. What would you do?

These are hard choices; one does not toss away half of one's brain carelessly; one does not hastily crack the heart in two. After some deliberation and divine intervention it was impressed upon me to hold the two together—the left and right side of my brain, the raging chambers of my heart—and my heart with my mind. It turns out that if I kept them bound together, it was better in the end (and more illuminating because of the sparks). The body functions far better when it doesn't divorce itself. The problem was how: How does one hold the fleeing auricles of heart together? How does one keep the dis-integrating mind in union? Just by trying really, really hard? No…

The thorn that was probing me, the steely wedge that was trying to split my brain and heart into warring factions was that violent thrust of *disunited man* that pits sovereignty against the volition of man. It seems this issue has always troubled *the body* of the church in one way or another. It has split many minds and broken many hearts.

100. I had always believed that one of the hallmarks of Christianity was this bright golden thing called freewill. It was lauded, placed in velvet upon a pedestal (so high I could not see it itself—that is part of the whole trick!), and spoken of reverentially as if its pedestal shot all the way to heaven to sit on par with God's throne. The trouble with pedestals is they crack. The trouble with high pedestals is the fall is long and violent.

This is to say, God's throne sits higher than man's choice. Yet because God's throne is higher, does that mean man has no choice—no!

To drain man of choice is to drain the world of moral responsibility and to inject evil into God!

Where sin abounds, grace abounds all the more—this is because sin is of men, of second order, and grace is of God, is ultimate. The penultimate can never overcome the ultimate.

I had always believed in the high power of the will—but something alien came into my head and heart—and the problem was not this alien, but somehow the landscapes of my heart and head. For when they were seen in this alien light, they were exposed as a kingdom of the self; a landscape of stone carved with pagan symbols mixed with Christian imagery—and in the center a great statue that looked all too much like me! It was not a lush landscape with a throne and altar for the one God.

In these trying weeks of little sleep, too much reading of man's opinion, and praying that consisted mainly of low groaning, I learned of God's sovereignty. The sovereignty of God is a very nice term to talk about to sound theologically astute, but when it comes to talking about human capability and our free will, well, God's sovereignty ceases to be desired—it is thrown out the stained glass window with hardly a notice to the smashing glass.

Many would give an easy "yes" when questioned whether God was sovereign; yet if sovereignty and human free will are thrown into the ring of discussion, quickly freewill is crowned champion. In theory God rules—in everyday practicality *we rule*.

But in truth, when they are thrown into the fight ring of man's design, the two only embrace and walk away laughing—for they are age-old friends. This being so, man who wants a fight, devises new definitions of both sovereignty and freewill, then unleashes them upon each other so man can sit back in his sin, or build his own stairway to heaven.

101. We have misunderstood free will—but this misunderstanding has come from blatant rebellion. We have sought to understand man's will upon deduction only, disregarding the revelation of truth in lieu of man's own judgment about what is possible and what is not.

Freewill: when did *free* come to mean *autonomy*? When did liberty come to mean *lawlessness*?

I believe we as humans have freedom of choice. I trust that this is reality because the Bible teaches it explicitly and implicitly from tree to tree (that is, from the tree in the Garden of Eden to the tree in Revelation). I believe in freedom of choice because Jesus endorsed it in word and flesh. I believe in God's sovereignty because Jesus taught it and walked it. What are we to make of this? One simply cannot read the Bible and not find the notes of human responsibility clearly.

One cannot (truly) read the Bible and not find a sovereign God, a God in complete control of His cosmos—a God unsurprised by the events unfolding, events He will use to bring His plan to sweet fruition. He is God who *chooses*, who has *called*, who has *known the end from the beginning*, who sent forth prophets and put prescient words upon their tongues.

From the first sentence, the keynote of all Scripture (*In the beginning God created*), to the last words of the last revelation (*Yes, I am coming soon*), God is ever announcing that all is His, and He will do what is His will.

Scripture is plain and makes no dilemma of it: human beings are responsible for their actions *and* God is sovereign—without Him we can do nothing. It is man who makes a dilemma of this unified truth.

Sovereignty/moral responsibility is as plain and painfully obvious as the sun; it is as intense as the sun and therefore it can never directly be looked at from our earthbound view and soft eyes. It is an obvious blur of light, a bright radiance that we never really see in focused fashion, yet see everywhere, and see by.

Let us live in this mystery's light while on earth, and not burn our eyes trying to define it—for we will only go blind and mad, never to see it again.

It is tragic that man has distorted the beautiful dance of *Sovereignty/moral responsibility*. The battle over this elegant truth is so ugly and fierce only because of its intended beauty and hope.

102. We should remember the Book of Esther when we start to grab and squeeze this sharp diamond of free will. Esther is a

literary marvel. Can you imagine a movie or a book that never once mentions the name of the central character? That never once sets the central character on the lit stage? Can you imagine such a story that, without this invisible and unspoken of character, the story's engine would shut down completely and run into the ground? It is hard to imagine such an idiot's story—one never telling of the central character by which the story stands and moves.

Well there is such an *idiot's story*; it is the story penned by a literary genius. It is the Book of Esther. It is an idiot's story not because the author was an idiot, but because it is written for two kinds of fools; the one who is so foolish as to not see reality; and the other so foolish as to believe reality despite overwhelming popular opinion.

One fool sees the light of the sun in and upon everything he sees—and for that he sees twofold and is wise; the other fool *only* sees an apple, a car on the highway, a sparrow, the blond hair of the woman he loves—and for that has missed the true beauty of each and remains a fool.

The Book of Esther is about the sovereignty of God. It is a story about God and how He works through and amidst human beings to work the wonders of His will. This is what the story is about, yet it is all done through the very valid and real choices of the people involved. The fool for God sees God's hand orchestrate the volitional history of mankind. The fool that disbelieves God only sees a story of interesting human interactions, a story devoid of a personal God.

I am indebted to my good friend Pastor Tom Hovestol for these insights into Esther.

Similarly, we should look to the book of Ruth. It also is one of the world's finest jewels in its crown of literature. One cannot read the Book of Ruth correctly without acknowledging the comforting movements of providence and sovereignty set amidst the movements of humanity and moral responsibility.

103. It is not *rationality* that has a problem with God's sovereignty and our moral responsibility; rather, it is *rationalism* that has a problem with such a tension. Remember the difference between the two: *rationality* is that which is related to man's ability to reason consistently; *rationalism* is the process of starting with the self alone in attempting to discover all truth. The first is Christian, and the second is the idolization of man—humanism.

Trying to comprehend the nexus of God's sovereignty and the will of man is like trying to pinpoint the synapse of a thought or trying to finalize whether light is particle or wave. One can either hold the two in tension or tear the two apart. The paradox of the tension is comforting—literally strengthening—while the tearing apart and isolating of the two forces us outside the bounds of Scripture, and for that, outside the bounds of reality. One can hold the two together and warm in the light, or one can attempt to tear the two apart and slowly go mad in the dark.

What we do know is that synapses very much exist, that light is mysterious, yet real and warming, and that God is sovereign *and* good—yet man is responsible for his actions, accountable for his decisions. We have the choice to dissect this living truth into a useless polemic or bask in its light that we are in dire need of. We have the choice…God help us.

104. I call attention to another tension: Sovereign *and* good. God is sovereign *and* good. Because of this there is hope.

Many people hate the idea of a sovereign God—this is because they do not hold *sovereign* in tension with *good*. To them, this sovereign God could be uncaring, bigoted, cruel, and capricious—He might be like man.

The idea of sovereignty divorced from goodness kicks against every stronghold of hope in the human heart. But to see that these two are wedded for eternity in an indestructible union is the only true source for hope—both in this world and in the next. In Jesus we see these two wedded, and He is our hope. We know God's will, for we know the life of Christ.

105. We speak of freewill as if it means *autonomy*—then, in our delusion, we also speak of God's sovereignty. As if one can have them both! Sovereignty and autonomy are the same; so humanity cannot be autonomous if God is sovereign. The two are mutually exclusive.

If by freewill we mean *freedom of choice under the authority and universe of laws that God has ordained*, then freewill is a hallmark of Christianity. But if we naively mean that we are totally self-governed, and can do absolutely anything we desire to do by our own strength, then this is an anti-Christ statement. It is more than that; it is an anti-scientific statement; an anti-reason statement.

We can do many things by the imagination of man and the tools of technology—but we cannot do *anything*, and we cannot do it upon our own governing. We are governed by the laws of the universe. We are governed by God. We are limited.

Yet, be careful! Because we are ultimately governed by God it does not mean that we don't rebel and cause ruin!

If you free a man from the laws of the universe he is no longer a man.

If you free a man from God's sovereignty you free man from all hope. If you free man from his God given gift of volition, you free him from love. And to free man from such things is to imprison him forever.

If science is free to do anything, then by definition it is no longer science. The scientific method is the border that frees science to function.

The Bible never claims that mankind is autonomous. Yet the Bible is unrelenting in holding us responsible for our actions.

Every painter is free; yet every canvas has its bounds. Freedom by definition has boundaries. Freedom is the possibility to bound about within given boundaries. One is free to be a great tennis player when there are rules and lines on the court—one is not free to be a great player if the court markings move about randomly, if the net height is in flux, if one can change the rules at whim.

There can be no master musician, no virtuoso, if there is no standard of time signature and no rigid staff lines to cradle the notes.

God's ultimate control does not resign us to be fate-chained androids. Our moral responsibility does not veto God's power. This tension is the throb of life—it is history—the story of humanity in God's singing cosmos.

As *the created*, we have been given power—but we do not have the complete self-governing power of *the Creator*. This is what Adam and Eve reached for, but they fell hard to the ground—dislocating their hearts and bruising their minds.

106. Jesus had something to say about this through His servant Paul. "Therefore my dear friends, as you have always obeyed—not only in my presence, but now much more in my absence—continue to work out your salvation with fear and trembling, for it is God who works in you to will and to act according to His good purpose." This is what is read in Philippians 2:12-13. The context of this passage is Paul writing to the church at Philippi to thank them for support and to encourage those who are being persecuted.

That being said, it is seen that it is God who works through the Christian, but the Christian who must work out their salvation. This is a mystery of will *and* sovereignty. It is a ribbon of beauty that we cannot untie. This passage, along with a mile more of Scripture, denies human autonomy and denies the human as android.

The very reason that we want to untie this *twining of goods* is not so we can finally believe, but because we don't believe! We don't want it to be true.

The tension of God's sovereignty/our responsibility is a challenge to our hot desire for autonomy. It is the same challenge as the tree in the Garden of Eden that stood to show man as creature and God as Creator. If it is true, if the tension of this mystery holds, then we simply cannot be god. Do you now see why we try so hard to tear at this union of goods?

107. The deceiver has used the good thing of freewill against goodness and has turned it into a bloated idol. Freewill has been inflated, engorged, and exploded into a monster. Like love traded for swollen lust, or hunger swapped for gluttony, free will has become a treasure of humanism. We should understand this word humanism.

Humanism is that which rejects divine justifications; it rejects revelation and finds truth centered in humanity itself. It is earthbound. It whines and wheezes that power resides in man's will; that man is the measure of all things. It is the reversal of the Kingdom of God—it is the kingdom of man.

Humanism has mixed good things with poisonous ones. It is sweet water with clear, oily arsenic. It is the ultimate form of idolatry— man at the center, making gods of what he chooses—making gods of mankind. It is the idolater becoming the idol. It is Narcissus wasting away, consuming himself.

This oily arsenic has slipped into the communion wine, has been poured into the eternal water that is preached by many *Christians*. Because many have not learned the Word of God, have not tasted it uncontaminated, many do not know where the water ends and where the arsenic begins.

Religion is like saltwater: the more we drink it the more we are burned by thirst. The water becomes a poison. The more *religion* we drink the more poison we swallow—all in the name of God. *Hail Christiandumb!*

Christiandumb says, "Here! We have water to offer!" And they do—but it is brackish water that ought not to be had.

The Gospel has become man-centered. But this is not good news! What could be more horrifying?

We have grafted humanism onto the splendid tree of the Gospel—and now some limbs that had pointed towards the heavens have bent and fallen, and like a weeping willow they now flop and bow to the earth. But the Word of God comes as pruning shears just as much as it comes as water to feed both leaves and roots!

108. Am I a Pelagian? No. An Arminian? No. A Calvinist? No. I am a Christian! I am a follower of our Lord Jesus Christ. If I constrain myself to the systematic theology of a man, I will surely cut myself off from *some truth* of the Gospel. For a man, even of the widest genius is only a man, and far under God. A man with the broadest view is far narrower in sight than God's tightest squint.

I am a follower of the one who was both fully God and fully man. I am a follower of the one who was both full of grace and full of truth; a follower of the revolution leader and obedient servant; a follower of the lion and the lamb; the King and the crucified. If our master was one of such great paradox why can't we as followers follow Him in this way?

I am not of Apollo; I am not of Paul—I am of our Lord Jesus Christ. Oh to live these words and not be the follower of men!

What if we were to reload the word *Christian* by following Jesus, and not define our relationship with Christ by another man who followed Christ? Is this naïveté—or obvious wisdom?

The shame is our own if our allegiance to Luther, to Calvin, to Wesley, or to any other man is greater than our allegiance to Jesus Christ the God/man. Let us live so on the day that all is revealed it will be seen that we have followed God and not men.

Much *ministry* preaches only one thing: How to be proud of your achieved humility!

We should move in humility. We should constantly be wary of overestimating ourselves. When we are strong then we are weak. Why is it that when we are weak we are strong? It is because the one we have to lean on is *the One* that can take us further then we could ever go alone; through His eyes alone we can see what remains veiled to our humanity. We must open our eyes to our blind spots and firmly acknowledge our frailty. When we *truly* know ourselves, we can't help but to be humble.

Only God can help us see ourselves. Only God can help dust know that it is dust. Only God can show us that we are earthy dust *and* the breath of God.

Only God can help us choose the good paths.

It takes the power of divinity for man to see his own frailty.

109. We speak much of faith—it tastes sweetly on the speaker's tongue; but tasting obedience is rather bitter to the same palette. It is like unsweetened baking chocolate.

Yet true obedience and true faith are two sides of the same coin. You cannot have one without the other—you cannot divvy them up chronologically—you cannot place one over the other—you cannot either/or them. Is not obedience trust? Obedience without faith is not obedience at all; it is rebellion disguised as a yes-man; it is religion not Gospel.

Faith and obedience—the two are held together. Truly, if you touch one, you touch the other.

We like to pit grace against works in a theological Coliseum. We do this because we hope one of them will win. If one destroys the other, the way to heaven becomes broad. Yet it is always a draw—it is a draw because they refuse to fight each other—they shake hands, then hug, and laugh together.

Faith and obedience cannot fight each other for their God is one; and so the road remains narrow. This frustrates us; so we continue to place them in the arena hoping one day for a wild and bloody fight, and an eight lane superhighway to heaven.

Works are the outflow of authentic faith. Works do not merit salvation, they only pour out of it like light spills from the sun. Sun rays do not have to try to be warm—they are warm by sheer nature. Sun rays do not attempt to be warm to stay sun rays. They are what they are.

Can we separate the heat from the light in a sunray that is resting on our face? They are inseparable. Can we separate the sun from its light and its warmth? To tear such things apart is to destroy both.

When we are saved by grace through faith, good works are there like humidity hugs a coastal atmosphere. Good works do not sustain faith—they are intrinsically part of faith.

Justification bears sanctification; sanctification does not bear justification. Being precedes doing.

"The work of the Lord is this; to believe in the one He has sent." Jesus Christ was sent to us, has called us, and has taken our sin upon Himself. The incarnation, crucifixion, and resurrection of Jesus Christ has

fulfilled all righteousness (met the standards of perfection), meted out divine justice, and given grace freely. Wrath and grace met on the cross of Christ and their collision exploded the love of God out to the farthest reaches of the world. We are called to trust in the one who did the great work of justification.

The only saving *work* of man is to trust in the saving work of Jesus. Many are the works born of man's gratitude in response to God's grace.

110. To Trust is to act. Actions reveal beliefs. To have faith in Christ, to believe in the one whom God has sent, means to obey Him. If our faith is an abstraction, a soft confession without any vindication through concrete action, then are we really believers? The Bible tells us that we are not; all reason tells us the same. So how can we be action-less believers? If we do not obey, we do not believe, this is why Christ says *you will know them by their fruit*. This does not make grace obsolete; it makes it obvious; grace ignites and sustains obedience.

"If anyone chooses to do God' will, he will find out whether my teaching comes from God or whether I speak on my own" (John 7:17). Action and faith, obedience and trust—they are like the auricles of the heart, the lobes of the mind.

Those the Holy Spirit has changed will bear the fruit of the Spirit. Those who are still a thorn bush will still draw blood—call them what you may.

An abstract Christian is exactly that—abstract, intangible, a mere concept. The world will not see you, Christ does not know you. An abstraction cannot be obedient or loving. Paul's theology was always practical, John's teachings on Christ, though he was highly symbolic and mystical, were always 'down-to-earth'. These men were realists. Christ was the ultimate realist. They had a theology of words *and* hands; their faith did not float about unattached. A Christian lives incarnationally, concretely, *in action*.

Oh the eloquence of action!

"Believe in the One He has sent" / *"If you love me you will obey me."* These are the words of Jesus.

111. Paul was intelligent, but more so, an apostle of Christ; he knew of our inane tendency to divide and conquer, to swing wildly from extreme to extreme like pious pendulums. So when he spoke of grace, he followed it with works—because naturally, works flow from salvation by grace.

Here is an interesting observation: The Book of Hebrews is often thought of as a book about faith and the book of James is often thought of as a book about works—and James follows on the heels of Hebrews—it is the very next book of the Bible. This ordering is rather interesting; though, I contend both books are about both faith and works for both are about Christ.

All that is Gospel speaks of *faith first* then the thankful *works* that flow from such wonderful grace.

112. Part of the attraction to the either/or delusion is due to the moss-growing sloth of our nature. Either/or-ism is an easy escape route. "If I go left, I definitely go left and I reject right—I don't have to think about it, or incorporate it into my life."

It is strange how *extreme* seems to imply difficulty and a lot of work, but more often than not the one-sided extreme is plagued with laxity—a mere falling.

Behind sloth is a zealous engine that works for what it wants; that pushes fervently against the Sovereign God.

It is easy to fall to either side of a tight rope; it takes grace, concentration, and muscle exertion to stay up and walking. There is a deep-rooted sloth in our nature that doesn't want to strain or work at something when an easy option can take its place.

Grace is easily twisted by the human heart—it is so beautiful that it can become dreadfully marred by men—the more valuable an artist's painting, the more horrible the defacing. "*Grace* you say! Well then, my work is done here! Sign the letters of resignation! Let your mind and hands slip into dark areas—we'll be forgiven, let's have at living wildly!"

There is a deep substructure of thought in the Western world that believes our existence should be centered and cradled within comfort and ease. *Either/or* often offers a path of least resistance to achieve this goal of cushioning our throne.

Given the way we bent and twisted ourselves, the deceiver often appeals to our comforts. When the deceiver comes, he comes in the savvy clothes of a short cut, not the knee-worn clothes of sacrifice. He has pomade in his hair and cologne on his chest, not dirt on his face or blisters on his hands.

And when the deceiver does come with blisters of labor or some ascetic task, it is because the labors are easier than saying, "I was wrong." For many, it is more comfortable to be in pain, than have peace that one didn't procure for themselves.

113. Don't be fooled—there is a great labor involved in the Kingdom of Heaven. We must count the costs and roll up our sleeves when grace opens our heart with the desires of God.

Like a racer in the Tour de France, the body of Christ must lean and swoop in order to navigate the winding hills of Europe, must compensate for sudden accidents, and must realign to stay the course—yet in all stay balanced, least endure a spiritual case of road rash, or worse, the tragedy of stopping wheels and the heartbreak of not passing through the Champs-Élysées to cross the finish line.

Like a racer in the Tour de France, if we as Christians are to cross the finish line our muscles must ache, our strength must grow listless, and blisters must sting our skin. If these do not happen, then are we in the race?

Balance does not always mean left, and it does not always mean right. It means going left when you are supposed to go left, right when you are supposed to go right. It is relative, but always in right relation to Jesus. It is absolute in relation to the Absolute one who speaks of the right way to turn here, then there, now this way.

All left or all right is nothing but falling—and we have already done that.

114. Comfort is another word bent and twisted by the world. Following Christ should be about comfort like many say—but there are two different dictionaries for the word comfort. The world's dictionary says: **Comfort** – 1. a condition or feeling of pleasurable ease, well-being, and contentment. 2. ease of life; no problems; fat bank account; elimination of stress; end of inner struggles.

By comfort we often mean a life of ease and pleasure. Yet comfort means *to strengthen*. It comes from the Latin word *fortis* which means strong. So as Christians we are to live a life of comfort; one in which we are strengthened by the grace of God as we experience the pains of life in a rusted world. So the pains of life remain, but with Christ we are strengthened through them. We are strengthened by the tension—and this is God's doing.

So we should be comforted—yet we must not maintain a polluted version of the word comfort. Our lives are to grow and be strengthened in the truth by God's grace and thereby learning to glorify Him—and this inevitably includes resistance, difficult times, and enduring what we would like to skip. We are meant to have relationship with God, and a great part of that relationship is being strengthened by our grappling with life and God.

Like Jacob we are strengthened by God showing us our weakness, showing us our frailty and that we cannot be blessed apart from Him, by any other than Him. It is in humility that we are truly strengthened, because the strength we gain is Christ's and not that of a grasping mortal human. Often times the strengthening, the comforting in our lives comes not as a plush job or gratuitous riches, but as a hip out of socket or some red itch that tests our resolve.

A life without resistance is a life of atrophied muscles, uneducated minds, and surrender to entropy; a sagging life without the healthy leanness of the truth. The children of God are led by the Spirit of God (the Comforter); they are to live a comforted (strengthened) life, not an easy life. We need to hear this refrain again and again: *The good life is not the easy life.*

An irony: A life buffered by creature comforts helps us forget we are creatures.

A life buffered by creature comforts, by easy friends, and Christiandumb is a toxic atmosphere. Rather, it is like no atmosphere at all! It is like the zero gravity of space that allows an astronaut to float easily upon the dark sea, but over time muscle mass is lost, strength bled, and the heart weakened. Without the gravity of resistance, we will be flaccid souls at best. Hah! *Safe Christianity*—it is a self-negating term! It is a non-reality. It is the child of pride!

We all want to live passionately, but we do not want to suffer; the irony is that passion literally means suffering. We want the glory without the trial – yet this is a law that no one can circumvent. We cannot live passionately for Christ without suffering. Suffering is the nature of rising in a fallen world, the chaffing of kneeling to a prideful soul. Suffering is the friction that comes from pushing against and resisting the gravity of sin.

115. What a contradiction we are: we fight sovereignty because we want control—yet in our control we pass the buck! We have a strange fear of freedom!

We fear freedom because we fear what possibilities crouch within our heart; because we fear the pressing reality of moral responsibility; because we fear there is a Beautiful Standard and because we fear the author of that standard is truly sovereign.

The deep anxiety of freedom is only healed by the Gospel of grace—by the good gift of the sovereign God.

A paradox: Proximity to God increases our awareness of our sin—proximity to God reveals that Christ is our righteousness and has freed us completely from our sin. We are not free until we are seized by our enslavement. We are not free until we know we are saved by one who rules over us as Sovereign.

What is man's part in salvation? Let's ask this: Is salvation good? Yes—no doubt. All Good comes from God. Salvation is of God. "But," we say, "God has given man choice, and this is good, so man has a part in his salvation!" Yes—but God gave the man the good. For all good comes from God. Ultimately, salvation is only of God.

116. God's sovereignty shines brilliantly above all things. Its truth means that He is the Creator and is therefore the basis for all worship. What does this mean to the self-worshipped? Among the self-reliant (the rebellious), sovereignty is utterly disparaged, considered a havoc to humanity, and deemed the most detrimental of things to speak or think of.

The intensity by which God's sovereignty is vandalized is telling. Do not think I am only speaking of those not in the church—I speak of those in the church as well.

The greatest comfort becomes the greatest terror; the greatest wonder becomes the greatest abjection. For when man attempted to be God, He had to, at the same time, desire and despise the very attributes of God; and by doing so, he held the shell but let go the heart of life.

The greatest joy, when inversed, becomes the worst horror; this is why the things of God seem like death to those who *think* they are living. This is why we must die in order to live; this is not sage-like word play, but the necessary remedy to an upside down mutiny of reality.

117. All this, though deeply important, has a certain silliness about it. It is like a child saying "Daddy, the sun is hot." It is true and of great concern to all life, but so obvious as to be *childish* in the saying. For God, by being the Creator, is necessarily sovereign; this means that we cannot speak of God without invoking His sovereignty. "Daddy, God is God." Yes he is.

To say *God is sovereign* is a tautology; it is not an option to be explored and debated. To speak of God means to have sovereignty hang in the air, to fill the atmosphere like oxygen, to swell and press against all of the cosmos like an unseen and vital energy.

How far have we fallen that we must say that God is God? For a *Christian* to argue any degree of sovereignty away from God is to argue any possibility away of their Christianity!

118. God, the Sovereign Creator: this is the center, the basis, the very origin of all worship. Worship: a movement of the will, the volition of man in acknowledging truth.

~The Beautiful Standard/Acceptance~

119. If there is no standard then there is no existence of beauty—merely opinion and a tossed about thin shell of a word. If the page of beauty is blank, then it will be defined by anything, and all becomes equal—cruelty, ugliness, deformation.

The Beautiful Standard is beautiful because it is the standard. Some call it natural law, some call it the Tao, and I call it the Beautiful Standard for it is exactly that.

How can law be beautiful? One of the subtle, but deep fractures of the fall is our collapsed ability to see beauty; sin spins us further into beauty blindness. This is why The Law of God is the Beautiful Standard—for it is the light of God revealing the sin that would steal the beauty of the Creator from the creation. What is more reasonable and beautiful than knowing who we are and how we are to live in relation with truth?

The Beautiful Standard will set us against ourselves—for we pretend to not know what we deeply know (the moral code written in the heart), and the Beautiful Standard will not let the dissonance lie.

This is why one will eventually call the beautiful standard *ugly* and *the prison of men*—for to accept it but disregard its giver is to never allow it to reveal the dissonance within—and therefore to never live in allegiance to it. When it does reveal that it has set us against ourselves then we will ban it, take it out of schools, wipe it off placards and invent philosophies that seek to demolish meta-morality. We will set up superstitious philosophies of relativity and set them about our homes and hearts as gargoyles to keep away the truth revealed by the Beautiful Standard.

120. The beauty of the standard comes in the stand against absurdity. Absurdity literally means *dissonance, incongruity, out of tune, and senseless*. Even in the most modern sense absurdity means *out of harmony with reason or prosperity*. The beauty of The Law of God is to

expose the dissonance of our existence, and align us with the Creator.

Rational thought is discriminating. If there is no absolute standard, then the only evil is discrimination, is discernment, is intolerance, and so the only progress is to crush all things to a flat moral field, to zero out evil and good.

God gave the Beautiful Standard because He is the maker of reason and order. Man seeks to destroy dissonance by flattening all things, by crumbling all to dust. God seeks to overcome dissonance by rising what is meant to be raised and lowering what is meant to be lowered—by aligning all to the order He created. Here again we see human tension leading to destruction, and God's tension of shalom putting all in right relation to another. Man destroys boundaries, God uses boundaries to unite. Freedom is founded upon boundaries. Diseases and insanities dissolve boundaries.

Think upon the word disintegrate—dis-integrate.

When man becomes the judge of good and evil, he must reject God for God is the judge of good and evil; when this inversion occurs absolutes and the Beautiful Standard are denigrated to mere opinion, matters of vote; opinion then becomes bigotry, for ones man's preference is another's oppression—therefore all must be zeroed out—no discernment is allowed, for it is considered oppressive. When man seeks to rationalize God out of the world, it is not God that is banished, but it is rationality. If rationality is banished, absurdity is all that is left—dissonance—anxiety—violence—gnashing.

But how does man judge good or evil if he has rejected the designator of Good? His judgment has become an arbitrary judgment, and if it is arbitrary then all judgment is equal and unfounded—it is all zeroed out; and with all zeroed out then reason has no place, because reason is discernment of the given order.

To call nondiscrimination or total tolerance a virtue or *the only virtue* is absurd, first and foremost; and, secondly, self-defeating for it is a discernment.

Man, in attempting to be judge of good and evil will eventually judge all judgments evil; he will call equality and tolerance in *all* things, and in this incoherence of existence, in this contradiction of believing the "truth" that there is no truth, he will destroy himself in violence after he has shattered the world around him. Unchecked tolerance leads to the violation of the entire cosmos.

Autonomy bleeds to absurdity.

The *age of information* slouches forward on the unfounded premise that all is equal, and that all information is neutral—and for it, it is a progressive tyrant. Information without discrimination is the disintegration of freedom, reason, and beauty—it is the total dissolution of humanity.

121. The Beautiful Standard is the unassailable safeguard of reason, rationality, beauty, and order—it is the will of the Creator. The Law is an expression of God's characteristic beauty.

Antinomianism or anarchy is not first a movement of hatred towards law, but first against the foundation of beauty and reason—to buck The Law is to set fire to all Rembrandts, to mar the face of beauty, to pour crude oil into the emerald Caribbean cove. It is to slight all creation because it disdains the Creator.

The Beautiful Standard is beautiful for it discriminates between rape and love, murder and the healing hand, disintegration and unity. If one acknowledges any form of beauty, then they acknowledge the reality of the Beautiful Standard. Beauty cannot, in the final synapse, be divorced from God.

122. To what can we compare a life without the Beautiful Standard? Imagine with me the Louvre. The aged museum director, who had given his life to the study and preservation of the

famed museum collection under his stewardship, fell into madness by way of certain ideas from a certain circle of thinkers. He claimed he loved the colors of the paintings to such a degree, that only he loved them truly, and he wanted them to be alive and free while others only hated the colors and kept them caged in their disdain. Taking the best painting from the museum wall, he threw the canvas and frame into a vat of ethanol—the colors lifted, spiraled around in an oily haunt, then the beauty was gone—only a grayish slick was left. In a moment of ecstasy he celebrated the liberation of the colors, and then upon seeing the voided canvass still framed and awash in gray, a visceral despair took over; he could live no longer, and so he took his own life. He could not live with what he had done; he could not live amidst the actions of his terrible conclusions.

123. It is when The Law is found beautiful that it then becomes the hammer—for we are found incapable of The Law—we are found incapable of beauty. This is the horror of the human situation—we work against that which is the ultimate beauty—the Creator.

The horror of humanity is the dissonance of our existence; Jesus is literally the harmony of the universe.

The Law is found to be a crushing hammer because it is *beauty unreachable*—this is why Christ is both the hard stroke of justice and sweet release of mercy. It is not unreasonable—the pain humanity feels—when we confronted with true beauty—for the sudden piercing is the most reasonable reaction of a sour heart confronted with its perfect origin.

124. The Decalogue, that is, the Ten Commandments, are more precious than a mountain rife with platinum veins, or an ocean tide of blue diamonds. The Decalogue is the voice of God calling to man to say "see, this is how it is! Do not deny what you know of yourself. Come, entrust yourself in Me."

The Decalogue is the voice of our true lover. "Listen," He says, "I will tell you of the lie so you may live by the truth." Who are we if we find no beauty in the Ten Commandments? *Whose* are we if we find the arms of benevolence only suffocating?

Some believe The Law is conical and confining, narrowing until we are smaller because of its bounds. But if the reality of existence is seen as upside down by we who are in the throes of the fall, then The Law is really the augmenting, amplifying, and radiating of our souls into greater and greater realms of existence.

125. This is tender skin—do you know what the Ten Commandments say? What troubles me about the modern Christian is that most professors of the faith would stutter after attempting to recall two or three—some pastors would stutter after five. We have fallen prostrate to such a different Gospel that we think grace is a word that allows us to embalm and bury the Ten Commandments. Grace is what allows us to live out the Ten Commandments. Jesus is the fulfillment of The Law. This simply means that He was the only one capable of living the way we as humans should (the way The Law said). Only He could harmonize *the is* and *ought to be*.

The Ten Commandments are quintessential; Jesus was the quintessential man. There is perfect unity between the Old and New Testaments.

Is law unloving? On the contrary, it is the voice of concern and compassion. It leads to love. Law is the buttress to grace. Anarchy is too weak, its self-gravity too thin to hold the bounding passion of love.

126. You cannot improve upon the Ten Commandments. They are written deep into the DNA of mankind. They are scripted into the spirals of galaxies and the spirals of solar flares and the symmetry of tree leaves—they are built into the divine language that speaks the universe into being. Yet we are ignorant of what is buried within our own DNA; we are unaware of what spirals over our heads in the menagerie of space; we stomp on leaves and pass by their telling symmetry—and we are blind to the Ten

Commandments though they are woven into the fabric of existence.

Murder on the farthest star still finds one guilty. Lust corrodes the heart in every atmosphere and under every alien moon.

127. God's law shows God's character. Jesus has not made obsolete God's character! No! This is a ridiculous interpretation of the New Covenant. Jesus is the radiance of The Law; by faith, by trusting in Jesus we are found in perfect accord with each ordinance.

The reason the world longs to abolish the Ten Commandments is they long to abolish God from their tiny universe. One must, by law of non-contradiction, hate Jesus in order to hate the Ten Commandments. When we buck a command we are rejecting the Creator and establishing our own self as Lord over Him. When we break a commandment we take a hard swipe at God, we swing another hammer strike upon the nine-inch nail within the feet of Christ.

When we judge a commandment of God as unworthy to be heeded we simply judge God's character as wanting. This is upside down—the standard of The Law is meant to judge us. It is meant to show us how collapsed, how dark, and how twisted we are. The Ten Commandments show us that we are not God, though we try to be. Here is the irony: we are judged because we have judged the commandments of God in not keeping them.

God does not establish arbitrary laws; to even speak of *arbitrary* in relation to God is nonsensical; He is the perfect arbiter and the establisher of meaning; this means that the true God, the Creator God cannot be capricious, but only benevolent and meaningful in every movement. God's laws are not capricious—they are extensions of His essence by way of His mandate. God's laws are good because they are the sheen of His glory. This means that God's laws are good because He says they are—this is because His essence is action—He is good therefore all He does is good.

Love the Lord your God; Love your neighbor. These are the ten laws in two. One cannot love their neighbor without first loving God. One cannot love God without then loving their neighbor. The deceiver tries to strip these two apart; to choose one without the other is to choose neither.
To choose one and not the other is to choose to shatter a tablet of The Law—and for that, the whole law.

If you have broken any of the laws, you have broken them all. How is this? The first law ("You shall have no other gods before me") is the foundation and the means for all the other laws; so when any subsequent laws are broken, the first law is already broken. This is because it is the first law being broken that leads to the breaking of all the others laws.

Every time we sin, every time we disobey God and shackle ourselves to slavery, we start by worshipping another god, a pseudo-savior—an idol of man, woman, money, prestige, etc. This means that we have broken all The Law, for we have discarded the glorious Creator for a mere creation! No matter what law we break, we throw them all out the window for we have judged God untrustworthy! We have declared the foundational law unworthy of obedience, and for that, the rest crumble into powder!

For 3,500 years these laws have presupposed and pointed towards the Savior. Before the fire of Sinai carved The Law into stone, their truth was heard in the blood. Abel's blood cried out for justice, cried out for Shalom. The earth has long groaned for redemption, aching within the hold of entropy. Adam and Eve fell because they broke the first commandment; they fell to idolatry—they themselves being the idols that were put in God's place.

128. The Ten Commandments were the official speaking of an *original* love, not the introduction of something new to the order of the universe.

If you do not see the Ten Commandments as love letters, then you misunderstand them. If you do not see the Decalogue as the light gathering leaves of our true roots, then you are a severed branch.

01. You shall have no other Gods before me.
02. You shall not make yourself an idol in the form of anything in heaven above or earth beneath.
03. You shall not use the name of the Lord in an empty manner.
04. Remember the Sabbath day and keep it holy.
05. Honor your Father and Mother.
06. You shall not murder.
07. You shall not commit adultery.
08. You shall not steal.
09. You shall not give false testimony against your neighbor.
10. You shall not covet.

Notice the first and last commandments are necessarily movements of the conjoined heart and mind; they are concerning the inner man's acknowledgment of reality, the trajectories of the will. Is it a surprise then that Christ would condemn both lust and anger? No! The Beautiful Standard has never been merely about the movement of hands, but the motion of the innermost man—and this is why it is so damning.

The Law in its brilliance is too bright, too revealing, too retina crushing to look upon—and so man fences The Law: he adds to it and creates distance between he and it by externalizing it. Each of these efforts at externalizing The Law is an attempt to run from the indictment its light brings, so that we can fool ourselves into thinking we can keep its commands.

If The Law's domain is first the heart and then the hands, then we are all crushed. Yet if its domain is of the hands alone, then maybe one can hold the hammer rather than by blasted by it.

129. Some look at law as that which binds freedom and mutes personal expression—some look at law as that which binds imprisonment and releases our God-intended personality.

In law there is freedom. It is not law itself that the world hates—for we as humans like the laws that let us be and let us do what we want to do. We like the laws that keep us comfortable. We like law—it keeps criminals in jail, it gives us power, it protects our assets, it allows us to make money and to keep that money. We do not hate laws in a general way; we do not despise law for being law; we hate law based on content.

What we hate is The Law of God—we hate His character that holds us accountable and reminds us that He is greater than ourselves. We deeply like self-law (*auto-nomos*, that is, autonomy); what we hate is ultimate law that is not up for veto or situational editing.

Man loves law that shows him the gavel holder; man hates law that shows him the judged.

The Ten Commandments were written on stone to remind us that our hearts are stone and incapable of the very laws; God became flesh to make our hearts flesh by fulfilling The Law for us.

130. Here is a great marvel: A lantern was given to a man who lived in great darkness—the glow of the lantern showed him that he was in a darkness that he had never acknowledged, because he hid from himself the disturbing darkness of his world. But now the lantern blatantly showed him where he was wrong and where he was right in his thoughts about the reality of the world. For this it brought joy and brought pain. Though it was beautiful, it increased his guilt for now he knew he must face his self deception and misguided views.

    Yet the lantern enslaved the man because he was now at the mercy of the lantern if he wanted to see—he had to keep it lit, protect it from disabuse, dote on it—if it went out, so too did his sight. But then came along a greater gift; a gift the lantern had alluded to all along. Then came the sun breaking into this man's low-lit world. The lantern still was there; its glow still glowing and speaking of the world around—but the brilliance of the sun superseded it, and made the glow superfluous—for something greater had came along; something brighter that washed out the low-light wattage. The sun came along not to shatter the lantern, but to fill the world with a greater light, a light that was complete and freeing—a light not dependent upon the hands of men.

Ask yourself this: Who relies on a lantern in the brilliance of a noonday sun?

It is reality denying for a man who is longing to see to cling to a light bulb and to defy the full spectrum light of the sun. Why then would we rely upon the works of law when one greater than The Law has freed us? Yet day to day, many called *Christians* attempt to look into the mysteries of God with only a meager lantern. Look church—the sun is shining—look into its great light to blind your moralistic eye and set you free in Jesus!

131. A Greek philosopher named Diogenes "The Cynic" walked about the Athens market place during the height of day holding a torch (or a lantern) and searching about. When people asked him what this absurdity was all about he replied, "I am just looking for an honest man." It is said that he never found an honest man, only the selfishness, deceptions, and vanity of mankind. Diogenes lived before the birth of Jesus Christ. One wonders what Diogenes would have said if him walking lead him to stand in front of Jesus? What would Jesus have said to Him? Might Diogenes have smashed his lantern and said, "Aha, now I can see for here stands my sight—now we are all seen as blind! Now the world has been given its true eye!"

Who is the honest man? The honest man is the man that realizes the lantern is not enough to light the world. The honest man is the one who realizes that he himself is not the sun, nor can he ever be. The honest man is the one who acknowledges that to be in harmony with God he must be saved by Christ, for Christ is that sun that has fulfilled and expanded the light given to man. The honest man is the one who sees the beauty of the law fulfilled graciously by the burn and beauty of Jesus Christ.

The honest man is only honest because the light of Christ has first shone upon him.

The law is beautiful—but the radiance of Jesus more so. How well can we know Jesus Christ, the one who fulfilled the Ten Commandments in perfect union with the will of God, if we do not know what those commandments are—and I am not speaking here of mere numbering. Our lack of knowing the Decalogue shows our lack in knowing *the Logos*—Christ Jesus.

The *Deca-logos*: the ten words. Jesus Christ the Logos: The Word

132. Why the law if we were to fail? This is why—to reveal the fall. Remember this, because it is often forgotten: the problem has never been the law; it is that we cannot do what it necessitates. The Law is only a spotlight on reality, *the ought to* of life set upon the high pedestal of reality to reveal the want of our reach.

The Law is an argument of reason that says, "Look here—see the distance between how it is and how it should be; see the dissonance between "you are the man" and "behold the man!" See the distance between heaven and earth! See that no stairway can be built by the hands of men!

133. If God commands something, does the command imply ability? If not, then why does He command it?

Why then does He command the cripple man to rise? Or for decaying Lazarus to shuffle forth in grave clothes?

Because the power is in His command, not in man's ability. The power is in the Word of God that creates and calls forth that which did not exist. The Decalogue, the Ten Commandments, is ultimately for the glory of God to be revealed—though in this The Law blesses humanity.

"How then, can they call on the one they have not believed in? And how can they believe in the one they have not heard? And how can they hear without someone preaching to them? And how can they preach unless they are sent? As it is written, 'How beautiful are the feet of those who bring good news! But not all the Israelites accepted the good news. For Isaiah says, 'Lord, who has believed our message?' Consequently, faith comes by hearing the message, and the message is heard through the word of Christ" (Romans 10:14-17).

134. "For this is the covenant that I will make with the house of Israel after those days, saith the Lord; I will put *my laws* into their mind, and write them in their hearts: and I will be to them a God, and they shall be to me a people" (Hebrews 8:10)

The fulfillment of the Beautiful Standard is how we are found accepted by God—but Jesus alone fulfilled them—He is the Beautiful Standard, and in this beauty man is condemned and redeemed.

~Disciples of Life~

135. Suffering is the perennial and pervasive revealer of *inwardness*—*inwardness* being one's entrustment to the truth. Why—because love is a spit-at stranger, a chastised alien in this world.

The light that sparks from the friction of suffering reveals whether one is a mere *admirer,* or a true *follower* of Jesus. It is the rasping of a coin across a slate touchstone—does one leave a mark or not? Are we coin or counterfeit?

Suffering pushes to crisis what quietly hides in comfort; suffering is a negative pressure, a siphon that draws out the poison or the nectar from within; it calls to light what kills the soul silently, or what nourishes the soul.

136. We should swiftly delineate *general suffering* from *Christian suffering*—or else one will mistake the Christian for the masochist. All will suffer to varying degrees for we live in an off-center world racing through space. Christian suffering is not the general suffering a Christian experiences (*as if they are exempt from the entropy of the world!*), but Christian suffering is to suffer for obedience to God's Word.

General suffering is a consequence of man's sin, and so it is universal—from melancholy to mass graves, from splinters in the thumb to genocide. *Christian suffering* is found when the sin of man takes action in hate against obedience to God—and attempts to kill God in another person.

Many say they suffer for their faith and proudly wear their golden martyr badge—but this suffering is usually just the ordinary and inevitable consequences of anyone born on earth. Let us be wise when we talk about suffering. Let us be compassionate and not offer cold comfort.

Like a cut to the flesh, suffering turns us inward, exposes what is within, be it blood, bone, love, hate.

In *general suffering* there is a collision that is often uninterrupted by pretenses—and there is an exposure of the correlation of the will and the reason. Because suffering exposes what is within, it highlights just where the entwined will and the mind place their trust. This revelation is a sudden exposure of the self—to be used either for good or ill, change or entrenchment. Pain, like a fist to a sponge, reveals suddenly what was held within.

137. When obedience (*not* fickle religious promises—*"If you take this pain away from me God, I'll never do X again!*) comes amidst suffering, then it is obedience to Sovereignty, and not obedience to self-origin. To obey the self is no grand thing; even an infant obeys himself, and so too does a tyrant! Ah! But to obey another even amidst being chaffed in the storm—in this is love!

Why is suffering linked with obedience? Because *general suffering* will reveal our rebellion that must be repented of; and *Christian suffering* is our faith in action, in friction against the world.

"He learned obedience from what He suffered and, once He was made perfect, he became the source of eternal salvation for all who obey Him" (Hebrews 5:8). But this is a difficult passage! How could Jesus learn obedience? How quickly we are to dispose of the tension of God/man—do you see how easily unbelief tears at the Word? He was fully both man and God; He had to learn obedience for He was human—and He could do it perfectly, for He was God.

Christ has walked through all that we will: He suffered generally for he was truly human; He also suffered for His perfect obedience to the will of God. He suffered for being Christ. If he suffered for being Christ, we will suffer for being Christians.

Does the Christian seek suffering? No, this is not love. The Christian follows Christ who is love—this will bear sure suffering in an unloving world.

Are we greater than Christ? The more like Christ we are the more the world will press against us like a vice. But here is joy—for let the vice press you further into Christ, deeper into self-resignation!

138. Suffering has two trajectories; it can lance us and drain us of ourselves and our inflamed self-reliance, or it can bruise our souls until they swell larger and loom more self-obsessed.

We all suffer: *if we do or if we do not* is not a question to be asked. Suffering in some form is the warp and woof of life in a fallen, entropic world. But what occurs in our souls when they are upon the forge—this is the question. Our souls, moving in progression to something more monstrous or heavenly, are moved along in either direction of this progression by our response to suffering and pleasure.

Because this world is a soul shaping forge, suffering can never be meaningless, yet it seems as though it always is. Because there is an ultimate either/or that we are headed to, all the adversity, pains, and heart aches are redeemed (in the joyous end) by them leading us to our good God—or they are made all the more miserable by the miserable master of *our self.*

139. When it comes to pleasure, there is a reverse reaction than with suffering: pleasure is almost always invested with purpose. This is because we feel it is our due, our right of existence. The error here is centripetal; that is, we find the meaning of the pleasure in our selves. Rather than set up camp and live at the meeting point of pleasure and ourselves, we should be acknowledging the double movement of the purpose of pleasure: it is centripetal (feeling the pleasure within ourselves) and centrifugal (acknowledging in gratitude that the purpose is to reveal the glory and the goodness of our Creator, the giver of pleasure).

Pleasure is for man—for man is for the glory of God.

140. A disciple of Christ is not one shielded from suffering, but one whose wounds have deep purpose in the fight for everlasting

love—wounds that are healed in retrospect when they are presented as white signatures of trust to the God who has scars of His own.

We are moving towards an ultimate either/or: all heaven, or all hell—all presence, or all absence of love. There is no floating island between, no atoll of both/and. There is no desiccated kernel of hell in heaven; there is no good seed of heaven to flower in hell.

One either lives in trust of Christ, or they don't. The nominal Christian is just that, *nominal*, because they want heaven and hell—and so they don't want Christ. Christ is an empty name to one who wants even the tiniest bit of hell.

141. It should be said, becoming a follower of Christ makes life more difficult—not easier in the conventional sense. But it also makes life *living*; good becomes truly good, and beauty becomes truly beautiful and no longer a mirage. It is the trading of ashes for beauty, of phantomness for substance.

But did not Jesus say "my yoke is easy?" Yes, He did, but most overlook that it is still a yoke. A yoke is for fruitful work, for focused exertion, for plowing the fields that will bear a harvest. More so, we overlook that the yoke is His. The yoke that we have, the burden we have to bear is the burden that Christ bore for us. Our strength is in Him, our meaning and our aim is in Him—in this way it is easy—a joy to bear.

We have been given a glorious labor. But when such a yoke is gladly upon us, the world is fast against us. As hate is against love, as arrogance is against humility, the upside down world is against the one who is up-right. Sloth is against *the glorious labor*. Pride is against the sweat of paradise. Easier?—no. Good?—yes.

We have been yoked with one stronger than us; one that can perfectly bear the load. In this we grow and become like Him.

142. Now this is an important thing—denying of the self. It is not a self masochistic thing; it is a loving thing. When we deny the self for Christ's sake we deny the falsity of ourselves as god, and place reality firmly on God. We pass the torch of authority, so to speak, to its rightful owner; we give back the fire we have stolen.

The paradox of true love is that we only show love for ourselves when we deny ourselves and glorify God in loving others; when we do this, we recognize the reality of God, that humanity is made in God's image (*imago Dei*) and only then can true love show all humanity, including ourselves, as loved and purposed for love. All this is possible because God first loved. And so, the paradox: only when we acknowledge we are broken can we claim we are whole. Only in kneeling can we rise. Only when we acknowledge that we are unworthy of love are we found to be the desired lover in the greatest romance ever told.

A true disciple will love in a way that makes the world angry.

A *disciple of life*, a true *follower* of Christ, will tacitly expose those who are voyeurs, those who are admirers of a Jesus of their whim and fantasy. The mere admirer will be exposed as idle and untraveled by those actually walking the good road. This means that the disciple will agitate nominal Christianity simply by way of their character.

143. There is a bizarre thought that floats about the spring waters of Christianity like a dirty plastic bottle. It is the belief that you can be a Christian without being a disciple. This is garbage (and recyclable garbage at that, for it comes at us in many forms). It is the thought that there are non-Christians, Christians, and then there are disciples, or *super Christians*. It is the misguided belief that being a disciple is an elite elective course once you become a Christian. This thought has *straight from Hades* written all over the label; but few are reading the writing on the bottle.

We are designed to be disciples. If we are not a disciple we are not a Christian. There are many good intentioned Christians who are not Christians. God will sort this out—not us.

What is called the *Great Commission* might as well be called the *Common Omission*. Many think that sin is merely what we do wrong; more often than not it is that which we wrongly don't do. Don't be surprised by this little twist—omission's tail is as long as history.

It is Eve that is commonly blamed for the fall; yet the Bible rightly lays the blame on Adam. What did he do? Only the most insidious thing possible—he stood idly by while the serpent spiritually raped Eve. Adam did nothing, though he was the one who had the direct revelation from God on what to do and what not to do. The Word of God considers this omission the greater sin. So if anyone ever slurs the Bible for showing women to be the source of all our woes, it only reveals their omission in reading the very text they have judged! Remind them of what the Bible actually says, and who the blame falls firmly on—humanity.

144. The word disciple literally means *one who learns, or grasps*. If we are not disciples then we are not learning—we are not growing in conformity with Christ; and if we are not growing in Christ who is the radiance of the infinite God, then we are not in Him and are of a dead origin.

Think of the fallen oak twig—once removed from the great tree it cannot grow. How can we be a Christian and not a disciple? How can we be a Christian and not be a Christian? This is no Zen kōan asking "what is the sound of one hand clapping" and seeking some esoteric meaning—it is only a flat contradiction and the idiocy is apparent. A Christian is a disciple!

Do we see that this broad road of being *just a Christian* is not being a Christian at all? Obedience is the narrow road—this is the only road for the Christian. A *Christian* who is not a disciple is a drying stick who calls themselves a living branch.

Why then obedience? Because it is the motion of love from a creature to its Creator; it is the expression of love between unequal parties. To claim love of God but shirk obedience is the claiming of a love between equal parties—*equality to God*—is this not the most unchristian thought possible? To not be a disciple is to not obey; do you see the gravity of the problem?

If you chose to follow someone, and you followed them for weeks, around every bend in the road and over every bridge, and then one day you stopped following and turned back, and it all became only a memory, could you call yourself a follower? Get from this what you will.

145. Most people want optimism, not discipleship. Optimism usually allows for one to stay where they are at. Discipleship calls for change; a disciple is usually taken to task because they are being taught by the master, being changed into something greater. Being corrected is what a disciple (though reluctantly) wants, because they want to be more than they are. Optimism flashes counterfeit smiles; discipleship gives heavenly groans *and* authentic smiles.

Tragically, there has been an over-extended leaning towards *optimism* in modern Christianity. Now, I must qualify my use of the term optimism: it does not mean hope in Christ as our Savior, or the joy that redemption brings; for these are always essential to the reality of regeneration. What it does mean is *a verbal and acted optimism that forgoes honesty and covers difficulties with a sick, sugary coating, especially in declaring humanity's basic goodness.* It is eating theological cotton candy all the time with no reprieve from its damaging pink sweetness. It is an act of substitution that trades a difficult truth for an easy-out.

This damaging optimism has stained pulpits, missions, writings, and other forms of sharing the Gospel. In fact, we might want to give this tainted optimism its own special name to distinguish it from true optimism—call it *optimiasm*; for *miasma* is the Greek word for stain or pollution.

146. A disciple is not one who merely has faith—but faith in accordance with knowledge. A disciple is tied to reality, not some fantasy; and for that, they are free.

It seems there is much talk about faith and belief. *Just believe. Just have faith* it is said. Why don't we hear the absurdity? Where are these words flying to? They seem to vaporize into the air.

What if I were to say, "Just be angry!" You would say "at what" or "why?" Or what if I were to walk up to you and say "Just doubt!" You would look at me with a screwy look and ask "doubt what?" So why is it that when we say *be positive, just have faith, just hope, just believe* we are not asking *in what* or *who* or *why* or *how*? All these nice sounding bits of spiritual wisdom beg for a subject. Faith in *what*? Hope in *whom*? Believe in *what*? And the *be positive* nonsense begs a frame of reference. Positive could mean up, could mean down. It could mean less, it could mean more. So what is it?

These trendy bits of pop guru *wisdom* need to be qualified—or quarantined. The Lord our God is our frame of reference. He is *the who, the how* and *the why*. How do we know the frame of reference?—His Word. And positive, well, is only positive if it moves us into closer fellowship with God. So it follows, positive could mean bankruptcy, a humbling and low paying career, a physical handicap such as a limp—it could also mean a jackpot in Vegas, healing of a tumor, or a career windfall.

147. There is a popular belief out there (let's call it the *The Secret*) that if we just think happy, positive things, then the cosmos will give us good things in return. (And of course by good things we usually mean a Mercedes Benz or a salary bonus or a famous face.)

This misguided belief says that if you ask you will receive. If you throw your requests out into the great buzzing cosmos, the energy will return to you and your life will vastly improve. The proponents of this will talk about god all whispery and *sacred-like*, but then call him energy as if he were something manipulated to run an infomercial kitchen appliance. They will stray from the biblical God but call their floating theories biblical because they will use dislocated words from the Bible such as sowing, or reaping, or heaven, etc. These same people believe that we can do anything—we just have to realize our potential and think and act positively about it.

All this hyper-spiritual fluff sells very well—it just sounds so happy and potentially prosperous—it sounds so Zen, so religious—of course it will sell—it is not love but spiritual lust! Spiritual pornography! It makes me feel queasy. It feels like happy thought vertigo—where is the grounding in truth? *Who cares, just prepare for the blessings you yourself stimulate!* "It's all just energy, just energy!" they say. But, my friends, it is hard to be loved by *just energy*. It is hard to worship energy when you use it to rev up your electric shaver or old green blender to make a malt. Let these people have their copper-topped versions of God. I will worship God who is **personal** and infinite; who is the Creator of the energy we know.

Saying that God is *just energy* is another way of invoking the Eastern thought that there is no personal god, but merely an *impersonal ground of being*. If this is true, why did Jesus call God *Father, Abba*? We cannot hold the *impersonal ground of being* worldview and the Christian *personal relationship with God* worldview together! We must choose one; now here is a wise use of either/or! These two must be slashed apart!

Attempts to de-personalize God dehumanize us. When we attempt to rob God of His glory we debase ourselves.

It is easier to *spiritualize* than to be a disciple; it is easier to piece and patch together a religion than it is to let the one truth reveal our fractures.

Energy has always been an easy idol. This is not a new phenomenon; it is a vogue new update to an old virus. There have been false gods of the river, the sky, and the sun. The powerful energies of fire, wind, and water, have always been a tool to subvert their Creator. Adding a smile of quasi-spiritual optimism and calling your god "energy" does not make it less idolatrous than throwing your selfish wishes and herbs into a sacred stream of river nymphs, or burning incense upon an alter to the sun god Ra.

Wide roads sell better than narrow roads. Discipleship is a narrow road. Wishing wells and the karmic energy of the universe are wide roads—super highways—eight lanes to speed about in within our Lexus frames of religion—air conditioning and leather seats to remind us "we're king and we deserve it."

Grace swallows karma like sunlight drowns out an old light bulb.

148. I am thoroughly an optimist—but a cynical one. The glass is half full—but if it is poisoned Kool-Aid I'd rather not drink it, regardless if it is half full or half empty. Many Christians drink poison because they are told the cup is half full; the cheery tone wins them, and they never look to see what they are drinking. No matter how pink a bullet is painted, I rather not take it in the chest.

This ill-optimism, this undiscerning optimism, this *optimiasm* would happen less if we were to dwell in the Word of God, merely "just read the Bible." God knows there are vipers that hiss sibilant scripture and quote it well—but we are to dwell in the Word, read it, live it, love it and absorb it until it seeps out of our pores like garlic oil from a garlic lover, like heat from a sun-blushed face. We are to dwell in it—literally, set up our tent amidst its landscape of truth.

149. The Bible is the most famous book in the world—it is astounding it is known by so few people.

I am learning to understand why the Bible is constantly shot at and systematically dynamited by both scholars and laymen—it is the same reason that we crucified Christ. The religious leaders sought to murder Christ not because he was ugly to them, but because He was the most Beautiful. "For He knew that for envy they had delivered Him" (Matthew 27:18).

Jesus was not crucified for being wrong; He was crucified for being right—being perfect. The Bible is swiped at for the same reason we violently shade our eyes from the zenith Sun; the beauty is simply more than our condition can take.

150. Here I set my face out for the world to slap; but I set it out joyfully. I believe the Bible is the very Word of God. A book of *life* for fallen man! I believe it was inspired in men by the exhaling of God. It is a book that holds the greatest gems of all literary traditions—who could out-write the author of Job? Who could shatter traditional thought with irony more smashing than the writer of Jonah? Who could shame the Psalms with more penetrating and beautiful poetry? Ecclesiastes—brilliant and blistering!

The Bible does not "burn my bosom" in some subjective proof of *authenticity*—but it does haunt my heart *and* my mind. Its words trace the corridors of my humanity like a man with a lamp exploring a castle, lighting artwork and cobwebs that have been there for centuries. Not only does it provide answers, it provides questions that are even sharper and harder to face than what I muster up in my own frustrations and spurious digs against God.

It is bursting with beauty; it is brimmed with blood and flinching tragedy. It is raw about sex, real about suffering. It is ripe with hope—yet it is a heavy history. It is excavated by archaeology, it is scanned by logicians. Its message is a comfort when one is dying; it is often troubling to the living. It is fully practical and profoundly mystical. It is balanced; self correcting. It is a psychological Rosetta stone. It is napalm; it is salve.

The revolution that takes place within its narrative evokes outlandish fury and surprising peace. It idealizes nothing, but shows everything moving towards perfection—a trajectory that outdoes the dreams of the naïve utopian. It exposes entropy with a harmonic voice of restoration. It is good news. It is considered to be too conservative and too radical. It sounds like the blues on a ragged old acoustic guitar in an empty bar; it sounds like gospel music in an engineered chamber hall. It is thought to be too hopeful, yet too earthy. It is considered too legalistic and too heavy on grace—that is, thought to be unfair.

It is supposed to be too ancient to be of any modern good; too modern to be written by ancient hands. It is too gruesome to be divine; it is too bright to be human. It is popularly ignored and continuously studied. It is a book that should either be burned on a raging bonfire as an offense against all humanity, or venerated as the Word of the Living God; you cannot set it somewhere in-between if you have truly understood what it says, what it means. It is a book of perfect tensions that lift up the peace and love of God.

151. "If you hold fast to my teaching, you are really my disciples. Then you will know the truth, and the truth will set you free" (John 8:31-31). Swiftly, Jesus disarms the dangerous idea that you can believe Him yet not obey. He knew the hypocrisy that was boiling in the hearts of men...

To trust something is to act upon it. It is painfully simple: If we believe Jesus, we will obey Him: "If you love me, you will obey what I command (Matthew 14:15). This is so simple—but it simply frustrates our masks and posturing, so we try to fight it.

If there is a separate category for Christians and another for disciples, then we can live the way we desire and still call ourselves Christians—without the annoyance of that obedience baggage. How convenient for man.

How are we to obey what He commands if we don't know what He commands? Could it be that we are supposed to seek the Scriptures for what He commands? If not, what are we to do—pull them out of the air?

We are to hear *and* do the Word. We must have right orthodoxy (right opinion) *and* orthopraxy (right actions). We are to let the Good News break free from our brain cells to flood into our heart's chambers, and let the radicalized heart pulse our hands and our tongues into right action. If the Good News is dammed up in our skull it will only make for a blinding headache and stiff, grumpy company.

"*Trust* the Lord, and do *good*," says Psalm 37. Remember, we must first *be* then we can *do*. Being comes before doing. In whom we place our trust will be seen in our actions.

"You error because you do not know the scriptures!" Jesus is still speaking these words—but they smack with twice the weight of responsibility, for we now have both the Old and New Testaments. If we do not see the Scriptures as those that point to Jesus Christ as our only hope, as God inspired words that tear down, dismantle, and shatter deceptive thoughts of man-centered religion, then we are in error.

152. To what can we compare modern discipleship? It is like an orchestra made up of those who play no instruments at all; and when the conductor sways and a song is begun, they stoically look over to a few in their numbers who do play instruments, and do it with passion. And when the song is played and the audience applauses, the orchestra of *no-players* exclaim, "What a fine job we all have done in playing that song." Would not the players sounded just as good without the *no-players* taking up elbow room and chattering through all the beautiful melodies that the audience needed to hear? Who then is the orchestra? And when does an orchestra not need to play a song? For an orchestra is to play—this is the reason for its existence, is it not?

Are we an admirer of the orchestra, or do our fingers rub and run across taut strings in following the conductor?

~Triune~

153. The Trinity reveals just how upside down the world is! Rather than seeing the mystery of the Trinity as reasonable, many tempt to use the mystery of the Trinity to discount the reality of God. This is the attentive playing of a song, the analyzing of melody and lyric, all in an attempt to disprove the songwriter.

Yet, it is the mystery of the Trinity that shows just how sane and rational Christianity is. It is insane to ask man to believe in a God that is like man; it is sane to ask man to believe in a God that is like God and beyond the minds of men. If God were to be God then His nature must be beyond what humanity can reason; yet the mystery is still reasonable because He is God and, by necessity, greater than, and beyond being captured by our minds.

Reality doesn't depend upon one's viewpoint. If I don't know how the pacemaker of the heart works, does my viewpoint of *"cardial mystery"* stop hearts around me? Does a heart surgeon's understanding of the pacemaker alone bring back the beats to the hearts I stopped in my unknowing? What a fickle and cruel world this would be!

If one must disavow all mystery to reasonably acknowledge reality—then we can know absolutely nothing. Tell me, what is energy? What exactly is time? How was the universe spun into motion? How does a thought relate to the grey matter of the brain? Can one speak exhaustively of these things and wrap them up? One who needs to know all before acknowledging something will never know anything.

The more honest we are, the more reasonable it is to climb up to a roof top and release the dam of pressure that has built in us for so long: "I don't understand!" The more honest we are, the more we will acknowledge there is a mysterious current under every wave we have ridden, named and catalogued.

The fact that true Christianity is resolute about the three-in-one nature of God is a peculiar pointer towards it being truth rather than it being a deception fashioned by man *who is so wise as not to invent something so foolish!*

The mystery of the Trinity reveals the coherency of Christianity and its insistence on reason. It would be unreasonable to claim that the essence of God is not a mystery.

Let us remember that mystery is not absurdity—but absurdity is a mystery.

The blur of the sun brings clarity to the world. If the image of the sun were clear to our eyes then it would not be blazingly bright enough to light our world, and all would be blurry and dark. It is often difficult, often impossible to see the source of light by which we see. Unaided, we cannot see the sun without going blind; unaided, we could not deduce the nature of God. Both are reasonable.

154. If one *must* rationalize away the paradox of the Trinity to maintain any religion (be it Mormonism, Islam, Jehovah's Witness, Atheism, etc.) then one simply does not believe in anything greater than themselves; therefore, they discredit their own Trinitarian-less faith.

Is a non-Trinitarian God always an extension of man worshipping himself? Well, is one ever *not worshipping an idol* if they are not worshipping the true God?

Is the Trinity balked at because the human mind cannot fathom how three are one, how one is three? If so, then one must reject any other mystery of divinity based upon our *not understanding*. The Muslim must reject the perfect omnipotence of Allah because it is beyond our finite minds; the Mormon must reject the miracle of prophecy; the Jehovah Witness must reject the sovereign Jehovah.

If one is to denounce the Trinity, it must be on reasonable terms—that is, it must be denounced in regard to revelation rather than deduction and what finite man thinks is possible—did God reveal or not reveal His essence in Scripture to be three in one? This is the starting point.

From the first chapter of Genesis to the cinematic mysteries of Revelation, the light of the Trinity suffuses and radiates all Scripture.

Many people claim that *rationality* is the reason they don't bow before God. They claim that "if God did exist He would not reveal something absurd, something illogical, like the tri-unity!" It is absurd to believe that God would not reveal a truth that seems absurd to us. Again—remember, *mystery* is not absurdity.

It is contradictory to believe in a revelation of God only as long as it is fully understood. Revelation is the revealing of a wonder, not the explanation of all mysteries. It is purely egotistical to think that a revelation will explain God exhaustively.

155. The Trinity has caused a great deal of commotion for control-minded humanity. Now here is the sharp point of this pen: Truly, it is not an issue of the Trinity being or not being true, being or not being absurd. It is that we do not understand the Trinity; that we cannot understand it—and this in itself is threatening to the human condition. One cannot accept the mystery of the Trinity without bowing to a God that is mightily above us. Belief in the Trinity presupposes humility. Hah! The very nature of God pricks the proud.

God is love—here is another mystery that is reasonable. The triune essence of God speaks to how He is love. Love has a lover and a beloved. God is love because He is a perfect relation with Himself: the lover, the beloved and the love radiating between. The Father, the Son and the Holy Spirit are eternally, and have forever been the perfect expression of love. Jesus glorifies the Father; the Father glorifies the Son; the Spirit witnesses to the truth of Jesus that is radiated by the Father. Jesus is the will of the Father—the will of the Father is to have His Spirit draw humanity to the wonder of Jesus Christ. Does this quickly spin out of our mental grasp? It does and it should—and reasonably so, for we are speaking of God, the author of reason!

Love is a subject-to-subject relationship; that is, it requires unity and diversity; it takes separation *and* consummation. All gods that are not *one in the mystery of the Trinity* are "wasting gods"—wasting away, self-depleting, as Narcissus and his empty self love.

The Scriptures are adamant that God is love—and for this they are adamant that He is triune. God is not a lonely God of the desert—lonely gods are bitter gods who have to rule by scimitars and politics.

Some have proclaimed that God needs us in order for Him to be love. No! This is not true—this is against His revelation. Our existence is a pure grace. God did not create us and this universe in order to have an object to love that He may become love; the Trinity precludes this. The Trinity reveals that our existence was born out of preexisting love—we were born of love; not of necessity for love to exist. And so we were not needed for God to *be love*.

This reveals a central reason why man commonly disavows the Trinity: for if the Trinity is not true and a god exists, then he needs his creation. He needs us that he may *be love,* for a lover needs a beloved. This, again, is the vaunting of man. It is a hidden-in-religion idolatry of man—it says that humanity is just as important and necessary as God. *"God needs us!"* This puts God in our debt!

156. Unity *and* diversity: a lover and beloved must exist for love.

The unified theory of everything—like the treasure hunter's Holy Grail, this great search of the philosopher and the physicist concerns the very lips of Christ. For the answer is in Christ—in God—in the

Holy Spirit. The Trinity is both one and many—and this is the foundation a *uni*verse that is *di*verse.

There is an *I-Thou* nature of existence that we cannot escape, for there is a *unity-diversity* in our Creator.

There is a difference between water and oxygen; and they are different than us, but a unity exists, and so we universally need them in each particularity. There is a difference between a lover and his beloved; yet a union exists. To speak, to merely make a sound, to even make a truth claim reveals there is a "one and many." All is not the same; though there is a unity to existence that allows for understanding and absolutes. There is continuity to existence—we live; life works.

The universal and the particular exist; they do and we acknowledge it by any movement we make. That is to say, we continually acknowledge this "philosophical thought" in our everyday life. There is a difference between a plum and us, and so we eat it because of our hunger. There exists both a thing called a plum and a hunger, but in us there is a specific plum and a specific rumble in the belly. There is coherence in how the universe is set up.

Every time we define something, name something and set it apart, we acknowledge the existence of the particular and the universal. *All is not the same and all is part of the universe.*

There is a kind of union beneath all things; even islands are connected to the earth. But there is a difference too; Jamaica is not Maui.

To collapse all into one (only universal) or un-connect all (only particular) is to make for incoherence. Maui becomes Jamaica becomes Mt. Everest becomes Kansas. All the letters melt together, all sentences pool into chaos. But this is not reality—there is order to reality and order means both *universal* and *particular*.

If we say there is truth, then there is a relationship between all things. The "relationship" is the universal; the "all things" are the particulars.

For those of the *philosophic bent*, this is not talking of the impersonal Platonic forms and ideas. No— it is just observing that there is relationship, that all is not insulated; that there is a necessity for there to be *separateness* in order for there to be *relationship,* which is a unity at its root.

157. God is personal, and in this, both *one* and *many* as the Scriptures reveal. It is because of this that *I* can exist, typing this for *you* to read—*we*, part of the human race—personal beings.

Any statement of knowledge is dependent upon existence coming from a source that is both one and many. If it was *one* alone, then diversity is a deception; if it was *many* without union, then there is no unity to even call it many! Either one stripped of the other strips the universe to a naked incoherence. No one lives as if it was one or the other—we live as if both.

Is all in life one? Or is it many? Such a question has hounded the philosophers for thousands of years—the problem of the universal—yet the disciples of God have found their peace in the answer. It is both. It is unity/diversity; universal/particular, many/one. I can think of nothing more obvious, rational and essential to our existence—yet it is a humbling and for that a hard and unwanted truth. And so the Trinity speaks to us of what we somehow know and act in accordance to—both union *and* division—but buck against because it is of God.

In wake of this nuanced but hulking truth, the Trinity is a necessary belief in acknowledging reality. The Trinity is not a road block, but a bridge beyond a gap we could never cross on our own—pun intended.

158. There is a necessary relationship between the infinite and the finite that cannot be overcome. The finite is to know of the infinite

(because we are made *imago Dei*), but to always fall in wonder to that which extends beyond oneself.

If God is infinite then we as finite beings simply cannot explain His nature. The finite will always be exhausted by the infinite—but this exhaustion is where the finite finds rests and anxiety falls away; the finite does not have to hold the world together—what relief!

We can know God for we have true knowledge, but this is never an exhaustive knowledge.

159. If we have faith in the revelation, then let us have faith in what the revelation reveals. There is no need to argue the Trinity if one doesn't first believe in the revelation of God! But if one believes in the revelation—ah!—then the Trinity is there waiting in its waltzing beauty!

The mystery of the Trinity is not a knock against the veracity of the Bible—it is a knock against the femur of man's pride.

"Then God said, 'Let us make man in our image, in our likeness'" (Genesis 1:26).

"'You are not yet fifty years old,' the Jews said to Him, 'and you have seen Abraham!'
'I tell you the truth,' Jesus answered, 'before Abraham was born, I Am!'" (John 5:58).

"For prophecy never had its origin in the will of man, but men spoke from God as they were carried along by the Holy Spirit" (2 Peter 1:21).

"When they saw Him, they *worshipped* Him; but some doubted. Then Jesus came to them and said, 'All authority in heaven and on earth has been given to me. Therefore go and make disciples of all nations, baptizing them in the name of the Father, the Son, and the Holy Spirit, and teaching them to obey everything I have commanded you. And Surely I am with you always, to the very end of the age'" (Matthew 28:18-20).

160. The purpose of this book is not to theorize, but to usher theory to the crisis of action, and have ideas ushered to the edge of obedience—for obedience is love and love is only an action, never merely theoretical. Love is an action because it is the movement, the great reality that throbs amongst the Trinity.

Love is incarnational—and therefore concrete in action. Abstraction without concrete commitment is a distraction, a deception that allows the poor to sleep on cold concrete and allows victims to stay in fear, unaided by fellow man who is *thinking* benevolent thoughts.

Love is a synapse that moves a hand to motion.

~ The Beautiful Correlation ~

161. All good comes from God.

We must remember, it is evil that is defined from good—for evil is the twisting of good—by nature evil is never from original stock. It is a pale and ugly version of what was beautiful and purposed.

You can have good without evil; you cannot have evil without good. This is fundamental, but deeply forgotten in our amnesia. When we realize that evil is a twisting of good then we acknowledge the Creator as good. God is not the author of evil. He did not create the twisted. This is lovely—this is not a thought to pass quickly over. Think about this and test this. Test all of these words and thoughts against the touchstone of the Scriptures.

Because evil is not of original stock, because it is a twisting of good, it correlates that evil is a poseur. It correlates that evil masks as that which is beautiful—an angel of light. And so, it correlates that Satan is the father of lies; he is the deceiver. Evil comes as beauty, as that which is attractive—herein lies the deception.

162. The reason we constantly try to explain and understand evil (as the philosopher David Hume asked "Whence then evil?") is to attach it hard upon an event, to attribute to it a meaning other than our own real guilt. Rationalization of evil is a metaphysical attempt at blame shifting. Like Adam and Eve, we long to pin the guilt on someone else. First we point at our neighbor, then society—ultimately we point at God. Isn't it said, "How could God do this!!?"

Humanity's great problem can be seen in the very issue of *the problem of evil*. We are constantly trying to justify God (call it theodicy, religion, etc) by resolving this issue of evil, by trying to rationalize evil into God's universe rather than just trust God and accept our due guilt. This is the evil itself! We are not to justify God—but He is the one who justifies us! Any inversion of this is an inversion of truth.

We must never think that Satan is the opposite of God; God has no opposite for *opposite* implies a type of equality. Satan may oppose God, just like humanity opposes God, but this does not make him or we *opposites* of the Creator. We flatter ourselves and the deceiver if we think we are opposites—we are not. We are creations of the one unparalleled.

163. This talk of beauty and goodness (and its twisting) has led us again to speak of tension. In the ancient philosophy of the Greeks, the great tension, the balance, is known as the *golden mean*. It is the apt middle between two extremes; one of deficiency and the other of excess. This is a balance born between two negatives. Really, this is a simple idea that sounds daunting because of the words *ancient, philosophy,* and *Greeks*.

An example of the golden mean would be generosity. Generosity is the middle ground between wastefulness (excess) and being stingy (deficiency). Here both extremes are a vice, and the intermediate is the virtue. Yet, there is another type of balance, of tension—one in which both extremes are good.

Where the golden mean of the Greeks was found halfway between two evils, we also ought to be concerned with holding two "goods" together in tension, like partners in a dance. If this seems strange, we must ask ourselves a question. Why must we always define virtues and balance in the framework of evil? As if goodness were chance and a secondary occurrence popping up between two intended ills? It is simply bad theology and insulting to God if we have to define His goodness by reference to evil.

We must acknowledge that "evil is defined from good—for evil is the twisting of good—by nature evil is never from original stock; it is a pale and ugly version of what was beautiful and purposed." This is important, for all this talk of balance, of tension, only comes out of Christ himself, and He was original goodness. Let us give glory where it is due—and stop defining good by evils.

Christianity knows balances defined by *the good*—by the gifts given to us by God. I have called these *benevolent binaries* or *paradoxical tensions*—but there is no real sense in renaming what it obvious—we can go the simple route and call them "two good things held together."

Remember the airplane wings and the scissor blades? They are two good things that when held together are beneficial, and when separated become dangerous or useless. The balance comes, not in finding a halfway point or a compromise between two evils, but rather in the simultaneous presence of two intended goods. One and a half wings is just as bad as only having one while you are in the stratosphere; it is two or no go.

I must admit, this is no innovative idea; there really is nothing new here; just something as beautiful and significant as the first sunrise to burst over the new earth. If one is looking for a new "step by step" theory on how to successfully apply Christian living to the current *isms* and *ologies* of the world, this is not that secret. Yet, if one is looking for another attempt at conveying what has been true from the glowing dawn of history, and will be until time and matter is folded up like a piece of paper, then this might be something to think upon.

164. It seems many people have become like the silly egoist who so loved to look at himself that he stepped closer and closer to the mirror until his nose was pressed hard against it, and he could no longer see himself or the world around him because he was too close and in the way. Well, it seems that we have moved far "too close" to ourselves and that we are often "in the way." We are enamored with ourselves. We have become so drunk on our *own ideas* of *what* Christianity is that we have little room for Christ's fully orbed goodness.

It is as George Orwell once said, "We have now sunk to the depth where the restatement of the obvious is the first duty of intelligible men." So here it is: Human beings have two legs, birds have two wings, and truth and grace are beautifully wed together in the Lord Jesus Christ.

165. God is infinite and humans are finite; this makes for very interesting relations. How can the two come into relation?

In our view from finitude, wisdom lives in tension. Wonders are perceived in the awareness of tension. Contradictions tear apart—they are the lethargy of what is banal, they are the slouching movements of entropy burying cities in sand and fracturing friendships.

It would benefit the heart if we understood the difference between a contradiction and a paradox. So often the heart simply doesn't care for this knowing—for it might lead to an indictment.

The law of non-contradiction states: One cannot say of something that it is and that it is not in the same respect and at the same time, in the same context. What this means is that truth by definition is exclusive. This is not seen merely by deductive methods (of human machinations); it is also exegetically found (revealed in Scripture). This is Biblical, for Jesus is *The* Truth, and there is only one way to the Father. There is one way—this is exclusive.

This is to say that A is not *not A*. What is cannot be the same as its antithesis. Every statement, every argument ever used relies upon this; even the argument to call it "untrue." The law of non-contradiction is foundational logic that is tucked into the wrinkled wiring of the human brain, and within the valves of the heart. The human being thinks in binaries; the heart moves in a double pump. Listen to your chest—you will hear. Does it pump or not? It does—the brain has just moved in antithetical thinking—does it or does it not beat? It is a two-fold beat? It is.

Both/and lives in the framework of an ultimate *either/or*. This means that goods can be held in tension because there is a right and a wrong way—there is an either/or standard that makes sense of given tension.

166. To what should we compare the exclusivity of salvation by Christ? A man built a beautiful building and filled its gallery with art so the people of his city could *grow* and appreciate the beauty. He worked hard and built the building large and creatively; he built a front door into the building so people outside could come in, and those inside could come back out—all at no cost to the people.

As the people were coming and going enjoying the art, the architect was approached by a grumbling man in a suit and spectacles. The grumbling man said to him, "You call this love for humanity, you who say you appreciate the giftedness of men? You only keep men from seeing the gifts! How do you expect all men to come into this place—for you have put up more walls than doors—that single door will only accommodate one at a time, you can never fill a building so large with such a small door. You don't love man, or art! For you only made one small door for a whole wide world!"

Just then a gallery visitor in tattered clothes overheard the conversation and spoke up: "Without walls, the paintings would be all on the ground, stepped on or stolen—the walls are needed just as much as those frames holding the pictures. Without walls there are no doors, without frames there are no pictures—without standards there is no love."

Then the grumbler in the suit and spectacles said, "Well then, I say there should be no pictures if there has to be frames or walls! How cruel it is for one to make pictures if they have to be framed! Cruel are the artists, cruel is the architect—cruel is anyone who destroys man's freedom!"

167. A contradiction is a un-truth, a stark denial of reality; a paradox is a truth beyond our immediate grasp, but true nonetheless. When God's ways are higher than our ways, we will inevitably taste paradox. We cannot fit the wide ocean of truth into our current paper cup of capacity; we can taste of the saltwater that gives so much life yet also dehydrates the man who tries to drink it all!

This is to say, we are to acknowledge paradox, but to capture all in our mind is to shrivel and make little of the world, and to kill the self by swelling of the brain.

If we deny the possibility of paradox then we claim all knowledge for ourselves, for a paradox is possible because we do not have all knowledge—we are not omniscient. If we deny the God-ward implications of paradox, we are either arrogant or omniscient.

Because we are not omniscient, it is surely possible for God to exist! We can only claim the non-existence of God if we are omniscient; therefore anyone who claims there can be no God is asserting them self as a god.

Paradox is not a God-of-the-gaps excuse to explain the unreasonable; rather, it is the only reasonable way to speak of truth in a universe that is even an atom bigger than the ego of man.

Many people enjoy attempting to disqualify the Bible on the grounds that it is self-contradicting. It is not contradictory, but it is paradoxical, habitually misrepresented, constantly taken out of context, or plain misunderstood because of moral, cultural and chronological walls—that is, by human finiteness. Regardless, if being contradictory disqualifies something from being true, then we as humans should be quickly disqualified to disqualify the Bible; for there is nothing more contradictory in nature then we.

168. We are meant to wrestle with God. Why did God rename Jacob *Israel*? Was it a whim? No, it was to reveal that those who were to be the people of God were to be wrestlers with God; people who struggled in honest relationship with God rather than ignore the Lord of the universe.

The name Israel means "God wrestler." God, in odd fashion that takes us by surprise, changed Jacob from a wrestler of men to a wrestler with God. Jacob, the deceiver who wrestled Isaac, Esau, and Laban for a blessing was now Israel who wrestled God—who found ultimate blessing in God alone!

A wrestler of men can boast in his own strength; one who wrestles with God will always fail. When we wrestle with God He always wins; when we wrestle with God we learn to love humanity. Our limp, our humility, shows our love. Only the wounded can worship. A paradox!

169. There is a bizarre thought in *Christianity*—and it is not a Christian thought! Like a child, I am the kind of person who learns and understands best through pictures and illustrations; so let us take an example: It is a beautiful spring day; the kind of day perfect for a walk when one is feeling contemplative and calm. The sky is brilliant and clear, the warm sun falls on your face as you search the atmosphere for a hint of turn in the season's moody weather. Nothing—not a cloud to hold back the silver streams of sunshine—yet, something catches your eye. Something like a silver piece of the sun falling towards you. As it moves further from the direct stream of light that is brightly concealing it, you see that this is no broken piece of the sun—but it is a silver airplane. It is an awkward airplane. In a moment, you realize that the airplane is acting rather unlike an airplane—and then, in an instant of interested horror, you see the plane has only one wing and an increasingly chaotic flight pattern. Unsure of what thrill seeker would ride as passenger on such a poorly designed machine—doubly unsure how the plane flew this far—you are quite sure that it will momentarily come spiraling down into the unsuspecting grass of spring.

This is a strange and absurd illustration—yet there is an even stranger thought within Christianity. It is the thought that *one* good is enough. Now a wing is a good thing, even great, but an isolated wing is a danger. Still, the absurdity can become even greater—which wing is better? It is madness that asks this question. I believe the only sincere way to answer this question is to be a passenger on an airplane, and at peak altitude ask oneself, "Which wing on the airplane is more important—which one can I do without?" The answer is simple—and can leave the bravest jetsetter in an uncomfortable sweat. Let us keep both wings.

One chooses between flying and driving; here is an either/or. One does not choose between the wheels and the engine of the car, between the left and the right wings of the plane. Here is the both/and.

170. Let me imagine other illustrations. Take for instance a marathon runner: which of their legs is more important? Let's sever a leg; one cannot honestly say that the right leg is more important than the left, or the left more important than the right. Which one shall we saw off? This is both gross and absurd. It is no stretch to say that if a marathon runner were to choose to use only one leg in the race, the crossing of the finish line is a big question mark.

How about the example of scissors? Spending time debating which blade is more important is both silly and devious—for in separating the two you would have two knives—the tool has become incapable of its intended purpose, and has become a dagger in the hand! What was meant for refrigerator art is now geared towards manslaughter.

171. Let's says there is a party to go to. When one is given directions to a party from a friend, rarely do they say, "leave your house, take all rights, and you will find the party." And in the same way, they will usually not say, "leave your house, take all lefts, and you will find the party." Any reasonable person will concede that directions usually consist of both rights and lefts.

Let's say I am responsible for the birthday party of a family member. In being responsible for the preparations I have given two friends the directions to the address of the party. If one friend had a bias for *the left*, and the other had a bias for *the right*—they very well may disregard the combined directions of left and right, and follow the *pure* paths of their bias. Not only would these two friends take senseless routes to the party—there is the likely chance that neither would ever arrive—and if they did, they would be very late, missing the food and fun entirely. I would consider them both foolish. Wouldn't you?

In a set of directions that includes both right and left turns, a purist for *the left* and a purist for *the right* will always end up lost—a purist for reaching the goal will end up at the party's celebration. Again, this seems like a ridiculous illustration; and it is—that is why it aptly describes the absurd imbalances in the body of Christ.

To seek the will of God is to be a purist for the goal.

The vertigo in the body of Christ is the dizziness of swinging between extremes, rather than holding those two extremes together in living tension—vertigo is the symptom of unbelief.

172. Paradoxical tension: Two seemingly irreconcilable truths that hold each other accountable; each keeps the other true and balanced and each relies on the other. The division of the two goods makes for isolated and relegated goods. Mysticism and pragmatism are an example. Mere mysticism leads to a whimsical God; mere pragmatism leads to a boxed God. Paradoxical tension holds the two opposites tightly so that a dynamo of life is created; and so Christianity is fully both. True practicality is always a mystery, and true *mysticality* is always practical when it comes to the realm of the spirit.

Christianity is not halfway between liberal and conservative; it is fully both. It is free to be conservative; and it is conservative that it may roam about freely. It is only in Christ that such paradoxical extremes hold tight to each other like energizing magnets—for it is not conservatism or liberalism that is sought, but Christ.

173. We error in thinking that wrong and right are accurately represented by an easy *black vs. white* contention defined by man who has torn apart life in order to find some semblance of control. As Christians our world has been infused with all the color of creation; colors revealed in purpose and destiny.

Existence delivers glorious highlights of cadmium white, and deep recesses of black—but to choose only one color would make a picture of depth and beauty a mere wash of flat color—like ordinary wall paint flung carelessly over a Rembrandt or van Gogh.

What this means is that we must not live by our one-dimensional external categories—what this means is that we must live by the will of God: black when He wishes to make like the night, white when He wants to make like the lunar satellite, or the pierce of a star through the velvet curtain of dark. Truth is Gold when He calls on the morning sun, yet silver when he calls forth the lithium light of the afternoon sun. This does not remove absolutes—no! It puts all the weight upon The Absolute!

Truth is absolute. God is the truth. God is The Absolute.

174. It is illogical to talk as if God could contradict Himself. What He says exists, what He does *is*. Contradiction is a term defined and derived from the twisting of truth. Contradiction is less than reality—unreality; God cannot be less than Himself. To suppose God could contradict Himself is to not speak of the true God. It is an error in logic, and for that, an error of heart.

Contradiction is the essence of sin—that which steals joy and undermines meaning and logic; it is to speak against that which is reality. God is reality; unbelief is contradicting reality.

Contradiction: To "speak against," from *contra* "against," + *dicere* "to speak."

To contradict God is to judge God; this is why there is no such thing as atheism—or rather, why atheism is a misnomer. When one contradicts God by denying His existence they have just enthroned themselves as a god. It is not that there is no God, but that there is a lesser god who is so much less of a god he doesn't even have the sight to see he has enthroned himself!

175. God's promises and words to us can appear contradictory (think of Abraham and God's promise about birthing nations through Isaac, and then God's command for the sacrifice of this

very same Isaac) Faith trusts God in the face of apparent contradiction (our limited reason and insight cannot resolve these); yet God in His eternal goodness remains true to His promises and Word—He shows the apparent contradictions to be perfect paradoxes, and shows Himself to be true and worthy of all worship. From Isaac came the nation of Israel. Abraham faithfully faced the apparent contradiction and found God to be infinitely true. Abraham found God to not be a God of contradiction, but a God of paradox, who was infinitely above the mind of man. Abraham is the father of faith.

What if there were a thin and slanted shaft of light, and we saw two tall silhouettes within it, moving and jostling about? We might argue all day that they were two distinct objects even if someone who knew more than us (someone who had seen in full light) told us they were one. When the full light is turned on and we see the two silhouettes as the legs of a standing person, wouldn't we feel silly about the complicated philosophies we invented to debunk or support the words of the voice we should have trusted?

176. There is a song lyric that says, "I am haunted by a perfection I can't define." We cannot define God—though we can know Him. God's goodness is far greater than any stone or poem could capture in a million years by a million Miltons and Michelangelos.

I am haunted by joy. Some people claim they are haunted by pain, guilt, and the dark inevitabilities of being human—this is understandable. I am too; but far less than joy. All are haunted profoundly by joy. What haunts us about despair is the inaccessibility of joy.

We are haunted by joy because it is uncontrollable, un-holdable, like the wind, and above all, desired. Though it is sought after, it is felt to be a phantom and its meaning somehow fleeting; yet this is only because we seek it on our own ability out of our own origin. We are crafted for joy; yet incapable of attaining it on our own. What is necessary for man cannot be fashioned by or wielded by man. It cannot be worked for—it can only be given.

Joy reveals dependence, reliance upon the Divine—and for that it is joy.

Joy is not phantom, some will-o'-the-wisp chased into the marshlands—on the contrary, it is incarnational. It is haunting, but substantive. It is no mere notion, but diamond-hard reality.

Joy is not a foolish fire, some illusion on the night's horizon—but it is the fire that fell to fallen humanity in tongues of flame within space and time; it is God with man, the comforter, the correlator of truth sent by the risen Christ.

177. It seems sweetly appropriate that the Spirit of God has been called the Holy Ghost. But this Ghost is real—active—more substantial than any tree, steel building, or garden rose. This Ghost is reality-dense, never captured or manipulated. He captures us through His holy magnificence. He convicts us through His beautiful perfection; we are magnetized to reality by the density of His beauty. He is *real* that is why He convicts us of our sin, of our collapse, our brokenness, our cold and stony hearts. But "Do not grieve, for the Joy of the Lord is your strength." (Nehemiah 8:10). We have a great reason for joy...

PART TWO
(178-182)

~The Keystone~

178. Man committed the wrong; God stood the trial. Man stole the fire; God underwrote the cost of the costly restoration!

Here was Jesus—*ecce homo*—*The Man*—about to be crucified upon the cross that grew from the seed of the fruit Adam ate! At that moment, He looked into the face of *that man*, of Adam's progeny—the *man of self-origin*. And what does man who ate and still eats of the knowledge of good and evil say to Jesus? "What is truth!" Pilate says, and so speaks as the representative of all untrusting humanity. Still, man does not trust the Word of God, but seeks to discover it himself, from within himself.

Could a man look upon rape and say, "What is evil?" To do so is sheer violence, utter hostility to the creature and the Creator. To look upon the face of Christ and say, "What is truth?" is also cosmic violence, also hostility to existence, to origin, to love.

Here we see laid bare the results of the ancient attempt at autonomy: when man seeks truth apart from God, he will inevitably disavow it, disembody it. He will eventually spurn it, mock it, and turn against it because it won't serve him, for it is greater than he.

Here we see in full fruition the dark fruit of unbelief and self-origin: truth twisted into absurdity, denied, emptied out to be used as a bullet casing, and loaded by man to manipulate and coerce for selfish gain. And so, rationalism proves to be the death of reason as well as faith. The rationalist loses both his heart and mind to ash in the very fire that he trusted in—himself.

Pontius Pilate, looking into the very countenance of truth, echoes the words of the deceiver, "did God really say…?" Pilate, looking into the incarnate face of reality, (for reality is ultimately a person) speaks again in Adam's tongue: "Truth! Hah! I entrust myself to my own power, my own rendering, for I am *as God*—I sit upon the judgment seat! What is truth except for what I decide! Are you not here for me to judge you?" And by this replay of the ancient fall, the cross was then raised, and the victory over death, over unbelief, was (in wonderful irony) won.

Because of Christ, faith in God is possible, reality accessible, the fall overturned, and once again, a life lived out of our true origin made available. We can now eat of the tree of life and reject the tree of self-reliance by entrusting ourselves to God— the Sovereign *and* Good, the Loving *and* Eternal.

To taste of communion, to taste of the flesh and blood broken and opened upon the cross, is to eat of the tree of life. Hah! The wonder of our God who turns the splintered beams of man's torture device into the boughs of the tree of life, lush with the fruit that, in eating, is the union of God and man!

179. The Lord Jesus Christ—the center and the circumscribe; the focus and the outer most rim of reality. The Lord Jesus Christ— the expressed image, the beauty and radiance of God's many perfections. He is God's joy, God's glory. He is God's greatest delight for He is the delight of His own greatness. And note, for this is important, that this is the very opposite of what we call narcissism.

Since God is the ultimate good, He must delight in His own essence; anything less would be unjust—and just-ness is a perfection of God. Simply stated, God is not narcissistic as we narcissists suppose and wickedly hope; for He is worthy of all admiration, especially His own. This wonderful perfection is how Jesus can be servant and King—and both fully. He is the expressed Lion and the Lamb of God's sovereignty.

180. "Jesus said to them, 'Have you never read in the Scriptures, *"The stone the builders rejected has become the capstone; the Lord has done this, and it is marvelous in our eyes?"* Therefore I tell you that the kingdom of God will be taken away from you and given to a people who will produce its fruit. He who falls on this stone will be broken to pieces, but he on who it falls will be crushed'" (Matthew 21:42-44).

Christ is the touchstone upon which reality is revealed. Upon Him we are seen as broken, disunited with our origin and drying up as a severed branch. But the broken, the poor in Spirit, the humble who acknowledge the truth of their need upon this stone are soon forged again upon this stone—the redeeming stone!

Those who will not acknowledge their fractures will be judged by He who was to save them—crushed, because they wanted to be god; crushed by the weight of reality; crushed because they did not heed the touchstone of love; crushed because they spit into the face of the Truth.

This is the Gospel of God: The Lord Jesus Christ, *The Keystone,* in His perfection, exposes all humanity as broken in order to save it, for He is love. Yet those that act as their own origin and deny *the Keystone* deny the very pivot of all history; they deny the mediator of reality and will be crushed by Him; crushed by the sheer substance and weight of truth—the weight of love.

Listen again to the first presentation of the Gospel—the *protoevangelion*: "And I will put enmity between you and the woman, and between your offspring and hers; he will crush your head and you will strike his heel." This is Genesis 3:15. It is the voice of God foretelling of a fallen world restored by the love of its Redeemer, who, though is stricken, rises again and crushes the deceiver and his children, *the self-deceived.* This is the ancient revelation of the incarnation, the crucifixion, the resurrection, and the ascension.

Upon Christ's cross Shalom was restored: man was united with Father God his origin; man was united with neighbor; the disunited man was united within himself; and all the glory of the work is revealed as God's. The upshot of this is the telecast of great glory, the wide-blown renown of the true God—both Creator and Savior—the basis and means for all worship!

This is what the Word has been saying all along: *Do not flee from reality, for in the flight you will only die, only destroy all the good I have placed within you. Live your life in accordance with Me—your origin, your source, your meaning and your end—I AM your life. If you accept my Word you will be revealed as fractured and scattered—but I will heal you through! If you deny the one who has made you and loved you, you will be crushed by the very love that has established you and the very foundations of the universe. To deny reality is to make a pact with death! Turn—live instead!*

181. The purpose of our existence is to acknowledge the person of this glory—to know Jesus—to acknowledge the visible radiance of the invisible God and to glorify Him by the means of His grace that allows us to be obedient. All else is grass.

The meaning of existence is to glorify God; the significance of our being is to ascribe worth—to worship what is true. Jesus is the center of all worth. Jesus is truth—he is the Logos: the ordering principle of reality. He is the cornerstone of the Scriptures, the foundation and the purpose of the universe; He is who the Scriptures point to, who the cosmos cries out to. Jesus is I AM; the heat from the burning bush. He is the stairway to heaven, the offering upon the altar. He is God, inviting us and enabling us into full origin. He is the fulcrum of reality that everything presses upon. He is the Lamb that brings redemption and the Lion that necessitates repentance—grace and truth! Justice and mercy! Holy, holy, holy, is the Lord Almighty!

182. One cannot separate the wounded healer of Christ from the loving Father; this is an ancient tension torn at over and over again like a thick scab. One cannot call God Father if not for Christ—He alone made the adoption available. He quickened our death into life; He transformed our slavery into freedom. If one denies Christ, then one denies the God of the Scriptures—one denies reality!

Jesus is the revelation of the glory of God; and only because of Jesus can "the righteous live by faith" (Habakkuk 2:4). Only by Christ could Abraham be the father of faith, only by Christ could Moses be the meekest man on earth.

Jesus is the living rendition, the en-fleshment, the embodiment of the words "Salvation is of the Lord" (Jonah 2:9). God saves; He saves us from our *thinning-out-of-existence* selves; from our flight from reality; from our tendency to tear the universe into phantom pieces and withered whispers.

The very name Jesus means "God is Salvation." In Jesus meet all the points of existence—for He is both Creator and Savior. He is what keeps the universe together: "For by Him all things were created: things in heaven and on earth, visible and invisible, whether thrones, or powers, or authorities; all things were created by Him and for Him. He is before all things, and in Him all things hold together" (Colossians 1:16-17).

Love has love won;
The Father fathered bastards come sons;
For you, I Am, came
To proclaim: "Tetelestai—Done!"
And upon the edge of the moan broke:
"Love has love won."

PART THREE
(183-359)

~All Hail the Mediator~

183. What is the joy of the Lord? Not *what*, but whom? Jesus is the Joy of the Lord—for Jesus is the manifest glory of God. This being so, Jesus is the ultimate joy for redeemed man. Joy comes amidst the piercing realization that Jesus is Lord, the Salvation of God—I Am that I Am.

Christ is the strength by which a Christian moves, by which he exists. "Do not grieve, for the Joy of the Lord is your strength." (Nehemiah 8:10). Such were the words of hope after Ezra read the Law, the Beautiful Standard that exposed all as broken.

When one is graced with the acknowledgment that we are our poison and God is our portion, that Christ alone is our Lord who saves us from ourselves, then a relationship with God is the most sweet and joyous possibility of our life—more so, it alone *is* life.

Who could separate the believer from the Sovereign God and His promise to keep them? None: for it is like asking what candle can washout the sun.

A disaster could tumble nations—and a Christian will grieve over the loss of life and damage done; they will cry, will ache—but there remains a strange but deep joy that knows no force of nature can tumble over God. Violence can steal the life of a loved one and a Christian will lament, will mourn over the cruelty and hard absence—but there remains a peculiar joy that knows no blade or bullet can separate us from our loving Father. There may be a slander of the most vile kind—and a Christian will weep over the venom that is in humanity, that is within the self—but there is joy in knowing that every mouth will be shut in the presence of God, and no injustice will be overlooked for all rumors will be dispelled and all reality revealed.

Did not Jesus suffer such things? And yet, as Paul says, "Your attitude should be the same as that of Christ Jesus: Who, being in very nature God, did not consider equality with God something to be *grasped*, but made Himself nothing, taking the very nature of a servant, being made in human likeness. And being found in appearance as a man, He humbled Himself and became obedient even until death—even death upon a cross! Therefore God exalted Him to the highest place and gave Him the name that is above every other name, that at the name of Jesus every knee should bow, in heaven and on earth and under the earth, and every tongue confess that Jesus Christ is Lord, to the glory of God the Father" (Philippians 2:9-11).

"Therefore, my dear friends, as you have always obeyed…continue to work out your salvation in fear and trembling…" for this is joy!

There is an unshakable joy in knowing that God will not be judged by spiteful clay but that He will judge all. When we recognize Jesus as Lord, we know the world is subject to Him; and since He is good, no earthly event can steal the joy of His eternal reign. In the end goodness reigns, and for that, all the past will be redeemed!

If Christ were our deepest joy, then we would never cry out to God, "This is unfair!" Grace means God can ask anything of us; this is why we often reject grace. We ought to count the costs for following a crucified Savior.

God is our salvation—over this atoms vibrate in awe; nuclear fission in the sun's heart bursts into molten delight; the ocean toasts the land in God's great honor; human lungs pulse in and out: *Yah-weh, Yah-weh*. Oh how often we curse God with the same breath that proves He is beautiful and real! Our lungs perform the automatic function of speaking the name of God, yet man denies Him…

184. It is the place of man to serve the servant—Christ the Servant King!

We give Jesus far less credit than He deserves. (This is the great understatement of my life!) Jesus was not only our Lord and our Savior, He was the quintessential man, the master communicator—a true genius. We naively think Him to be simple and dopily smiling—a benevolent village idiot of sorts—saying nice moral things, snippets of wisdom to tuck into our memories for when someone acts rudely to us.

One such example of this is the common view of the Beatitudes and the Sermon on the Mount. It is often thought that Jesus was just quipping, just bouncing around to whatever random word of wisdom popped into his backwater-town mind. But this is not so. The Sermon on the Mount was no lollygagging string of niceties, but a purposeful and directed discourse that would shame any Greek politician's best rhetoric.

Like we so often do, we rip texts into simple nuggets for us to polish and show off—to quote proudly and assure others of our favored position in God's Kingdom. But we must tread carefully—we must not use God's words for our purposes. Stripping Christ's magnum opus apart is akin to shattering Michelangelo's David with a wrecking ball and then saying how wonderful the jagged pieces are that you carry around in your pocket.

The Sermon on the Mount is full of form and purpose; that being so, it is no accident that the famous Beatitudes begin with "the poor in spirit." For this is where Christianity starts—brokenness. Christianity starts with the revelation of our desperate situation. It is out of this acknowledgement, out of awakening to our helplessness that comes the possibility of humility—come the possibility of the other Beatitudes.

185. How does one *achieve* humility? It cannot be achieved—this is why the Beatitudes start here. It starts with grace. Never has one's own hand made one's own heart humble. All the Beatitudes hinge upon trust in Christ and self-resignation.

One knows the truth because one is in the truth; one never moves into the truth by knowing of the truth. This means that we are saved not by the stretch of striving, but are saved in the bend of humility. One is saved not in personal ascension, but in the descent of the Divine One.

Salvation is of the Lord—this is the literal name of Jesus. And since salvation is of the Lord, humility is from the Lord. Humility is not a work—it is the great anti-work. Humility is like trying not to think of a great pink elephant when you are told not to think of a great pink elephant. The more you try at your task, the more you fail. It is something that cannot be attained by grasping—but only by losing your grip.

Humility is not earned by trying; rather, humility is the outpouring of brokenness. Like juice from a crushed grape, humility seeps out of a crushed spirit. It is from this juice that the wine of Christianity is fermented.

Humility is key, for salvation is of grace alone. What does this mean? It means that salvation is for the poor in spirit—those who have come to resignation—those who have been pushed and pulled to the absolute farthest reaches of their being only to know they are dust; for those who know their desperation. It simply means that salvation is for those who know it is only of God, for they can do nothing without Him. And so it is, as Jesus says, "Blessed are the poor in spirit, for theirs is the Kingdom of Heaven."

When we know we are nothing without God, everything changes. When we know we are clay, then God makes us anew with His light. "God be merciful to me a sinner!" Such is the true response of man to God. These things are beautiful to look at. These things we should play over and over again in the theater of our mind.

The true condition of man: reliance upon the Creator. The man fully alive is the man in full resignation.

186. There is no darkness in Jesus at all, only light.

Because God is perfect, because there is no darkness in Him, the more we look upon Him the more we realize His perfection. The deeper we are allowed to see into Him the more we die, the more we then live, and the more the wonder multiplies. Because He is infinite, this eternal amazement at how good God is never ceases. Each microscopic look unveils another telescoping universe of beauty. A relationship with God is an upward spiral of wonder; every turn a surprise of joy.

The more we look into the infinite good, the less we know we are good.

187. *A perfect and just God gave grace to those deserving of death by inflicting the just punishment upon His perfect innocence while absorbing the wrath—thereby maintaining true justice while dispensing grace.* That is heavy talk for this buoyant truth: undeservedly we were saved; the hero has taken our bullet; the hero has sucked the killing poison out of our veins (a poison self-injected), and in doing so took the damage upon Himself. Such words fall short of the marvel they speak of; it is like telling someone that the flames of a pink and pearl sunrise are "cute" or saying that the way summer light brings the Caribbean ocean to mesmerizing life is "nice."

Unless God were to die for our sins, He could not be *both* just and merciful. Only through suffering could justice and mercy kiss. Only through God taking the force of His own wrath could the guilty be justly pardoned. Only through death could there be life. Only through Christ's self-imposed restraints could there be true freedom. This is the great paradox. Salvation demands the held tension of justice *and* mercy.

Christ's solidarity with humanity was necessary—otherwise the cross was an absurdity.

If God were to grant mercy without the cross of Christ bearing it, He would no longer be just, and therefore, not holy. Think of this, truly think of this: Without the cross of Jesus Christ grace would be unjust; but because God who demands justice took the just punishment upon Himself, justice is served (holiness is maintained—God stays consistent and true to all His revelation) and grace is mediated out to those who acknowledge this love revealed in God's self-wrath/self-sacrifice. Here we catch a glimpse of presumed contradiction sparking into paradox.

In order for the narrative of the Bible to stay consistent and to make sense, Jesus has to be God. Only one who was fully God and fully man could bear this divine salvation of mankind. For only one who was God could be perfect and fulfill the requirements of the law; only one who was fully man could accept the punishment that humanity was due.

If Christ were not fully God, the cross, the sacrifice of Jesus would be impotent within the framework of reality that God has created and revealed. Only God is perfect; and humanity is flawed—this is why the Gospel is good news—the miracle of the incarnation made the impossible possible. With God all things are possible; salvation is of the Lord (Matthew 19:26; Jonah 2:9).

188. Jesus is the wounded healer. It is not just a nice theological thing to say that *God knows our pains*, or *has felt the pressure of being human*. These things are not known to Him simply because He is God, but because He is God who became man to suffer with us in order to save us from death and the dislocation of His presence.

He knows human pain, not theoretically, bur experientially. He has felt a splinter enter the meat of His thumb; He has felt spit stick to His face; He has felt sorrow vice-grip His chest muscles. He knows how it tastes to lick the desert off of dry lips; to taste the oil of a pressed olive; to laugh deeply with friends until the ribs ache.

How can I not follow the innocent one who said "forgive them" as His nerves were snapped by nails hammered through muscle? Even in His deep pain, light poured from His wounds. The wisdom and mercy of Jesus are beyond what the world could bear. He is the God with wounds; because of the cross we can follow Him. When Christ was lifted up, we were humbled. We can only follow Him because we have been humbled.

"Forgive them, for they know not what they do." All that poured from Jesus was brilliance and love! In this one prayer, Jesus shows both condemnation and mercy towards those who screamed for His crucifixion, towards those who glowered at him from the rock of Golgotha. They are guilty of not knowing they are blind to the truth before them, yet Jesus prays that they may see. In His love, in the action that was the incarnation, condemnation and mercy met.

189. The incarnation of Jesus was not a mere tool to get our attention; it was an extension of God's character. The incarnation is God's displayed humility; it is love in serving action.

True love is that one would die for His friends. Jesus told us this; Jesus showed us this. Jesus was showing us the love of the Father. Jesus was showing us that God is love.

Love is not God like a lot of backward people say; but God is love. There is a great difference between the two. Love could not die for us because it is god, but God could and did die for us because He is love. One is an impersonal abstraction; the other is a real person; one a thin notion, the other, the pivot of reality.

Jesus' love was majestic and pure; and for that it made men mad with anger and insane with jealousy; not because He brought the confusion of madness, but because He brought the clarity of truth that exposed the mad human heart.

190. The heights of human worth can be measured by the depths that God would dive in order to rescue humanity. There is no greater descent than God becoming a man of sorrows, a carpenter of Galilee hung grossly upon a cross.

Suppose one dropped a penny in a puddle—they might pick it up. Supposed they dropped the penny in a two foot tidal pool—they might pick it up. Suppose they dropped the penny into the deep of the wine-dark Mediterranean Sea—they would count it lost and move along. Suppose one dropped a penny into the deep of the great Atlantic Ocean—surely they would not dive for the lost copper? But suppose one dropped a priceless jewel, the world's most treasured of treasures—puddle, pool, sea, and ocean would be braved to rescue it. Now suppose a beloved bride or child fell into the deep! God dove through puddle, pool, sea, ocean, heavens, and cosmos to redeem humanity from the dark depths, the green-black depths of human sin. The incarnation, crucifixion, and resurrection are the unimaginable attestations to human worth.

Humanity has worth because God loves humanity. This is important: we are not loved because of our worth; we have worth because we are loved.

So here is the wonder: we were coal dropped into the deep sea, but God dove, and when He came up we were a diamond in his hand. Surely we are not *worthless*—though we are *unworthy* of the great salvation that lays hold of us.

191. Jesus was a laborer who confounded the intellectuals; He was an intellectual who comforted the laborers. He was a child who taught the priests; He was a priest who loved the children. This is my opinion (but reasonable speculation), but I believe Jesus had scarred hands before He went to the cross; he worked with the plane, the hammer, the chisel, the saw and all the roughness of wood. It is comforting to know that this leader of men and angels, this majestic Lord of ours, felt the splinters of a fallen world—not just the extremity of the cross. There is a credibility and practicality

to Jesus because of His working hands. He was not a man of lofty ideas and ungrounded thought; rather, He was a man of lofty realism and divine practicality; a God with sweat on His brow, dirt on His feet—laughter *and* sorrow on his lips.

The Kingdom of Heaven is as real as and more real than any timber Jesus planed and notched to frame a doorway.

Is it not ironic that a carpenter would be nailed to cut timbers? Why such tremendous irony? What depths of beauty there are in the ironies of God—of poor men upturning the world, of foolish things shaming the wise, of death breeding life, of lions lying with lambs, and the anointed one called "the friend of sinners."

192. God both gave Jacob a limp *and* showed him the stairway to heaven. To know Christ is to know your deficiency. To know Christ is to know your only hope. What was the stairway to heaven—this very bridge between man and God? Again, not *what*, but *who*!

By Christ we can hold truths in tension. Christ is the co-relation, the correlation of man and God. There is no correlation without the cross of Christ. There is no beautiful tension without its offensive crossbeams, only lethargic contradiction. The cross offends our warped desire to live in inert contradictions and shrug off the implications.

"How much more, then, will the blood of Christ, who through the eternal Spirit offered Himself unblemished to God, cleanse our consciences from acts that lead to death, so that we may serve the living God! For this reason Christ is the mediator of the new covenant, that those who are called may receive the promised eternal inheritance—now that He has died as a ransom to set them free from the sins committed under the first covenant" (Hebrew 9:14-15). Christ—the co-relation! The one who is found amongst the Trinity, the one who gives man eternal life, yet lives to exalt the glory of God! Christ—the one who takes the blunt of justice, the one who justifies!

Correlate these passages: Genesis 17, Genesis 22:10-22, John 1:43-51, Galatians 3:16—Jesus the truth, the pearl gate, the very gate of the City of God!

The gates of God's City, each a large pearl! The pearl—a treasure born of suffering—of sacrifice! Christ the Pearl of Great Price! Correlate Revelation 21:21, Matthew 14:45-46, and the Passion narratives.

193. Where the finite and infinite meet, paradox is found, just as white foam is found where surf crashes onto shore. As long as we live out of ourselves, centered in our finite nature, than any meeting with the infinite will be violent and tearing; yet when we live from an infinite center, the Christ life, then paradox is healing and necessary as oxygen to the lungs.

God does not tear His universe into pieces. So Christians, as followers of Jesus Christ who is the fullness (*pleroma*) and image (*eikon*) of the invisible God, ought not to be guided and torn by false either/ors that compromise truth by choosing certain goods over others; such counterfeit antitheses cause the fabricating of contradictions.

194. The follower of Jesus will not choose between faith and reason—to do so is unreasonable *and* unfaithful (See there!—we hold *those* together in tension often!). The hard divide of heart and mind is the flailing of man, not the creativity of God.

To live a life based on belief is not simple-minded nor an idiot's crutch. Belief itself isn't narrow-minded or silly; rather, it is the belief that is held which is up for debate. Scientists believe string theory, quantum mechanics, and unknown operators can resolve the apparent contradiction of light being both particle and wave.

This does not show them to be simpletons, but it does show what they believe.

So, to say it again: belief does not equal *unintelligent* or *superstitious* or *simpleton*. It is the content and trajectory of the trust that reveals such things.

Every intellectual life is carried by some foundation of belief, some assumption, some set of presuppositions. Some people use beliefs to hold their unrealistic, contradictory world together; some hold beliefs that are paradoxical but reasonable and true.

This being said, there is no battle between faith and science—this is an admired myth. Yet there is a battle between trusts, a war of faith vs. faith. When we acknowledge this, then we can start to address each faith reasonably and see how they correlate with reality and see if they are internally coherent.

195. All scientific thought is based on belief—but it seems no one wants to reflect on this because of what it might mean to their world view. If one discredits following Jesus Christ because it is rooted in a belief, then they must discredit the scientific method for it too is rooted in a belief.

The scientific method is rooted in the belief that the scientific method works to show truth; it is rooted in the belief that mathematics will stay constant and not sprout fickle wings and up-away; it is rooted in the belief that the sun will not rise in the West tomorrow because it never has; it is rooted in the belief that the replication of results means reality.

I am not arguing that these are silly beliefs (I do not believe they are silly at all); rather, I am stating that they are assumptions—beliefs that are not verifiable. Why? You cannot test the validity of the scientific method by way of the scientific method—that is circular and self supporting—and thoroughly unscientific.

And to take this a step further, most scientific knowledge we state to be true, we believe simply on word of mouth, on some verbal authority—for who has retested every scientific experiment to see for themselves the veracity of the hypothesis? Sure, we could commission an experiment in order to see for ourselves—but we don't because we go by trust.

There is just as much faith in labs of science as there is when one prays to God. Some take the words of Einstein, Darwin or Crick as authoritative; some take the words of Paul, of Moses or Jesus as authoritative. Whom do you trust? More so, why do you trust them?

196. Faith holds mystery and reason together at the heights of their energies. Mystery is reasonable in a world that lives day to day looking for answers of why we do not sink, yet floats easily on a sea of questions. We try to divorce these two but it does not work, for they are a bride and groom deeply in love—one in white and one in black.

Simply look at the pattern of discovery; for every discovery made, more questions abound. For each answer in a single cell there is a new body of questions gestating.

In trust the heart rejoices and the mind receives.

197. What if our relationship with God were put into a book? Why would most Christians' books be found in the self-help section of the bookstore, instead of the adventure book/superhero section? For a world that is enamored by the idea of the superhero—from the Grecian Hercules to the American icon of Superman—rarely, when it comes to our relationship with God, do we apply the rules and logic of the superhero.

Let me state it bluntly: The whole point of super-heroism is that the hero can do what needs to be done, but what we cannot do. A child knows this; it is enacted out daily in all the fantastic games of cops and robbers, knights and fiery dragons. It is when the heroine has fallen from the highest skyscraper and helplessly plummets to her sidewalk-death that the hero arrives. It is when the police and army are bested by the villain and his half-wit creeps that the savior comes and sets the world right again. It is when all defenses are broken, all hopes are hopeless—such is the time for a hero.

The child longs to be the hero simply because the hero is special, somehow sacred—and they have the abilities to do what others ordinarily cannot. What would be so super about Superman if everyone could do what he could do? What would be so mythic about Odysseus if he could not think and scheme different than all the rest? The child knows these things; why do the religious forget them? –because they are religious, not realistic!

198. It is absurd to believe a drowning man could throw himself a life preserver; or that a stranded woman could send herself a rescue vessel; or that a man in a deep well could pull himself up by his own bootstraps. It is in dire straits such as these that the idea of a *savior* makes perfect sense.

Does it not seem inherently wrong for a man to say he is his own savior? Yet with iron tenacity, humanity always attempts to take some kind of credit for whatever salvation has occurred. But if one can swim—then swim to the shore. Such does not make one a hero—rather, a person that can swim. If one can build her own boat—then build it and forgo the costly efforts of the Navy. If one has the rope and cowboy skills—then lasso oneself out of the well. It is in these instances that one can understand and even appreciate the strength and ingenuity of humanity; but such things have nothing to do with being a hero to the self.

198. You see, the problem comes not in understanding man's abilities; but rather, in understanding the situation man is in. If a champion swimmer jumped out of a flying airplane without a parachute, a lifetime of the best swimming lessons would not be any help in his situation.

If a physicist was unlucky enough to find himself mid-round within the boxing ring, he might quickly calculate the odds of getting pummeled—but there is a sad inequality of situation and the ability to overcome the situation at hand. What needs to be understood is the *instance that humanity is in*—and here is the rub.

If a man bellows from the tides, or marks a giant SOS on an open beach, or screams from the belly of a well, and soon finds himself rescued by one who is quite able, is such a rescue due in any way to the ability of the one in peril? No. To cry for help somehow falls short of "saving oneself." It would be a vain and intolerable person who prided *them self* in *their* own rescue by lauding *their* powerless, pathetic cry. "*But I yelled…*" Hah!

Help comes from the hero. To claim a hand in the heroism is rather foolish—semantically or by way of plain common sense. Yet each day, myriad religions seek and claim some portion of salvation's heroism. In countless ways, we attempt to wrestle the glory from God; and never are we more creative and ingenious than when trying to claim the glory for ourselves. Truly, we are deceived if we believe our situation is one in which we do not need a hero.

We find ourselves in a great instance which we do not have the ability to overcome. There is no force of muscle, no abundance of wit that can maneuver us out of our dire sin. Salvation comes in the mysterious moment of true humility.

It is when our greatest attempt falls curiously short that the greatness of grace spans the vastness of the divide. Must one seek; Yes. Does one's seeking make God find him; No. God has reached out to man. It is He who opens the door, He who searches for His sheep. We must always bear in mind, it is not one's knocking that rattles the lock loose and unlatches the door; it is God's graceful hand from the other side.

A vagrant cannot find audience with the King—the King must call for the vagrant. The vagrant's reply to the King is merely a matter of response; but in no way does his acceptance claim responsibility for the royal meeting. Yet, such analogies are endless and make little sense until one finds themselves hungry and homeless, or drowning and crushed by an iron sea. As Christians, there ought to be nothing more clear and obvious than the gravity of our human situation—and the greatness of Christ that overcomes it. We are the tramps. We are the sea torn. We are in a great instance in which we have not the ability to overcome; we are the helpless in need of the hero. Gracefully, the Hero has offered us His hand.

The gravity of our situation calls for grace.

Repentance is the acknowledgement of being found.

199. There was a man in a deep ravine. He had fallen from a great height—from a high and beautiful path that wound around a mountaintop garden. When he had fallen (trying to reach some luscious berries, too close to the edge, I'm sure) he had mortally wounded himself. His body was wracked and broken; shortly, he grew weaker as he lay without food or water. Emaciated and barely conscious, the man lay in the steep and unfathomable ravine.

Now there are different versions told of how the man can get out of his dire ravine:
-He can die. This is a rather bleak version.
-He can scream for help with what little voice he has, and curse the ravine.
-He can try to lift himself up with what little strength his broken body and delirious mind have, climb the daunting and sheer cliff, and make trail for home (the mountain's top). This is just as bleak as the previous options in his current condition.
-He can hope his ancestors will one day evolve wings so they don't find themselves in such unfortunate circumstances; meanwhile he will pass away knowing that his demise is *good* for the process of natural selection.

-He can pray to the Hindu gods, and come back in another life as a spry mountain goat who wouldn't have such a problem.
-He can find Buddhist enlightenment and become one with the swallowing ravine, swallowing himself by saying there is no ravine, there is no pain, all is all.
-He can try the consumer and popular version of Christianity (Christiandumb) and pray to God, hoping God will teleport him out of the ravine—or rather, out of the ravine and onto a fully loaded yacht.
-He can do the true Christian thing and scream for help as he is praying to God for deliverance.

There are other options—but these are the oft spoken ones. There are two that I am very interested in. One is the consumer Christian version, and the other is the biblical Christian version. In the consumer version, God hears the cry of the ravine-man and teleports him out of the ravine onto a yacht, into a Bentley, or to keep the metaphor steady, the scenic penthouse at the top of the mountain.

In the biblical Christian version, here is what happens: The ravine-man prays and God hears him. As the ravine-man is screaming for aid, a *man* sent by God hears his plea of helplessness. The Hero prepares supplies, ties a strong rope, and climbs down to the now unconscious man. He gives the ravine-man water and nourishes him with food. He bandages his wounds, sets his bones, and holds him close when the chill of night sets on. He encourages the man and exercises him until he is strong. Then the hero climbs up, and when at the top, He grabs a strong hold of the rope. He instructs the ravine-man to climb the rope, and as he does the Hero pulls up vigorously on the rope, and offers instruction on where to and where not to step because of loose and dangerous rocks. The Hero has saved the man in so many ways, yet the man could be said to *have climbed up the rope*. The man is now somewhat strong enough to journey to the top of the mountain—though only while leaning on his new traveling partner. No doubt he'll still have dangers to face along the way to the mountains summit, but he now has a helper.

Would a man who escaped such a fall ever say he saved himself? No; his gratitude runs too deep; his own efforts too impotent. This man knows what a Hero is.

200. What odd or cruel thing is this Christianity that says "repent," but yet says we are dead in our sin? What is this that petitions us to choose God, yet tells us we are morally incapable? That tells us to fight for what is good, but we must lay down our arms? Is this a cruel joke, an insufferable contradiction, or the necessary and mysterious meeting point of the infinite and finite—the communion of God and man?

It is not illogical to trust; it is a reasonable thing to trust who is trustworthy. It is unreasonable—no, insane—to distrust the one who is only good and only true, the one who cannot lie.

Surely truth is greater than the human mind alone, just as it is greater than the human heart alone; yet still truth is greater than both put together. But when the desire of the heart inflames in unison with reality tasted by the mind, then correlation with reality is there and pulsing. For trust is where the heart and mind come into agreement.

All have a faith, a trusting in someone or something; so all hearts meet with their minds—but not all desire, not all zeal of the heart is in accordance with reality. The heart and mind often lie in bed together deceived, pulling the blankets over each other's eyes, trusting in what diseases them. They may be in bed together, but neither can rest with the other because neither rest in God.

"Therefore having been justified by faith, we have peace with God, through our Lord Jesus Christ" (Romans 5:1).

Faith is trust, but what is trust? Trust is acknowledgement of what is real. Acknowledgement (to *accept*, to *admit*) is a function of desire, and desire the predisposition of the will—and the human will a facet of the diamond that is the imago Dei.

So, only in Christ who is the truth, will one's heart meet their mind in true accord. Until then, the heart and mind are a fragile alliance at best—both untrusting the other and sparking anxiety. The heart, the seat of affections, which is against itself (for it was made *imago Dei*), will then be half against the mind.

Faith is not an escape from reason, but is the touchstone that shows our communion with truth, our relationship with reality. Faith in Christ is not the cancelling of mind, but the correlation of heart and head, of desire and design. But faith in man is the cancelling of mind by way of hardening the heart.

201. Is God love? Is He the sole source of love? Then who can implant love into the human soul? God alone! A Christian is one who truly loves—so who can make themselves a Christian? None save God!

God is the sole fount of all that is good.

~Unity~

202. There is a broken synapse between the Old Testament and the New Testament—but the break is within man, not the perfect arc of the text.

Imagine reading a good novel—and then being wrongly told it was written by two adverse authors. Now you cannot read it or think about it the same. You start to look at the text with wary and *conspiracy theory* eyes, looking hard for contradictions, oppositions, subtle discrepancies; and buzzing through it all is a nagging feeling of discontinuity. This has happened with the Bible.

Many people see two different Gods within the Scriptures—one violent and one velvet. There is the thundering disembodied voice; a stringent law giver who prefers fire and wind as favored vehicles for manifesting Himself to a scared humanity. He is considered the great cosmic kill-joy. This is a powerful God— *wrath, justice*, and *judge* are the words that best describe Him. Then there is the New Testament version—*suffering, servant*, and *savior* are the key words now. Here is a God who speaks gently of grace and forgiveness; God with us in flesh and history.

This divine schizophrenia reveals much about the fractured "god" of man. Fallen man has put at odds the perfections of God! And not only this, but he has used God's own words in *the tearing apart*!

203. Let us not forget where Scripture twisting was first heard. Do you not recall? No, it was not in desert conditions where the hard wind blew and the dust dried the skin—it was not in the desert of the exodus or the wastelands of Jesus' temptation —it was under shade and the cool of leaves of Eden; it was amidst fruit and plenty. "Now the serpent was more crafty than any of the wild animals the Lord God had made. He said to the woman, 'Did God really say…?'"

Let us be watchful in our comfortable places and easy days.

The words of God have been misused and maligned since the garden days.

To many, it is as if God used the 400 years of silence between Malachi and Matthew as a time for regrouping after recognizing His plan for dealing with humanity was less than par. No! This strips both the law and the cross of mercy of their meaning!

Let it be said, Christ was no back-up plan. The way of Christ's cross was planned from the start—a good reading of Genesis will reveal this truth.

Many are ignorant of what the New Testament means to communicate for they don't know of the Old Covenant.

The Old Testament and New Testament work in harmony—they are not dissonant like the awkward chords of a beginning guitarist. If we don't find them in union it is because we are not in union with the Word.

The Old Testament is riddled with a gracious God: A God of immense mercy and tender love; a God who whispers; a God who desires intimacy with humanity and longs to hold His bride. When anyone typifies the Old Testament God as one of mere wrath and vengeance, they are only painting a warped, caricature.

Also, when anyone typifies Jesus as a feel-good, bubbly God who dawdles around sprinkling healing like fairy dust, they too are drawing a horribly inaccurate caricature of God. In Christ we see a God just as concerned with sin and justice—count how many times Jesus uses disturbing phrases like "weeping and gnashing of teeth" in regard to those who do not obey God!

Yet we have tamed the Savior who came to bring fire and a sword as well as grace and sweet redemption. Truly, the power of His teachings was shocking, unsettling, and challenging. Nevertheless, His words have been softened, and are believed to have been delivered with a cool smile and syrupy tone. In an exchange of the truth, the great challenger and "offender" of fallen humanity has been turned into a non-offender and self-esteem booster.

In an absurd trade like that of an army of angels for a squirt gun, Christ's strong words and methods have been swapped out in a diminishing trade.

Christians, as Dorothy Sayers has so vibrantly put it "very efficiently pared the claws of the Lion of Judah, certified Him as a fitting household pet for pale curates and pious old ladies."

204. It is humanity that is in need of editing—not the Gospel. The scriptures are to judge and read us; not for us to read and judge them.

The Bible is in pieces in the minds of men, and for that, it is seen to have no heart, no gravity in which to unify a worldview.

Many have a hard time reading the Bible correctly largely due to the fact that they do not see it as a cohesive narrative. Instead, they see it in floating clips and phrases—bits of dislocated information that seem to knock into each other like ice dregs in the North Atlantic. A cold knocking about that offers no warmth, no fire to humanity.

205. To what can we compare this fragmented view of Scripture? Imagine someone throwing at you disconnected and cryptic bits of Dostoevsky's classic novel *The Brothers Karamazov* for most of your life. Imagine the bits of narrative and Russian history incessantly being used to teach you and guide you—but there is no context to decode the attempts. Such idiocy would only confuse, frustrate, and make one passively angry.

The truth the novel was meant to impart never hit its mark, nor was the novel ever enjoyed for its artistry, simply because the context and narrative was violated. The author's tale was now only disconnected facts hollowed out by their isolation. You would have no real relationship with the story—just wounds from its angled bits and pieces being thrown at you.

Then comes along someone who loves the book, who says the author has taught him and changed him—"Yeah, right!" we say in cynicism. For how could that insane smattering of words mean so much to him...*he must be lying!*" And we walk away bitter, leaving Dostoevsky to the hypocrites, or to the weak-minded who need a crutch...

We are often taught the Bible as *a clutter of truth*; as haphazard facts instead of an anchored story that gives an overarching meaning, a sense of continuity to history and our lives.

206. The anchor, the magnetic core of the Bible: Jesus—He is the center by which all holds. "The Son is the radiance of God's glory and the exact representation of His being, sustaining all things by His powerful word" (Hebrews 1:3).

The purpose of the Bible—Jesus. If one does not know Jesus, they do not know the Bible. If one does not preach Jesus, they do not preach the Word of God. This *preaching* does not mean shouting "Jesus" at, or throwing Bibles at people who sleep-in on Sundays or have a cigarette in their mouth! Nor does it mean simply slapping Jesus onto a bumper or silk-screened onto a shirt.

"You diligently study the Scriptures because you think that by them you possess eternal life. These are the Scriptures that testify about me, yet you refuse to come to me to have life. I do not accept praise from men, but I know you. I know that you do not have the love of God in your hearts. I have come in my Father's name, and you do not accept me; but if someone else comes in his own name, you will accept him. How can you believe if you accept praise from one another, yet make no effort to obtain the praise that comes from the only God? But do not think I will accuse you before the

Father. Your accuser is Moses, on whom your hopes are set. If you believed Moses, you would believe me, for he wrote about me. But since you do not believe what he wrote, how are you going to believe what I say?" (John 5:39-47).

They knew the scriptures, but they did not *know* the Scriptures. They read the book wrongly.

Every book of the Bible groans when this dry-rub of *legalism* is invoked. Every book of the Bible cries out for an unfathomable redemption—an undeserved salvation. Each book is like a spoke, pointing into the hub that moves them, or a ray pointing back to the sun that sparked them.

207. Without Jesus, the Bible is a Frankenstein script; it is parts and gaunt limbs—pale religious arms and legs brought to artificial life by the will power of men. But this is not the actuality—for Jesus is the blood through the organic story; the marrow and the flesh of a personal, coherent universe.

When the Bible is brought to *life* merely by the imaginations of men, like Frankenstein's monster, it will turn upon them until one is lost to myth and the other dead. Is this not what we see: a book of myths and spiritually dead men?

Because the Bible is perceived to be *in pieces* by most people, it becomes a weapon of choice. (Remember, the first dagger jabbed at the truth was a twisting of God's word!)

When a kitchen knife is taken out of its context of the kitchen and finds its way to the school playground, something is wrong. Because the Bible is not seen as a narrative, it is often manipulated and pillaged. Many feel justified in pulling out a verse or two from the loose string of beads, and doing with them what they will, what pleases them at the time—playing marbles with them, throwing them harshly at a neighbor, etc. And so, people feel justified taking the kitchen knife to the playground and calling themselves Christians.

Because of this *fracturing of narrative*, one can *prove* anything by the Bible. I don't know what you could not *prove*! You could *prove* the Loch Ness Monster, I'm sure, if you just bump around certain scriptures of Jonah and Job! You could *prove* there is no God; there is a God; or there are thousands of gods and each lives on his own star. You could *prove* communism and capitalism. You could *prove* Mormonism or Hinduism. You could *prove* transubstantiation and symbolic communion. You could *prove* and approve of being totally smashed on Vodka, or being a bone-dry teetotaler. You can *prove* Jesus had a son, a daughter, a grandson, a granddaughter, a dog named Indiana, or a gold fish named Methuselah. How? By twisting it of course! I'm sure it can be done—that is, if it hasn't been done already.

You may laugh, but take this seriously; it can and does happen. Devise a fish story, throw in some embittered archaeologists looking for some airtime, reference an obscure text, and next thing you know there is a special on The Discovery Channel about "*The Lord's sacred goldfish Methuselah*"—and that is why the symbol of the fish is so important to Christianity! And there you have it—*proof* of this insane concoction every time you see a fish symbol on a Volvo or Toyota. There will be believers. What will be believed is unbelievable!

208. This troubled me for a long time—this whole division issue: denominations, cults, sub-denominations, sub-cults, sub-cult-denominations—it seems so devious and childish. "*Fine! I'll go and make my own club then!*" How are so many fractures possible? They are possible because the Bible is seen to be fractured—the illumination of the *guide book* is shooting off in a thousand different directions and it has no center! This has happened not because we go to a fractured mirror, but because we go to God's Word with fractured lenses. The light of The Book is not bad, but the light of the eye is.

Few play by the literary rules of normal reason when it comes to the Bible.

The deceiver, it seems, knows much about Judo. In Judo, one uses their opponent's momentum against them. So here the deceiver has violently pushed forward the truth of the Bible as a *special book*: *I will make it so special that no one treats it like a normal book; I will make it so special that it must be read like no other book—it must be read illogically, out of context, and twisted about. I will make it so special that they think it is whole, even torn into pieces! Let them forget God in the memorizing of all the bits and pieces! Let the special become absurd!*

We have become so pushed forward and off-balance with the religious *special-ness* of the Bible that we think it un-godly to read it normally! We read it abnormally and absurdly, and we read it wrongly.

It is characteristic of inverted-man to go to the book that is the expression of reality and deal with it deceptively. Let us not be surprised. If we are surprised, then we are dealers in deception.

Imagine what we would think of someone who read *Macbeth* like the Bible is read. They would step up to the front of class and tell us about their creepy, bizarre and obviously wrong interpretations—and we would scratch our heads in weird wonder. One might first check to see if they were on unregulated meds, or surrounded by a purple haze. But straight away, it would rightly be said that they are wrong in how they are reading the famous play of the bard.

Would this be judgmental of us? Would this be intolerant? Or would this be compassionate? That depends on our graciousness—and as Christians, we should be full of truth *and* grace because Jesus was full of truth *and* grace. We do not need to belittle, but we do need to stand for truth; so we must contend and correct.

We must remember that it is insanity not to call people out on their destructive madness. We are more mad then they if we call their insanity sane; or worse yet, we are murderers if we watch someone committing soul suicide and do nothing.

209. We read the Bible wrongly when we either/or it as a sum. What does this mean? Well, do we read it literally or do we read it symbolically? Do we read it spiritually, or do we read it historically? Can you see? These either/ors are devious because in them we feel we have to make a blanket choice—but when we make that choice we amputate something important.

Imagine doing this with a public library: "Are the Books in the public library metaphorical or literal? Are they poetry or biography?" This is absurd; yet we do it with the Bible, which is a library of books about God and man. *Bible* comes from the word *biblios* which means *books*. Let us read them normally—with head *and* heart in motion.

Here is a suggestion—let's read the Bible like it is *meant* to be read. "*Ah! But how was it meant to be read?*" we might ask. We must pay attention to genre. When it is poetry, read it as if it were poetry. When it is doctrinally focused, then read it as if it were doctrinally focused. If it is meant to read like history that is because it is history and we should read it like history. When it is wisdom sayings, let us be wise enough to treat it as wisdom sayings and not mathematical equations.

When the text is symbolic, let's treat it as symbolic—if we don't, then as fast as one can say "low budget B movie," we will have a Jesus with literal horns and seven eyes running around with a sword for a tongue—a divine mutant! Should we regard Jesus as all seeing (seven being the number of perfection) and full of authority (horns are symbols of authority), or go with the mutated reading making a monster out of the Messiah?

Now quickly, before the stones come flying—I must say that because something is symbolic, poetic, parabolic, etc, it doesn't mean it isn't historical and true. Let us be reasonable; "Come now, and let us reason together" (Isaiah 1:18).

What would you do with the man who read a legal contract as metaphysical poetry, or a love note as a tax time news letter?

210. There is a violent hobby among many *Christians*, it is called proof texting. Proof texting is really pretexting. What is this? This is religious bet rigging. It is loading the scriptural dice. It is manipulation and molestation of the Bible. It is done every day, especially on Sundays, in plain sight, applauded, admired, studied and rarely ever questioned.

A pretext is an excuse; it is a concealment of the truth. A pretext is wholly anti-Christ-like. It is lying by excluding. It is commission of sin by wielding omission.

There is a little saying that speaks to this addiction of the self-gravitating heart: *a text without a context is nothing but a pretext*. This simply means that if you strip a verse from Scripture (without the context to show what the verse actually means) you can twist and maneuver the isolated verse to *seem to mean* what you what it to mean. That is, you read *into* the text your meaning, not read *out of* it God's truth.

Now, all this is to simply say: "There is no God." I just *pretexted*—were you listening? This is the very opposite of what the Scriptures say. The Scriptures actually say, "The fool says in his heart 'there is no God'" (Psalm 14:1).

When we pretext, we trade a truth for a lie—but it sounds *oh so good* in its religious lingo. This obvious secret is a skeleton key that (partially) unlocks the riddle of multiple denominations, sects, and cults. When this key is turned, no longer do we question the Bible for being suspect, or unable to convey its message, but we now must question the man or woman who is spinning the Bible like a toy top for amusement.

A broken mirror becomes a myriad of daggers.

A broken mirror turns a beautiful face into a monstrous image.

Yet the mirror is not broken; it is the lens of our worldview that is fractured, and therefore casts this fracture upon what it looks upon.

Here is an irony: The looking glass of life, the Scriptures, shows us as broken not because the glass is broken, but because the glass is whole, and it accurately portrays who and what we are: broken people. Yet, when the broken eye looks at the mirror, it does not see man as broken!

211. There is a tendency to think verse numbers are sacred; that they are holy hinges of God's Word—and therefore they allow us to dislocate the joints of Scripture. Maybe if we understood that verse numbering didn't appear until a man named Robert Stephens introduced the numbering in 1551, and chapters were introduced by Cardinal Hugo de S. Caro in 1238, then we would think differently about our cut and paste tendencies.

These numberings were not meant to be divisions, but rather to make for ease of reference. Numbers were meant to help us see the truth, not to keep us deluded.

If numbering is holy, then what will become of all the heathen Christians who read a verse-less bible until 1551? Poor Paul; poor Augustine! Too bad for them—if only they had these near-arbitrary numbers we have ...

212. I make these points not to be a nit-picker, but to remind the reader that the Bible is a story of epic purpose, and that with the

advent of the numbers, we often lose the visual representation of the text as a story arc, and as long sweeps of narrative motion.

The Scriptures are not a mail order catalog, an internet order form, or a numbered fast food menu to pick and choose from (*yes, I'll take a John 3:16, maybe a half portion of Psalm 23, and two of Proverbs 3:5 please. And make sure there is no Job or Jeremiah in there, I hate Job, and Jeremiah is far too salty for my taste!*) This is outrageously unethical and unfathomably shallow. If we pick and choose God's Word we choose to pick ourselves out of eternal life like a thin-rooted weed. For in picking, we are judging God.

If we misuse and amputate Scripture we do violence to Jesus. If we marginalize Scripture we marginalize Jesus. If we have a low view of Scripture we have a low view of Jesus.

If we forget the Bible is a story (a true story) then we can forget it is about a person (God) and forget it is about a relationship. If we forget it is a story then we will turn God into an object, an idea, a thing, a theological factoid, rather than see Him as He is—the lover of our soul.

The deceiver knows that the more he can un-relate and unhinge the Scriptures in our minds, pull them apart like the limbs of some cadaverous thing, then the less inclined we are to see the love in them; the less likely we are to see the relationship between God and man. If the form can be pulled apart at will, then it is a short step to pulling the message to thin fibers that can then be snapped one at a time in the individual's heart and mind. Snap…snap…snap…

It is easier to run from God within religion when His Word is dislocated and unable to *run* and *move*. It is easier to play at being god when the Scriptures are like toy blocks instead of a sword that divides even spirit and soul, joints and marrow.

Relationship is where meaning and mystery meet. The Bible is the communiqué of a presence—not merely a cluster bomb of facts. Presence transforms; facts merely inform. Arguments are not enough—but the presence of the Spirit is what changes mankind.

The Bible was written for man to see how upside down the world is, and how it should be up-right—this being the case, the Bible will be called upside down and be used to disprove the existence of God; this is reasonable given man's condition.

~The Culture of Death~

213. To what can we compare a culture that has normalized death? A cryptic old man would walk to the center of town every day; up and down Main Street he would walk and scowl. As he did, he would pull aside the first child he saw, hold them by their arm, and slap their face; then he would walk away with the same unmoved countenance and saying nothing.

When he first did this there was an obvious uproar; when he did it again there was complaint; and when he did it yet again, there were some whispered rumors. Then came *the horrible hush*—for time passed and all came to know the man and the strange ritual of roving and slapping in silence. All became familiar with his slow steady walk, tuft of white hair, hollowed cheeks and lean grabbing fingers—and so they would say, "Here he comes, that old man again!" And every time he grabbed a child, slapped them, and walked away slowly, the town would all say, "There he goes, that old man—that's just what he does! He's done it for as long as we can remember. What's there for us to do—that's the way it has always been around here."

Eventually a catalog of jokes was made about the man, some named him an anti-hero for being "free in his expression," others tried to befriend him by taking up the art of slapping as well, and others attempted to ignore him to no avail.

The man's absurdity was only outweighed by the town's absurd normalizing of his behavior. Do you hear it? The chorus singing, "There he goes, that old man—that's just what he does! He's done it for as long as we can remember. What's there for us to do—that's the way it has always been around here"?

Death is abnormal—though our culture insists it is part of the great chain of being. We all have had a cradle, we all will have a grave—"it's just the way it is," they say, with an uneasy grin and an amazed stare that anyone would say otherwise.

Death is not part of the original nature of be-ing, it is the result of man's do-ing!

214. In every corner of our buzzing culture we find evidence of the desire for eternal life. The shimmering celluloid of cinema, fame inducing internet trends, the dark sparkle of rock stardom and the vanity fair of media-hype—they are all around us. Our hi-speed culture is inundated with evidences of Easter. How is this? These odd things are concrete evidences of Easter's veracity?

Take a look: We worship youth over years; tame the language of death with easy euphemisms (*passing away, no longer with us, gone to a better place, etc*); cryogenically freeze ourselves until 2050; replace our organic parts with plastic ones; live as though invincible; deal with death in the self-removed, vicarious realm of television and movies; pursue fame to preserve our names in the annals of history; and when our mortality shows, we cover it with make-up. Each one of these attempts at immortality is a denial of death, and an attempt by a paper army to keep a juggernaut at bay—they are tragic and sad attempts to hold back an Atlantic tide with just one's hands and a plastic bucket.

These attempts at fooling the Grim Reaper are impulsive cries from the deep of the soul: "But we were meant to live forever...I must live forever!" Such attempts at circumventing death speak to the reality *and* necessity of Jesus' resurrection. The problem is not that we want eternal life, but that we want it *our own* way, by our own strength. But our ways are external futilities, like trying to get oneself out of the Grand Canyon by pulling up on one's own boot straps—there is much effort no doubt, but no movement closer to greater heights or eternal life.

Let us remember the intimate tie between *the Passover* and Easter. At the epicenter of Easter is Jesus, Lamb and Lord, who took our sin and our death; at the heart of *Passover* is the same—an innocent life sacrificed so death would pass over those under the blood. God has graced humanity and given us true life through the death of Jesus Christ. The Passover was not an arbitrary event in history—it was a prescient moan of victory from the cross of Christ.

Our culture begs for immortality, yet strangely we often "pass over" Easter and forget that behind the pastel façade of eggs and fleeting sweets is the sacrificial lamb that has taken our sin and was hammered by our deserved death blow—and in the strike of justice He has forged for us eternal life. Let us not pass over Easter, but let us remember *Passover*; and to all the misguided buzz about eternal life, let us exclaim *"He is Risen!"* for only then can we rise with Him. Jesus is the Passover.

An irony: by attempting to escape death through circuitous routes of securing eternal life, we as humans highlight the reality of our sin and our desire to be free from it.

Death represents more than an end to earthly pleasure—it is the possibility of facing accountability.

215. As a joke is meant to help us cope with a disturbance, glamorizing death is our device to help us cope with the inevitabilities of a world that is saturated with death. We glamorize the grim—it is our way of placing reigns and muzzles over our anxieties; it is our way of establishing a type of "control" over the inevitable hand of death. The glamorization of death is like the nervous laughter of an accused man.

Though we reflexively turn from death when it comes to us in person, we fast look into its gaze when we look through the glass of the voyeur's lens. We cope vicariously; that is, we look into our sin through the buffer and distance of *a lens* (be it a photograph, a movie, television, or even the lens of an author's pen. We are drawn to the glamorization because of what we have become—and we are repulsed because of who we are meant to be, but are not.

Because we are made to thrive upon eternal life, but have spurned that life, we gaze into, and are repulsed by the ashen face of death. We seek life but we seek it in the form of death. We feel alive when we dare-devil ourselves over a cliff, out of a plane, or amidst the fear of an adrenalized sport. Modern models, those the media puts up as paragons of beauty, are mandated to look skeletal and emaciated—dead women walking. Our movies have morphed from adventure tales with casualties to casual murder tales for the sake of adventure—men as meat being ground to pieces.

Could it be that we are attracted to death, but are disturbed by the very attraction?

An irony: The more we deny evil, the more we will be enchanted with death and its gruesome incidentals; the more we recognize our sin nature, the more we will see into beauty and taste of a joy once hidden.

By running from death we acknowledge the "unspoken abnormality" of the world: that we are sinners, and that we really don't want our *due wages*. The wages of sin is death. Our denial of death is a backhanded evidence of our true nature. The further we run from the light we have turned our back to, the longer the shadow grows that we run headlong into.

216. There is a strange and common symptom of the elevation of man— it is something counterintuitive and often overlooked. This strange and common symptom is low self-esteem and deepening self-deprecation. Pervasive in near every sphere of life is the praise of humanity—it is the accepted standard.

Think about how parents talk of their children; think about how we often regard ourselves. A parent, when confronted with a young child's rebellion, deceit and blame shifting will wonder "Where did they learn to do that?" as if it were something foreign to the human race. Often, as things don't seem to go our way, we wonder, "Why isn't this working out for me, I'm a good person—I deserve it?"

And all the time, as we champion our vaunting good nature, there is a growing dissonance on the inside. What are we to make of modern suicide rates, depression, low self-esteem, and the trend of self-mutilation called *cutting*? What are we to make of the rising numbers of premeditated violent acts among the young, among those coddled and affluently comfortable?

Somewhere within, something tells us that we are not what we claim to be; something undermines the very tower of Babel we attempt to build with bricks of self-esteem. As man's self flattery skyrockets, so too will its shadow of self-deprecation.

As the idol of man is raised higher and higher, its shadow will extend further and further. Like pain to warn us of physical danger, depression and self-deprecation are hazard lights on the dashboard of the soul, saying stop driving this idol of self! Could it be that they are not the devils we thought? But rather angels who wrestle us into obedience for our own welfare?

Anxiety is an *angel* that tells us to take heed.

217. There was a town that found in its proud leader great qualities. They gathered to build a statue to honor him, but it never seemed to be finished—only it grew taller and taller. On the day that the first granite crown was to be placed, the entire town huddled beneath its height and cheered, not realizing the whole town now lay in a cold, long shadow; not realizing that the foundation could not support the height, and not realizing they stood in the very spot that that the granite would fall upon and crush them. They applauded as the crown was set; altogether forgetting the voices of the *killjoys* who shouted from the jail cells, "Stop! Take down this idiot statue of man! Be careful! Before it... "

218. The Medicine that is Poison: If we were to watch a child try to balance out a teeter totter by adding more and more weight to the heavy end, say, by adding more and more rocks, we might question that child. We might recommend a check up at the doctor's; maybe a mental evaluation; maybe administer some meds. And that is exactly what we do: we give meds—and that medicine is the self-esteem movement. The child has repeatedly been told, "Good job!" in reward for absurd efforts, and therefore not only continues

in the absurdity, but tackles it now with more effort and energy as to gain acceptance from those he loves. The child moves further and further in the wrong direction, and all the while confused by positive social responses, and the continual frustration of his goal.

Like prescribing milk to settle someone's stomach who is lactose intolerant, the more we have given them the medicine, the more damage that is done. The more we play to the human ego, the greater damage we do. Appeasing for a mere moment, we risk eternal suffering.

Medicine has become a poison simply because the disease has been misdiagnosed. Humanism believed the disease was that humanity *knew not its greatness*—and so had to be goaded into the self-worth it deserved. Christianity calls the disease humanity's fallen nature, and offers a dose of reality.

We must never be surprised by our own potential for evil. If we are, then we have misunderstood the message of grace.

The Christian is not surprised by death; but the Christian life is a sustained movement against death.

219. I do not live at peace with death, for that would mean living at peace with sin—but I do not fear it. I defy death and what it means; but I defy it only by faith in Jesus and His righteousness. Any other defying of death is condoning it and participating in it (for unbelief is sin the wages of sin is death). By Christ alone does death receive its death blow.

We are not called to accept death, but to conquer it through faith; for someday "There will be no more death or mourning or crying or pain, for the old order of things has passed away" (Revelation 21:4). Death is disunion—faith overcomes that which is disunited.

"Jesus said unto her, I am the resurrection, and the life: he that believeth in me, though he were dead, yet shall he live: And whosoever lives and believes in me shall never die. Do you believe this?" (John 11:25-26).

When we die to ourselves through the crucifixion of Christ, we begin to live; we become the living. The living will never die; The Lord is the Lord of the living. The dead die; the living live.

Like the flood that Noah and his family floated upon, the baptism into Christ both judges and preserves. Baptism's death is justice, for wrath is what all humanity has earned. Its preservation through rebirth is salvation—that which we are graciously given because God is love.

From the blood of Abel came the cry for justice—but from the blood of Christ came a two-toned cry: justice/mercy!

220. Is there Hell? Yes. Is there Heaven. Yes. Is Jesus the only way of salvation? Yes. Are these unfair? Intolerant? Let me ask this: Is it unfair that justice be done? Is it not good that mercy be given? Is it not good news that the broken, collapsed, and twisted have been saved from their caved-in and twisted-up selves?

We think hell is unjust only because we don't understand grace. We think hell is cruel because we have a cotton candy view of grace and a sickly notion of love.

Maybe we could call hell a horrible idea of a disgruntled religion if God punished from a distance (maybe)—but we cannot, because God himself died for us; because He put Himself smack into the middle of the fray. He tasted the grit between his very own teeth.

Hell is just because God was killed for us—perfect love did not exclude Himself from His judgment. We cannot curse hell because God cursed Himself in our stead. And so, to deny the love of Christ is the offense that makes hell just; it was always the offense, it will always be the offense.

Hell doesn't make God *not good*, but it reveals us to be guilty—guilty of a multitude of crimes culminating in spurring the ultimate love. We don't like this, so we don't want to deal with it. Denial does not change reality.

Do all you want to soften the un-hip, intolerant word *hell*; try appealing to various *spinnings* of Greek definitions, and try twisting the facts of our own souls. But Jesus, the most pure and perfect, the most humble and wise, the brave and loving—the good—spoke unabashedly of Hell's reality.

Trying to debunk hell is only an attempt at debunking a sovereign and good God who is both just and merciful. Debunking hell dissolves grace; there is no need for grace if there were no justice, no penalty for that which is wrong. If we weren't so hypocritical and dishonest, we would realize that we long for what is both just and merciful—and God is both.

If we long for justice, then by necessity, we desire that there be a hell. But do we long for universal justice? Or are we merely selfish? Do we only shout "justice" when some line of hurt traces its way to us?

It is pride that believes we are worthy of heaven; it is humility that acknowledges hell.

All deserve hell—does this sound horrible? It is horrible, and it is our fault. But the good news is that there is grace; there is the heart of Christ that lay upon rough wood. Grace saves us from a deserved hell. Love saves us from deserved death. Love wins. Love wins. Love wins. Love has love won.

When we understand the atrocity of idolatry we begin to understand the justice of hell. Idolatry is deicide; it is the attempted murder of God. How does one punish the attempted murder of God?

Does a capricious God put us in hell for stealing a piece of candy? A song? An inheritance? Or maybe for telling a white lie—a black lie? For adultery? For the shedding of blood? No—we deserve hell for the sin that underlies all these sins—the sin of unbelief—the heart's desire to put a bullet into God, into the one heart of true and infinite love.

It is the warped root of our *sins* that makes us deserving of hell—it is the *sinful* heart that necessitates hell. But again, grace trumps death, love bests the ill-aligned heart.

Is eternal punishment unfair for the heart that desires to murder infinite, eternal love?

221. Death is the perennial and pervasive reminder that we live in an abnormal world; and when we turn from it, another sallow stalk springs, another creeper vines tangles into view. There is no running from this *eternal footman* of death; so this pale figure has become embraced and glamorized. Sequins have been sewn onto his shroud, and we have watched his sweeping movements in the limelight—elegant, he sweeps and dances—and we are induced into sleep by his lipless romantic grin.

Wake up, O sleeper! Wake up and dust off the sequins! Believe! Believe…rise from the dead, and Christ will shine on you!

~Denying Humanism/Embracing Man~

222. There is an oddity about Christianity—this oddity is that it both denies *and* embraces the world. This is possible because the Christian worldview starts with a God who is both infinite and personal.

Following Jesus stands fast alone amidst the world's religions because it alone both truly affirms life *and* denies the world. (It stands fast alone because it is not a religion—but a relationship with our Creator.) Christianity alone stands against the world for the world. Christianity is a bold and humble double movement.

I follow Christ not for lack of better choices, but because Jesus alone is the most brilliant and the only way; yet it follows that other "paths" are wanting, flawed, and in error.

How is it that only Christianity both *affirms* and *denies*? Don't other religions do the same thing? Only Christianity can truly affirm and deny because only Christ can hold the two in tension—only He could love enough to die for the unlovable. There is no stance that shows greater love and greater disdain than the cross; the posture of all other religions is akimbo: hands on hips, slightly disapproving –and self-righteous.

Religion tries to love the world, but its moralism won't allow it to. It is because Jesus is both the just and justifier, both Creator and Savior, that

Contra mundum (against the world): This is how we love the world.

There are a million miles between the Gospel and these other religions. There is a great divide between these things called religion and the relationality of the Gospel of Christ. Now let me spend some time discussing some manifestations of the religion.

223. I believe a humanistic Christian is greater deceived than an atheistic humanist. Both are oxymorons, but one is a pretension under the name of Christ! (A humanist cannot be atheistic because their god is man; a humanistic *Christian* is not a Christian.)

Humanistic Christianity is deeply troubling and widely spread. It is a greater deception because it is a deception done in the name of Christ; it is undercover rebellion (and even undercover from itself). It is subtle and violent—it is deadly because it is a cancer masquerading as a cure. It must be exposed and dealt with.

224. This is important: there is a difference between *humanistic Christianity* and *Christian humanism*.

Humanistic Christianity is a religion that strives (undercover) to ever push God to the margin in order that humanity may take the throne of glory. It is counterfeit "Christianity," and it is concerned primarily about human comfort, ego stimulation, self-esteem, and self-deception promotion. It poses as a love for God, but it is only a lust after godhood because it is only *love* for the self. It is attractive because it seems plush and sweet. The God of *humanistic Christianity* is man.

This *humanism* is a pandemic in the Western church—and it is a category five on the Pandemic Severity Index for sure. Yet, it is so slippery, so momentarily sweet, and it looks good—so it is often swallowed.

Humanistic Christianity is Christianity with the heart ripped out, and therefore, devoid of a functioning mind. It is only an insipid shell, horrible, because like a corpse, it is not what it should be. It is not Christianity.

All devils are angels; this is why the great level of danger. If a devil looked *the devil*, self-preservation would turn us away; but because a devil looks the angel, our self-seeking holds onto its wings, not considering the heights it will take us (or drop us from), and consuming whatever fruit it will give us (no matter how waxen).

225. *Christian humanism* is a different term, but an ambiguous term—so we must be wise with it. It can mean something good, but it can quickly disintegrate into the "insipid shell" just discussed.

Christian Humanism often refers to the belief that we as humans have freedom, individuality, dignity and that these are essential to true Christianity. It is a view that believes strongly that we are made in the image of God (Imago Dei). It also believes that education and the arts are valuable, pivotal, and necessary to the human condition because they glorify God. This is an orthodox view. But we must be careful; sometimes the terms *Humanistic Christianity* and *Christian Humanism* are confused, and swung around like a drunk slings around his drink, cracking into things and spilling his addiction onto others. Better to just call it Christianity, and let the weight of glory be God's, not ours.

226. *Skeptical humanism, secular humanism* or *humanism* is a belief that shuns revelation and God and gods of any kind. It retorts, *"Gods you say!* The Greek pantheon, Yahweh, Allah, Brahma—all hogwash!" It trusts in science, rationality, self-determination and the power of the will. It trusts in white knuckles and mental prowess. It is a belief that man is responsible only to himself, and that there are no transcendental justifications, no divine love, no ultimate meaning, and there is nothing beyond the sun (metaphorically speaking). It is the religion of the atheist and often the agnostic. It is the belief (yes, it is a faith) that man is god. It is the religion of *rationalism*.

227. There are two basic beliefs: The belief in God the Creator; or the belief in the only other possible god—call it rationality, evolution, Gaia, Molech, bubble-gum Jesus, Shiva, sex, or Zeus— but the real name of this other god is *man*. We are either a humanist (self worship disguised by irreligious and religious dressings) or a

Christian—that is, one who acknowledges the ultimate sovereignty and Glory of God the Father, Jesus the Son, and the Holy Spirit.

This is why orthodox Christianity speaks so well and so often upon the distinction between grace and works. Works is the mechanism of salvation for he who is god—the humanist finds salvation in his works; the Christian trusts only in the works of God.

I will say it again—for it is such a foreign concept to most, though it is under our very noses, under our very skin! The battle that we face in the universities, in the city streets, and in every small town is the same battle that was waged in the garden; it is not a battle of faith against science, but of faith against faith. Faith in God the Creator or faith in man the creation—this is the fray.

228. I am a Christian because I am a horrible god. There is only one good God; all others are false saviors, plastic messiahs, and tyrants playing the saint.

Unlike the secular humanist, I do not believe the universe is the result of the collision of time, chance and matter. This humanism is too cold as it and we all spiral through an arctic universe—our only tie to each other the vast tomb we will all die in. Humanism is too disturbing in a world that is disturbing. Humanism offers no hope to the disturbance we know life to be. Humanism offers no answers to our desires for perfection, to our haunting hungers.

Humanism's greatest advocates, its most well-known priests, lived and died tortured lives—never eating of peace, never attaining the power of human will that they spoke of. It is a religion that is spoke of, but never truly lived (for in the end, it has to steal commandments from God to get along here on earth).

Though Jean-Jacque Rousseau, Friedrich Nietzsche, Bertrand Russell, and Ayn Rand were all bright lights in *their universe* of overwhelming darkness, they are sad and isolate shadows in a world of light.

Yet, they were shadows of humanity that Christ died to illumine with His love and eternal life—yet the proud gravity of humanism and pride is strong like a black hole. They chose to kick at the one who could heal their dim souls. These "bright lights" of humanism were blind, lost within themselves, and passionately longed to share their loneliness. And today, their disciples are many far and wide, are blind, are lost within themselves for they follow the futile wanderings of the blinded ones, of gifted souls gone mad.
*Now some may say, "*So and so* was an *antihumanist*—their philosophies differ!" Okay then, we'll just say they had different ways of being their own god—and for that, were humanists.

We as Christians ought to know the names mentioned above. Look them up, look into history and read about them if they draw no connections or thoughtful responses. Most likely, if we do not know these names, then we are unaware of their worldviews that have infected our culture. If we are unaware of the thought that manifests itself in our society, if we do not see the great cultural opposition to the Gospel, then likely, we don't see it because its glaze is over our own eyes, its infection creeping over us—and for the darkness we cannot see the darkness. Often, the disciples of such people as Jean-Jacque Rousseau, Friedrich Nietzsche, Bertrand Russell, and Ayn Rand have never even heard the names of their depressed-masters.

229. The irony of the secular humanist! "Free! Free of God! Free to live any way we damn-well want to live!" they say in triumph. But, when one rationally extends the *logic* that has set man free from the annoyance of God, then one realizes that the universe is only a machine of matter, and so too is man only a machine and nothing more. Therefore, man is biochemically, mechanically determined even in the smallest of movements—he is not free at all! Nothing more than a deceived android!

I agree with humanism's view that the world is an inhospitable place where there is much cruelty and pain; but I do not agree that this is all there is, that this is the best possible world. I do not agree that humanity's only commonality is that we will suffer and die, leaving only sad monuments and ruins in our wake. It is the biblical stance to believe there is redemption and hope.

I do not believe evil is natural to the universe we live in. It is a parasite. It is a falling away from the original. The Bible tells us this, as well as the dissonance we feel inside when we are confronted with evil. "It should be otherwise" is both whispered and shouted within our souls as we stand at a July funeral and bury another friend; as we talk to a senile parent staring into space for a lost name; as we weep with a rape victim; as we mourn in the ash-wake of another human engineered catastrophe. Can an honest person look into the world and ignore the embers and scars?

Humanism's *realism* caves heavily into pessimism. It assigns beauty to randomness. Meaning is sucked out of the world like soda through a plastic straw—though there is no one to suck it out. The concept of thinking and reason become nothing more than colliding oddities of energy in our already accidental brains. Love becomes only a tool for survival of the fittest, and therefore, is not love—the word love being emptier than the sucked out soda can.

Can there be beauty without order or rationality? If so, then there is no standard; then this means there is no differentiation, no difference to define by—and the distance between beauty and ugliness dissolves and the two mix into a greasy smear. Beauty requires the existence of the particular and the universal; the one and the many—and this means differentiation. Beauty exists. Humanism melts beauty.

Humanism says there is no meaning or purpose, and that we must make up our own, that we must *will our meaning*. This relativity of "personal truth" needs to be tested. Can we do and be anything we want, as long as we will it?! If this is the case, then we have *no right* to restrain the will and power of the murderer, the rapist, the genocidal tyrant, the common thief. In practice who would let this be? And if this is true, then each vote for virtue and justice is a useless breath, a wasted ballot—or worse, equal to evil. There is nothing good, there is nothing evil. There is only will. There is only power and force. Does this describe reality?

230. The great 2 + 2 = 5! Humanism is the great case of 2 + 2 = 5. In George Orwell's seminal book *Nineteen Eighty-Four,* 2 + 2 = 5 is the concept of *illogical reasoning* that the prevailing oppressive social structure uses to brainwash people to keep them herded away from the truth. If you are told something enough, told it is true, and others believe it, you too will eventually believe it, though it is a blatant contradiction and therefore false.

In Orwell's novel, this concept of believing in obvious untruths is called *doublethink*. Doublethink is used to brainwash the main character into thinking two plus two makes five. In Orwell's own words doublethink is explained as:

"The power of holding two contradictory beliefs in one's mind simultaneously, and accepting both of them. ... To tell deliberate lies while genuinely believing in them, to forget any fact that has become inconvenient, and then, when it becomes necessary again, to draw it back from oblivion for just so long as it is needed, to deny the existence of objective reality and all the while to take account of the reality which one denies—all this is indispensably necessary. Even in using the word doublethink it is necessary to exercise doublethink. For by using the word one admits that one is tampering with reality; by a fresh act of doublethink one erases this knowledge; and so on indefinitely, with the lie always one leap ahead of the truth."

231. Humanism is the great *doublethink*; and with irony, humanism levels this charge against Christianity. Christianity is a sweet explosion of paradoxes, but humanism is a whimpering puff of frustrated contradictions.

Here is the great 2 + 2 = 5 of humanism: *There is value to human life yet human life is the accident of time and chance, merely evolved random protoplasm*. The modern humanist will shout all day long at a rally for human rights, they will weep over the loss of a loved one, they will donate time and money in the wake of a tragedy. Yet there is no reason for them to do any of this. If we are nothing more than inadvertent electrons and random collections of protoplasm, then there is no inherent worth in a human life. One cannot believe in a meaningless universe and yet believe in meaningful life.

If it is a worthless universe then all human life is worthless, and the rally shouting for human rights has nothing to do with rights. The humanist proclaims an insignificant universe, yet, significance of human life—doublethink. They claim there is no right or wrong; then they stand up to vote for amendments that they deem right or wrong based on the value of human life—doublethink. Two plus two makes for five.

It is the Christian who, because they love, can put their finger on the nerve of doublethink.

I follow Christ because I believe $2 + 2 = 4$, so to speak; because human life is intrinsically valuable. It is intrinsically valuable because it was made in the image of God.

232. For the secular humanist, it was chance and time that brought about human life. But what goes unspoken is that chance is a chain that binds all possibilities; yet meaning and design are the artistry that propels all possibilities. Chance can do nothing; it is not an active agent. Chance means "to fall out of". Nothing can fall out of nothing. Possibility does not fall out of nothing.

Purpose alone gives us significance; we are significant by design. Without purpose given by God, all is idiocy, all is an absurd garble, life is merelygartblehu lly nndijhwxx%^ !!~01j. Meaningless.

How can we even invoke the *meaninglessness* of our universe without disproving it by the very meaning of our words? By the very reasoning in our minds? It is like waging a war against the alphabet while using essays and words and sentences as weapons against it. It is madness, like cutting the ocean with a knife.

233. The human worth to the Christian is sober and consistent because the Christian world view acknowledges that we are made in the image of God. To a Humanist, human worth is relegated to magical thinking, *doublethinking*, because human worth runs counter to the worldview of evolution and chance. The two are incompatible. A human being cannot have worth in a worthless universe; we cannot have significance if all was unintended. There can be no truth, no wisdom if life is "a tale told by an idiot, full of sound and fury."

There is no room—no possibility for love—in a world spastically turned by the random fits of humanism. Evolution cannot account for love—it can account for self-preservation and falsely calling it love—but true love is absurd in a world without God. Most Humanists believe in love—therefore, they live in the invisible prison of doublethink. They are constantly beating their heads against the unyielding truth of the universe.

Anxiety is the dis-ease of humanism. Anxiety is the friction of the grinding contradictions that are our beliefs. It is a messenger to them…

In day-to-day life humanism steals the virtues of the Christian God, and then refutes the God from whom they came. It wants the fruit but also wants to chop down the tree because it has a distaste for the roots (and yet absurdly expects more fruit). The virtues they have stolen do not fit into the humanist ideology.

These virtues must be stolen! Hah! Love, compassion, worth, and respect cannot arise from the proto-slime. Slime plus time equals old slime—not the wonder of the human body, not the mystery of the mind. One slime plus two slimes *ad infinitum* does not equal human dignity. One *goo* plus two *goos* does not equal a mother weeping over a lost child, or the tears of an unrequited lover.

And so humanism destroys language; destroys science; destroys love; destroys everything including its own steely platform. Nothing can exist in a meaningless universe because there is no meaning to *meaninglessness*, there is no meaning to *nothing*, and there is no meaning to *universe*.

234. The irony of humanism is that it attempts to explain everything, and in doing so, can explain nothing. It looks for meaning as it debunks the word *meaning*.

If we deny the Creator we are forced to explain the world in a way that denies the dignity and worth of humanity. This leads to lives of pleasure without purpose, self over community, relativity of truth, chaos over order, love as an absurdity, the loss of sanctity of human life, and the wholesale butcher of humanity in deed and thought.

It is as the writer Dostoevsky said, "If there is no God, all things are permissible." If we value human life, then all things are not permissible. When we do away with God we do away with human dignity, we level right and wrong, and we prime our lives for war.

"God is dead" many say—meaning that man has become rational enough to do away with silly myths. This can only be said if man is dead. Man is dead, that is why we so often believe that God is dead. The man alive knows that God lives.

If our world is enthralled by skeptical humanism, then what we need is to become more skeptical; more and more, further and deeper, we need to plunge headlong into doubt until we doubt our doubting ideology, until we drown in it, until we doubt the very construct of modern *normalcy*, until we doubt ourselves—then in this humility of a fully doubted self we can come to know God.

This is to say, the only solution is faith in God.

"There is no such thing as truth"—how could this statement be true if it is correct? Why should I live by this self-refuting statement? This is the madness of postmodern relativity, the madness of humanism.

235. The famous humanist playwright Samuel Beckett wrote: "The major sin is the sin of being born." In reality, the major sin is not that we are born, but that we are not born again; but that we choose to stay rebels in light of all that is good. The major sin is spurring truth.

Christianity, though it speaks of sin, warmly offers true human dignity. Ironically, it is the humanist that says "all you speak of is sin; you steal the dignity from all humanity." Hah! If they had an honest mirror and honest eyes they would see their fatalistic view of *born not as a sinner, but as a sin,* being spoken out both sides of their mouth—and behind their lips a silver-tongue. It is the humanist who cuts the dignity away from humanity—not God.

This wolf's cry of humanism: "All you talk about is sin," is merely a red herring, a subterfuge to try and steer others and themselves away from Christianity and away from a perfect God. It is not an honest critique. They wail about human dignity not because they are defenders of human dignity, but because they are defenders of selfish desire. They want what they want and use human dignity as a false defense and a bartering chip. What is meant by human dignity is *freedom*, and often what is meant by *freedom* is permission to be selfish. Selfishness is often confused with freedom. What is meant by *freedom* is often *no accountability*. Yet this is not freedom, it is chaos.

It is *selfishness* that deconstructs and schemes against human dignity. It is a suicide bomber. Talk of sin is an attempt to disarm the selfish dynamite.

Humanism affirms the world—and falls into hedonism and irrationality because it does not also deny it. Buddhism denies the world but doesn't affirm it, and therefore sinks into a detached irrationality and cold heart.

236. I am not a Buddhist—this should be rather obvious by now. I am not a Buddhist (neither a watered down Hollywood version nor a traditional Buddhist) for many reasons. Let's start with Nirvana. I am not a Buddhist because of the *deathless lake of Nirvana*.

I cannot believe that the purpose of life is to blow out all the fire of desire and be absorbed in to the great universal lake of oneness. Why can I *not*? This allows for no one to be an individual; it does not allow for an I-Thou, lover and beloved. In short, this stance does not *coherently* allow for the radiance of love. It offers a suffocating detachment. For there to be love we have to be separate beings. Jesus and the Scriptures are clear that we are to be one body, but that we are also to be individuals; it takes individuals to make a community. Heaven is the community of the saints in the presence of their God.

Christianity seeks a living body, but Buddhism seeks only a million severed hands. What is more grotesque than millions of severed hands unable to shake each other, unable to help each other? Buddhism's deathless lake of nirvana destroys the individual *and* the community. It destroys the blood and the heart; it destroys the bloods relation to the heart. Buddhism does not correlate to reality—and so I will not entrust myself to it.

Buddhism believes that evil and suffering are part and parcel to our current existence. With this, the Bible agrees—but the two take totally different routes from here, for they come from opposing origins. Buddhism (again, we are speaking of traditional Buddhism not hip quasi-Buddhism) goes the way of full detachment. It attempts to kick itself free of the earth. Buddhism seeks to extinguish desires and bleed the individual into the universe. There is no I—only it.

237. Buddhism is world denying. True Buddhism is more than putting some bamboo in your deco kitchen, attending expensive religious/business seminars, and trying to quiet your mind between corporate meetings or performances. If he were still living,

Siddhartha Guatama (Buddha) would very much detach himself (*his non-self*) from the popular caricature of Buddhism that is finding great popularity in the western world.

True Buddhism is radical in its separation from the world—not integrative and readily merging of a Lexus and Beverly Hills mansion with the "middle way" and the great deathless lake. Historically, Siddhartha was a great prince of unthinkable wealth who left his family, royalty and luxury behind. It is ironic that such a founder would find favor with the wealthy in-crowd who further burrows themselves into luxury and wanton excess. Maybe some misunderstanding is about?

Fundamental Buddhism is the abandonment of everything. It abandons the lovely ocean inlet along with the terrible tsunami; it abandons the red velvet petals along with the blood drawing thorns; it abandons love and the lover along with relational dysfunction. It abandons hope with despair, compassion with passion, joy with the doldrums. It has not the strength to hold onto anything lovely while abandoning the unlovely and *unreal*. It destroys a diamond not because there is a flaw of dust within the diamond, but because there is a bit of dust somewhere in the world! This is neither wise nor good.

238. The Buddha's last words were "Strive for your own salvation with diligence." One may say that these words sound like Paul's words. Yet Paul and Buddha move in opposing directions—as far as the East from the West.

Buddha moves towards self-salvation through the power of will; he speaks of salvation coming to us by our own means. Paul speaks of salvation that comes to us from another's grace— yet within that grace, we are to work it out, cultivate the fruit of the given salvation with reverence and responsibility. Yet even in doing so it is not our own efforts, it is God working through us.

Buddha says *look within*, Paul says *look up to God*. Buddha says "your own salvation," Paul says "salvation is of the Lord." Buddha told his disciples "follow no leader;" Paul tells us to *follow Jesus*. Buddha sat under a tree, and under its canopy of leaves he found enlightenment. Christ hung naked on a tree and it shook the pillars of the cosmos.

Buddha sat down under the Bodhi tree and said he would not get up until he obtained enlightenment. I believe he wouldn't have gotten up to help a dying passerby—for his enlightenment was of most importance. The *Dharma*, the doctrine of Buddhism is one of detachment, not of love; Christ on the other hand, got off His cross, and got up to help all the dying passer-bys in the world.

Christ, while on the cross, was concerned for others and even secured care for His mother by telling John to watch over her! Christianity is attached enough to love the world. Christianity is a tension between two worlds; it rests upon Jesus who is the very bridge—the very stairway to heaven that Jacob foresaw.

There is today what is called *Engaged Buddhism*. One might argue that this may be the truth; but I would simply say that engaged Buddhism is not what Buddha taught; it is not *true* Buddhism. It undermines its own religious tradition. It is syncretism and Buddha himself would reject it.

Syncretism is pick-and-choose religion; a buffet line of do-it-yourself salvation. It is the melding together of various lines of religious thought.

239. Different, yet sharing of some similarity to Buddhism, is Hinduism, another thick branch of the Eastern family of faiths.

Hinduism believes that the world is *maya*, or illusion. The world is simply a dream of the god Brahma—we do not exist, we are just a wisp of a dream that will snap-out like a candle in a hurricane as soon as Brahma awakes. There is only Brahma; we are dream mirages. Such an ideology makes for no movement to change the world which is mere illusion, but only a detachment from it; human dignity is a reverie apparition; sciences become, literally "the stuff dreams are made of" and the end-goal of existence is to disappear as pollen into honey. Both Hinduism and Buddhism deny the world and move to detach themselves from its perilous passions and dreamy illusion.

Buddhism and Hinduism are wholly world denying—and Humanism is wholly world affirming. These religions offer no cure to the plague that each one diagnoses. Christianity denies *and* affirms the world—it seeks to change it *and* transcend it. This double movement makes sense of corruption and the hope of redemption; it makes sense of the terms *ought to* and *should be*.

Affirmation/Denial: In it/Not of it.

True Buddhism or Hinduism is a hard stance to take—not because hard or difficult is unacceptable (hard and difficult are often the true way), but because world-denying is unacceptable. It is unacceptable to zen-out from the world while the world lights up in flames, runs down into desperate cries, panic, brutal loneliness, and whimpering desperation. It is unacceptable to pass by the beaten and unconscious man lying on the roadside. It is unacceptable to not cry out at injustice.

Let me note that there are benevolent actions in Buddhism and Hinduism; but they hang upon the religion like loose clothes—they are not the essence—they are not fundamental. Strip these humanitarian actions away, and the naked frame of Buddhism and Hinduism remain. Strip them from Christianity, and you rip the skeleton right out of the body, killing the organism.

Christianity stands on the goodness of God that makes for human worth and necessitates charitable and loving action. This means that we cannot relate rightly to God if we relate wrongly to humanity. The difference between the Dharmic religions and Christianity is the difference between clothes and bone; between option and essence.

Just world-affirming (humanism) is not acceptable either; it may hit and miss with helping others here and there, but it is a frigid world that makes for selfish hedonists, cold hearts, get-what-you-can exploitationists and a confusing battery of floating relativistic opinions. There is no anchor—even science stands to be dismantled as the search for truth is useless in a truth-less cosmos. There is no invisible sun to hold all beauty and benevolence in orbit, so the world spirals into the far reaches of the crypt of the cosmos. There is no single authority.

World-denying leaves a person dissolved into a deathless lake and unconscious of the suffering plight of others; it is tuning out, smoking up, reclining in affluence, falling asleep in apathy. *World-affirming* lets us shiver as best we can in a useless universe where we will only die, trying to get warm along the way by the temporary friction of sex, fame and power. Neither option provides adequate impetus for love and for social action.

240. Christianity is a worldview held together by beautiful tension: followers of Christ must be world-denying *and* world-affirming. This standing against the world (*contra mundum*) for the world is a bridge of redemption. It is the promise of summer in a long desperate winter. It is the promise of healing to a stabbed and fading planet. It allows for hope to exist, yet does not Pollyanna-ize the reality of life.

The Christian worldview sees darkness as darker than any religion does, and sees the light as brighter than any religion. Why? Because it has two good eyes. The better the vision, the better one can delineate shade from shine—the contrast is brilliant, not feathered and fuzzed together.

Being born again in Jesus Christ is not a birth that makes the world either more *happy* or *sad*—rather, it is like the contrast knob on a television, computer screen, or graphic design program; the dark gets darker, the light gets brighter, but both at the same time.

Christianity takes the muted colors of life and emblazons them with brave radiance. In light of the truth, evil becomes more insidious and revolting, good and beauty become more magnified and intense. Sorrow increases; joy increases; but the blasé grey of despair is come undone.

As Christians, we are to be the culture makers, not the cocooned. It is in making culture, in exacting influence by being within the world, yet by being of another origin, that will make bridges of fellowship and synapses of evangelism.

Following Christ is neither ascetic nor indulgent. Christianity affirms the goodness of the creation that is the human body, but also restrains the body from being ruled by its self-destructing and God-denying desires. The Christian worldview sees creation as fundamentally good, but fallen. There is an impetus for restoration, and for stewardship.

At the center of this *denying* and *affirming* worldview is the cross of Christ, is the wounded God who rebelled against the rebellion of man by suffering the sinners wages Himself. The tension of the cross takes stinging pain and diffuses it like light rays into laughing redemption.

Do some research; look at the faith of those who are the founders of modern science—look at the worldview of those who started the first hospitals, the orphanages, and fought vehemently against the slave trade. It was the Christian faith, the Christ-entrusted that fought against the world for the world; that fought against the slavers for the slaves, against the sickness for the sick, against the tyrants for the children, against ignorance for the truth.

Christianity's tension of both denial *and* affirmation are the two hands of a midwife, the two tongs of forceps that birth science, compassion, social justice, heavenly assent, earth care, sacrifice, individualism, community, romance, faith, hope and love. Religion drains the world of such things, and makes us choose *one over the other*, killing one good to allow for another.

241. If these passages sound intolerant and *narrow* let us remember that Buddhists, Hindus, and Humanists all believe that only their view is correct. That is why the Buddha taught the way of enlightenment; that is why someone wrote the Vedas; and that is why Bertrand Russell penned the *Humanist Manifesto*—each to share their exclusive claim of the truth. If you don't think this is true then ask a Humanist why he is not a Hindu; ask a Hindu why she is not a Buddhist; ask a Buddhist why he is not a Christian. Each will defend their view, and in doing so, will state their claim on truth while proclaiming others are *not the way*. Just something to think about for a world that doesn't like to think about their contradictory world views.

You can make yourself a Buddhist, a Hindu, or humanist, but you cannot make yourself a Christian. One can join any religion, yet only God can make one a Christian. This is grace. All *faiths* are not basically the same.

If someone says that *all faiths are basically the same*, they do not know of the faiths. Think of it like this: All trusts are not basically the same; there is trust in man or trust in God—religion or Gospel. What should be said is that "all religions are basically the same." Thank God that Christianity is not a religion!

242. To what can we compare most modern talk of Jesus? In the front window of the book store on Main St. there was a book with a bold title printed importantly on its leather cover—but inside all the pages were blank. The book had no content, no words, and so a reasonable book lover said to the bookseller, "There is no content, just this title! There is no way to tell whether this is trash or a classic for the ages! Is it a romance, a comedy, a textbook? What good is it?"

    The book seller said, "Well, but it is selling like hot cakes—and everyone is talking about how great the book is, so I will surely sell it!" Clearly frustrated, the book lover said, "But what are they saying about this book—it is empty! They are talking *nonsense!*" The book seller answered, "Oh that is why they buy it of course, for they can all talk about the same book, but make it say vastly different things! Everyone likes it because it lets everyone say what they want to say!"

~Worth of Worship~

243. Worship has to do with origin.

Worship is a continual return to the center. This requires strength, love, resistance, tension, open hands, and counterbalance—all of which only come through grace. Every movement of our existence ought to be a motion towards our center, our Creator.

Worship is derived from the words *worthy* and *ship* that combine to mean: the condition of being worthy, of honor, of renown. The renown—the fame of God!

Christ is our cause and our end—and for this, *worth*ship must be our core and fringe!

Because worship is center-based, of *original* concern, it can never be compartmentalized. It must flow into all we do. It can never be in a margin alone, for it must be throughout the Christian existence. If it is in the margin, upon the edge, it is also at the very center.

In the body of Christ, worship is not an appendage, not a finger, not a hand, not even our arms or tongue—worship is the blood that is found in the heart, the mind, and every extremity. And like the blood, worship is always in return to the center, seeking vitality and renewal in the heart of our existence, Christ.

Because worship is truly center-based, it is necessary that it is also the circumference. The integrity of the center holds the outer rim, the rim purposes the center. So, worship is both centrifugal and centripetal. It is introspective and communal, lighting the soul and radiating into the ambient culture.

Jesus is the center. Jesus is reality. He is the image of the invisible God. He is the radiance of God's glory. He is the truth. He is the center in which all things press upon—the embodiment of our origin; He is also our end, our rest—the Omega.

We worship, or we worship; one is life—the other, death. This means that we are designed for worship; never do we not worship. Is this confusing?

244. Why was Cain's worship rejected by God while Abel's accepted? On what grounds was one offering rejected and the other accepted—surely there was meaning to this?

"In the course of time Cain brought some of the fruits of the soil as an offering to the Lord. But Abel brought fat portions from some of the firstborn of his flock. The Lord looked with favor on Abel and His offering, but on Cain and his offering He did not look with favor. So Cain was very angry and his face was downcast" (Genesis 4:3-5).

"Then the Lord said to Cain, "Why are you angry? Why is your face downcast? If you do what is right will you not be accepted? But if you do not do what is right, sin is crouching at your door; it desires to have you but you must master it." (Genesis 4:6-7).

The problem at its crumbling core was not merely fruit vs. flesh; it was a matter of trust, and for that, love.

The evil was that Cain did what *he* thought was right; *he* judged what was good and what was evil rather than entrusting himself to the command that had come from God. In response to the sin of origin, God had ordained that a sacrifice of life was to be the way for man to commune with the God he had broken from. This precedent was set forth when God killed the first animal in order to clothe Adam and Eve.

As Adam and Eve trusted their own selves over God's warning "do not eat of the tree," Cain trusted his own decision of what worship was worthy—and he chose to give "some" of his fruits of the soil rather than what God had called for. Cain chose to spurn his origin just as His parents did—he did not entrust himself to God; therefore, the problem with his worship was that he trusted in himself. He was still eating of the fruit of the tree of the knowledge of good and evil.

One cannot worship God when they are worshipping themselves. We worship, or we worship; one is life—the other, death. This means that we are created for worship—never do we not worship. It is who we are: worshippers.

Because worship is an issue of trust, we perpetually worship—but are we worshipping what is true?

Unlike Abel who was forced to look upon death and his own darkness of heart, Cain would not look upon the consequence of his fallen condition (the slain animal, the mess of blood and death, the symbol of the communion break, the symbol of the horror of rebelling against one's maker in a murderous way). And like his parents, Cain hid from whom he was: a fallen man (his sacrifice was fruit and vegetation from the ground just as Adam and Eve hid themselves behind easy fig leaves). He hid from God by lying to Him: "Then the Lord said to Cain, 'Where is your brother Abel?' 'I don't know,' he replied. 'Am I my brother's keeper?'" (Genesis 4:9).

Cain did not come to God in worship—He came to God to hide from Him. He came to him in the deception of religion, "Here am I to worship (to hide in your shadow)!" The problem with this is that God casts no shadow! So where is one to hide? There was no repentance in Cain, there was no love for God, for love is founded upon trust.

Cain's anger came from wanting to be as God, but he was God's creature instead; the dissonance of his rebellion and the truth was his anger—and this anger murdered the first man. We kill man because we want to be God; we kill man because we want to kill God.

Is it no wonder that worship has shed so much blood! Spend a moment or two in the leaves of some history books and you will see the wars religion has waged. There is a truth to the world pinpointing religion as a source of war—for religion is the deep impulse of man (don't make the mistake of not recognizing atheism and naturalism as religion). Where the world errors is calling Christianity a religion—for it is the antidote to *Homo Religioso*, the religious man.

All hate, all anger, all war at its taproot is of the ultimate either/or of existence: We worship, or we worship; one is life—the other, death.

The shadow of death uncoiled from the first movement of humanism—that is, man's self-worship.

Every bayonet and bomb is born out of how man bows.

Sin crouches and desires to have us if we don't entrust ourselves to God—what is this sin? It is the spiral of unbelief that exponentially leads further and absurdly into the self as one's source for truth. Un-trust in the truth will corrode the mental faculties, destroy the body, and destroy collateral life. Read the first three chapters of Romans and you will see Paul expose this spiral of sin that crouches and desires Cain—and everyman.

God said to Cain, "If you do what is right will you not be accepted?" But what does this mean "do what is right?" It means to trust in God; or as Jesus said, when the people asked Him what they must do to do the works God requires, "The work of God is this, to believe in the one He has sent"—to entrust ourselves to Him (John 6:29).

Cain was to entrust himself in the word of God and in the slain lamb as a sacrifice—is this not what we are supposed to do? Is not Christ the Lamb of God? So why church, why do you offer leafy greens of self-reliance?

What was the purpose of the animal sacrifice for the clothing of skins put upon Adam and Eve—it was to recall the tragedy of pride, and to look forward to one who could reunite us with our Creator, our origin—it was to trust in Jesus Christ, the one both fully man and fully God who could take the necessary wrath upon Himself, die in man's place, and reestablish the trust of man in His Creator.

245. The word *repentance* means to change your mind—to literally turn it around and walk it 180 degrees the other way. We must turn from ourselves towards Jesus, from our self as origin to Jesus as origin—then we will find ourselves, and our purpose—we will find meaning rushing into our life like warmth into a resuscitated body, like sap into a grafted limb. Because our compasses are wrong, because that heavy magnet of selfishness has spun the needle 'round, we need to turn, to repent of the path that is only leading to drier and dried lands—to badlands with broken wells.

Repent: to reorient, to re-origin one's mind; to turn one's mind from the lie to the real.

Repentance is when the caved-in heart's collapsing spiral is reversed, and explodes in a bloom, upward and outward, growing greater in the acknowledgment of being a creature of God.

"My people have committed two evils: they have forsaken me, the fountain of living waters, and hewed out cisterns for themselves, broken cisterns that can hold no water' (Jeremiah 2:13). Mankind has hewn out his own source of life, his own futile origin, because he has separated Himself from his Creator.

246. The purpose, the meaning, and the significance of my life is to glorify God forever—in such is eternal joy. The purpose of life is to acknowledge God in all things and to rely on His water alone. Purpose is only found in true origin.

The glory of God and the joy of man are one. Glory of God/Joy of Man.

Humanity has a deep seated hunger for joy simply because we are meant to be filled with the warmth of joy. Just as we hunger for food or thirst for drink there is an appropriate satisfaction for each hunger. As we are designed to eat food rather than aluminum foil or asphalt, and as we are designed to drink water and nectar rather than crude oil or mercury, we are designed to find joy in the glorifying of the Lord rather than the vaunting of ourselves. Joy is synonymous with the glorification of God. The two are intertwined.

Our joy is consummated in the praise of God.

Joy comes from a person. Joy has to do with identity, with the name given to us by the one who defines us. There is only one true definer, one purpose maker; there is only one authentic joy for there is only one Creator.

Happiness comes from good things. All good things have come from God. To grasp at happiness without a reference to God is to twist the happiness and debase it, to amputate it from its source, to diminish it. Cleaved from its source it is always less substantial, and more of a phantom. And so, happiness is often a phantom limb; it is never really a part of us, just some vaguely familiar 'ought to be' but is 'not quite'. It leaves us with phantom pain and a phantom ache we cannot massage to relieve.

God is the full fountain of goodness; not a portion and not a tributary, but the whole fountainhead of goodness from which all glory flows and will inevitably be returned to.

247. When we do not glorify God and find no joy in the radiance of God, it is akin to spitting on the trees, or flowers, or at the oceans of creation in the posture of contempt. We spit at and flip-off reality—we say "your purpose is nothing, your existence is

worthless." For the purpose of the heavens and the earth are to radiate the glory of God.

If one does not believe in God, no sunrise can be *truly* beautiful, for the event is hollowed of all meaning and signifies nothing; it can only incite a kind of lust that seeks to consume and dominate it, for there is to be no relationship with it because the feast of light is not an expression of a personal Creator, but mere happenstance.

All forms of naturalism (the religion of evolution) can only incite a lust, a mentality of consume and conquer; but never can naturalism birth a love for creation. For love only occurs between personal beings; that which incites an expression of love must come from a personal being, must be purposed and signify the relation between the persons. For one to be a naturalist and feel a love towards nature is a misnomer—they can only lust after that of nature which somehow makes them feel powerful in its consumption. Their gaze over the wonder of the ocean becomes a rape; their meditations upon the mountain ranges are a violation of their enduring strength.

248. What does this mean to glorify? What is glory? We must see this word for what it is and do away with the caricature of what it has become. It has become a filler word; a religiously loaded exclamation: *"Oh glory to God!"* we say, without really thinking what we are saying (except that something nice has happened to us). It has become a word lightly used, and it has become a *light* word— insubstantial, thin and frail like cellophane paper.

Rather than a loaded and hallowed word, it is a hollowed word. It is unloaded, ineffective, a blank, and therefore can be shot into the air without power and efficacy; and it is shot often; so most think nothing of it.

When I was a child I watched a movie version of Washington Irving's classic tale "The Legend of Sleepy Hollow." As a child I never would have guessed that I would learn something about the glory of God from the scrawny and chronic scaredy-cat of Ichabod Crane. It was a lesson in contrast.

Ichabod was the ultra-thin school master who moved into the hollow and then was terrified away by the Headless Horseman. Ichabod's name is a Hebrew word. It means *the glory has departed*. The root word is *Kabod*, this is the Old Testament word for glory. Now Ichabod was thin, flimsy, and vanishing—he disappeared and became nothing more than folklore, a vaporing legend. This is the diametric opposite of what glory is.

Kabod comes from two possible roots; the noun *kavad* that means to be heavy or to make heavy, or the noun *kaved* which signifies weighty or heavy. And so *kabod* or glory means: a heaviness, a greatness, weighty—substantial. This word aims at something that could be called "the density of reality". When something is light (not in reference to illumination) it means, flaky, insubstantial, less real, lacking and wanting.

The meaning of glory that has been emaciated, the true meaning of it is a reference to reality—abundance, not lacking, dense, substantial. All this is a reference to what truly is, the Absolute of existence.

The density of reality! God is the most real, the weightiest, the heaviest of all. We must not think in mere physical terms, but in the scope of reality which is much larger than and encompasses the material things we know. God is not like a phantom—He is the most real; the maker and melter of the densest rock or iron.

To glorify God is not just to say nice things about Him, but to ascribe the greatest reality to Him, to see His existence as the ultimate existence, the necessary existence, the highest reality that the reality of everything else is subordinate to.

His existence is fundamentally sounder than anything material we know: more than titanium, more than an entire metropolis of sky scraping buildings; from Him came all the reality we call material. He is reality—there is no better way of saying it than reality Himself said it—I Am. Moses asked the Fire Sprout in the desert the name of He who was sending him, the name of God to tell the people in slavery. The Fire Sprout spoke: "I Am That I Am."

Jesus too said, "I Am". The heat that Moses felt from the bush was the heat the disciples felt from the face of Christ.

Though the Spirit of God is called the Holy Ghost, He is more substantial and real than the material world we know; He moves the heavens and can change the face of the earth as well as the hard packed soil of the human heart. This is not to say that the physical realm is not real as many religions do say; it is only to say that God is the ultimate reality.

249. To glorify God means to acknowledge the rightful place of God; to acknowledge that He is the fount of all goodness, the center of reality. So to praise God is not to mouth pretty words, but to acknowledge what truly is. It is to be the ultimate realist.

Many wonder why God would need the lip service of His creatures. He doesn't. Many wonder and speculate about God's vanity in desiring adoration. Yet, praise is the acknowledgement of reality—God's concern for His glory is about the truth of all existence. God is goodness, and like anyone who is moved by something beautiful, something good, it is longed to be shared and held in like view by another.

Lovers tell each other about the beauty of a silver sunset they are watching, sharing verbally the joy they are taking in. A friend calls you and tells you about a song he has heard, how it has moved him, and how he wants it to move you too—so he's coming over and bringing you the album. We as humans long to share with others what we see to be good.

God wants us to share in what He *knows* to be good and true. This is purely a beautiful thing—there can be no vainglory in God, because He is goodness. There is nothing selfish in God, because He is love. There is nothing dependent in God, He is self-existing and doesn't need us. This last bit may be hard to swallow for our pride, but nonetheless it is true. Now, if we think it through without reacting rashly we might discover that God not needing us only proves His love for us. He does not love us for some self seeking purpose, no ulterior motive, but rather He loves us because He chooses to love us; it is His will.

He wants us to live in reality (not an image or illusion), to share the love and benevolence of who He is—and to avoid that which runs counter to good. The call to glorify God is what saves us from ourselves; it graces us away from all that is death. Now this is love.

We are designed to reflect reality—we are meant to see, acknowledge and shine back the glory of God that is reality. When we do not we become more and more phantom, like thinner and thinner vapor.

250. Man has a glory as well, but the height of man's glory is less than and reliant upon God's glory. This is necessarily true because all goodness comes from God. Man's glory is his reflective capacity, his imago Dei. It is interesting that a synonym for *reflective* is *weighty*. Remember, the glory of God is weighty.

The glory, the dignity of man, is rooted in his nature to reflect the glory of God, to bear the radiance of the ultimate reality, to exude the love and the goodness of God. Our glory by nature is secondary, never primary. We can only show, only testify the sun as warm and illuminating; we ourselves are never that great flame-dancing star. This is why pride is absurd and in the end futile, for it wants not to be illuminated, but to be the illumination by which everything else is seen. It cannot be, so it is an impotent fight against reality. It denies what is good by trying to be the good itself rather than a bearer of the good. It is akin to loathing the sun and stars and with a seething pout say "but I wanted to create the universe."

God is the source of all goodness. This is what it means when the Bible speaks of Jesus as the Alpha and Omega. The means and the end of all are He. If He is the Alpha then all good flows from Him. If He is the Omega then the purpose for all things is His glory. He is what pushes us and draws us forth in a stream of beauty. The purpose for all of creation is the glorifying of God. Creation is a communication of God's being. Every delta, gamma, phi, and lambda that does glorify God is due to God. He is the means.

How it ends and how it begins, the Alpha and the Omega, He is the means and the end to how it ends and how it begins, the Alpha and Omega, He is…

Yet He is no bounded circle, rather, He is bounding good! And so life is no retrograding arc, no circular fate like many suppose; no karmic circle of life, no ritual of repetition, but it is a breathing and expanding history. It may have its rhythms, its sub-cycles, but it is no tape loop or eternal echo chamber—it is a growing melody with ever new lyrics of praise.

Jesus' mission on earth was to bring salvation to all humanity; His mission was to glorify God; they are one in the same. The joy of humanity is the glory of God. The glory of God is the joy of humanity. The light and the heat are one.

251. Again, this has brought us back to grace. Grace is wholly of God. How can we earn salvation? We cannot rise above our nature. Salvation is good—it is love in concrete action. God is the source of all that is good, He is love; so it follows that salvation is of the Lord! Grace is the only way. God is the only way. When we understand this, when our eyes latch onto a small sparkle of what God's glory means, of what it means that all creation is meant

to glorify God, then grace suddenly throws open its wide bright wings and breathes.

Salvation comes by grace through faith. We must trust the reality of our redeeming God—when we do this, this trust will manifest itself into our actions and become obedience—as when the rays of light from the sun bathe the earth and grow the foliage and plumes of gardens. When we put our faith in Christ over ourselves, we acknowledge the goodness of God that is reality and shine with His radiance, discarding our paltry *shine* and abandon ourselves as the greatest reality.

If we look at the laws of God in light of this grace, we then understand that the laws of God are freedom from *phantomness*, and the way to a greater register of reality, a greater density of being, eternal life—because we know God's character, His name, and reflect His eternal glory.

Many people set their face against Christianity and the Bible because they say it is a binding list of rules, of silly archaic laws that constrict them. Such justification (and that is what it is) to live a lower life is lunacy; it is like saying that "I don't want to be encumbered by the realities of gravity, the weak nuclear force, the strong nuclear force, and the electromagnetic force." If one wants to buck these "oppressors" then they will only destroy themselves, the pleasures they seek, and the so called freedom they desire.

Freedom lives within the bounds of benevolent rule as the ocean lives within the bounds of continental shores. And with this in sight we can truly call the Ten Commandments and the summation of the law "to love God and neighbor" as truly beautiful; more beautiful than any man or woman or sunburst or starlight.

Without boundaries all is permitted; and the first to be dissolved like salt into a tsunami is *freedom*—freedom, whose very roots and etymology are words such as *love, joyful, not in bondage, beloved,* and *friend.*

252. I have always been enamored by the sun. It is more than an engine for sweet summer days. It is a powerful symbol that no human can ignore—it works its way into our rhythms, it colors our very skin and thoughts. Its spears have sunken deep into the human psyche for good reason. The sun has a purpose outside of the material necessity of planet earth; it has a purpose for the human soul. It is more precious than most people think.

We think of it iconically as a golden orb with triangular rays. It seems to me that from our view on earth it is more platinum than yellow-gold. Its platinum white streams give function and form and depth to the flat wash of blackness that would be otherwise. Its radiance a bearer of joy (literally, the lithium in the sun's light enters our eyes and makes our bodies happier through the alteration of serotonin levels). The sun's glory—its reality, its worth—are seen in the glow of the sea; the shine of a diamond; the manifold of color seen; the blush on warm human skin; the depth and brilliance of an eye's iris. By its light everything is known. By its light all warmth comes (for who could ever conceive of fire or lamps without the sun first shining?). By its light the special qualities of all things come to life. It is one light—yet the revealing of many good and beautiful things.

We are moody like the moon, irrational, dark-sided, and lunatic. An ordinary rock, without the grace of light, rotating 'round, just a cold satellite. It is the sun that gives its shine to the arctic moon. The moon, no matter how fast it was to spin itself, could never set itself alight. We can never set ourselves alight; it is not in our constitution.

Each day and night we have been graced with a drama in the skies telling of grace, of God's fountain of goodness, of redemption.

Do not the celestial bodies speak of God—are they not the signature of his reality written in swoops and curves upon space? "The heavens declare the glory of God; the skies proclaim the work of His hands. Day after day they pour forth the speech; night after night they display knowledge. There is no speech or language where there voice is not heard. Their voice goes out into all the earth, their words to the ends of the world. In the heavens he has pitched a tent for the sun" (Psalms 19:1-5).

253. Worship is the wine from the crushed grape; it is the oil from the pressed olive. It is the acknowledgement of our purpose and design. Grapes are for wine; olives are for oil; we are for God.

When we live in the light and freeing gravity of what it means to glorify God, then it transforms what we, in religion, have called worship. If we *only* worship God when the stage lights are buzzing and the sound booth is running with compressors and amplifiers humming, we are bound to only reflect for men—it will be a cold-burn and mechanical light, like a soft LED, no matter how hard we try to be ablaze.

The worship and praise of God must then be holistic, total, unceasing. It must be a unified life—like white light it is one, but varied in its spectrum, igniting all the wonderful colors in the world. Worship is the reflection of God's original glory, yet it is shined outwards through His people in infinite shades and hues.

Worship is a great growing mosaic that will forever expand through us, by God, to reveal the portrait of His infinite love.

Why are we always partitioning our worship as if it were a computer's hard drive or our financial portfolio? Notice we are always compartmentalizing what is mechanical or what is purchased—what is used for self gain. Compartmentalized, partitioned worship cannot be worship. It is an *act of worship*, with an emphasis on *act*—it is posing, posturing, and self medicating more than it is an honest acknowledgement of reality.

Worship is acknowledging God's worth. Worship is the only right response to the reality of God's nature. How can reality be flipped on and off like an appliance? Worship must be unceasing like breathing, always dynamic and flowing as the blood in vein and artery.

254. When we worship without knowing the Word of God, without knowing His character, we participate in some kind of phantom worship, some disembodied form that has no content. It is a worship that has words, multitudes of words but no meaning. When we lip the words "you are good" just because *it is good for something to be good so we should say God is good*, we are not really worshipping God. We should call God good not because we want to worship Him and good is a good thing. We should call Him good because He is the good, He is what defines all other goods—anything that is good is some reflection of Him. Goodness is who He is—it is the character of His love. Goodness does not define God; God defines goodness.

255. We must be honest with ourselves and peer intently, deeply, and see if we really love to worship God, or if we love the mystique of a concert setting or the synergistic enchantment of a choiring crowd. Are our worship rallies self indulgent or reflecting God's effulgence?

To speak of worship only in reference to music is to distort music and destroy worship.

Worship music should be an expression of our life with God. It should have minor 7th chord laments, slow sweeping love songs, buoyant melodies with an emphasis on the upstroke, complicated and majestic chord changes in Gospel style, the ambiguity and spontaneity of jazz, the drive and heart-pulse of modern rock, the honesty of blues, and the craft of classical composition. It should have chorus highs and solo lows; dissonant despair and clarity of hope. All this at once? No; but in due time.

If we limit praise music to a snappy and sappy song, then we demean God into a cheap, quick thrill of a god; a cosmic pat on the back to perk up our Sunday blues. Praise and worship ought to reflect our dependence upon God no matter the elevation of our mood or circumstance. It is not blasphemy to weep to God, to cry out in white knuckled frustration—but it is ungodly to take these intimacies to another rather than your God. If you cannot take your salty tears and your white knuckles to God, then is He really your God?

256. What does it mean to worship in "spirit and truth?" Does it not mean that spirit is truth; that spirit is more real than the sand beneath our feet or the stones of the building in which we stand? It means that God is real and He knows the electrical rhythms of your heart, the synapses of your mind, and that if you feign worship He knows. He sees through your Sunday armor. Doesn't it mean that God is not bound by a body and building?

God knows the attitude of our heart no matter the posture or the place. Remember this, O church, one cannot hide from God though covered in the clouds of the sky or in the deepest ocean recess—one cannot hide from God even in the church—one cannot hide from God in worship! Remember Cain.

Spirit and truth: Does it not mean that we are broken and we are dependent upon God—this being the *truth*; and that we need help to even see our dependence upon God, that we need to be born again—this being the *Spirit*?

Worship is the acknowledgement of reality. Only God can show us reality.

257. Be warned! Many use the platform of worshipper, of worship leader, to pursue worldly desire in a 'God-like' structure; to chase fame among men under the protective umbrella of "serving God." We must be wary of wanting to be a superstar-servant. If we want to be seen by men for our Godliness, then most likely we will—we will have our rewards and they will pass away like dew into the afternoon heat, or like fame from a one hit wonder. We can gain popularity; but it is often at an eternal price.

"Dear children, beware of idols" (1 John 5:21).

The true servant-superstars are never even really seen—this is because they are drowned out by the light of the sun.

We must tread carefully when our feet are on a platform. When we are on a stage we must tremble. If we start to burn with unauthorized fire we could burn the whole place down—and not in a good way. We must burn only with authorized fire; we must praise God with an honest heart and without posing. Let us remember that platforms are usually hollow, and stages usually vacuous underneath. The star stands on the hollowed stage; the servants kneel on hallowed ground.

Remember this, church: God is a consuming fire *and* an everlasting love. Choose one over the other and you choose to worship a false God. Choose one over the other and your worship is idolatry. When the two are held together in the heart, by the Spirit, arrogance and self-importance melt away.

Be careful you *bright stars* of Christendom. Be careful of what you become when the lights of the stage are on you—be careful of what you become when they are off of you. Be aware that you are known by the One not mesmerized by mood lighting and the booming, intimidating power of a sound system. Be aware that the stage is lifted up; it is set higher than your audience—do not be like the stage you walk easily on. Walk with trembling on the stage, for you do not deserve it. Do not be higher than those you speak to—you are not.

Remember that the light that shines on the superstar is the light of man, not a shaft from the heavens. Remember that you are no sun—you are like the moon. Whatever light you have it is not yours, and if it were removed you would be a cold rock spinning in space, just a silent satellite. And like the moon you have a dark side; do not forget your need of grace when you are in the favor of men. Beware of your human charisma; it smiles defiantly into the face of grace. It can feel worthy of drawn attention, feel worthy of offered praise. Your charisma can smile over lies, and lie to itself about doing so. Your charisma can become a caricature of itself. Remember there is only one priest—there is only one mediator, and no matter how golden your tongue, how handsome your face, or how powerful your voice, you are not He.

We must repent of seeking vain glories; of seeking echoes and images of the one we love the most—ourselves.

Wonder why you are liked by everyone. Wonder what you have compromised in order to have everyone hug you when you walk into a room. Wonder why you find yourself smiling when you feel like a smoldering volcano inside. Wonder why your message is received well by the world.

True love is *usually* not highlighted in the limelight; it is in the bearing sun of day during the long working hours; it is in the candlelight of intimacy where no one else will ever see; it is in secret service. Our relationship with God ought to look more like a faithful laborer or monogamous lover than that of a posing celebrity in a camera's sharp flash.

Save us from ourselves…

Our greatest need is to be dismantled. This is the prayer of the righteous: Dismantle me; I cannot overcome myself without You!

258. *And the Fire that Forms*

Fell me with your sweet hammer swinging;
Show me in pieces with your lavender-aflame,
Loud-calling under my chest, thunder,
Singing laughter deep-tackling the night,
Foil flashing the sky once dark, opening its vault
And exposing light that is light.
The sledge that strikes is made to form,
To forge and carve this un-tempered steel;
This bent and flat unwieldy tool!
Oh, that trembled light that comes, that breaks
The norm, the known; unknown from the sky it breaks—
It is meant to charge, to balance
To bring hard-burn, and ash, and seed
Into wanting soil new life!
Then and only then,
Only when I am truly trembled (must I so shake?)
Only when the storm of the world is found
Not foreign, but at home, windy
In my veins, and the dust of ruins
Felt on my tongue resembles the ache within;
Only then do I catch a quick up-spark,
That glitters the dark down and breathes
Flames jumping alight, violet a flight!—
Only then does the glory of God move through me
Back to meet its original glorious light—
Only then is the glory shown when my soul finds limp
From this wrestling, inner thorn
Of sky vs. sky
Of white slapped hard against night,
Exposed when life is second born.
And the fire that forms—joy.

259. We are built for worship; but if we suppress the truth of God, then we will be forced by our own upward-thrusting nature to find a substitute. Much worship is the worship of a substitute—this is why, under big smiles and honest intentions, it is often driven forward by envy, by the pride of ambition and unbelief in the Gospel.

Worship is holy—this is why it can be so subtly evil and be *campy* evil. When we worship out of the tree of knowledge of good and evil, we can have honest intentions, but unknown to us, they are wicked, wrapped up only within themselves, for it is a worship that comes from man, not from living through Christ. We cannot worship out of anything other than the goodness of Christ.

260. Hope: The sovereignty and goodness of God; the Creator and Savior. What else can give hope? If God is both sovereign and good, than no matter what evil we spit into the world, it can be redeemed. There is no corruption that cannot be used for good, no action is outside the authority of God—and so His plans cannot be overturned.

Salvation is not upon the shoulders of men! This is worthy of worship! I say it again: Salvation is not upon the thin shoulders of men! This is relief to the despairing soul!

~...the Church~

261. The decapitated church has no pulse.

Maybe it is true that there is *a lot of common sense in the Western church, in Christendom*—but there is a substantial lack of rationality. There is too little rationality, and too much rationalization.

The church is the community of those who can truly weep and laugh; for only the church knows the dissonance between what we are and what we are meant to be, who we are and who's we are intended to be, because only the church knows Christ.

262. The real church will always be seen as paradoxical: the most pierced with sorrow, the most arisen with joy. True humanity is fully orbed in the church; this is alien and odd to a phantom humanity that perceives flatly from a self-ruled vision. The unreal church will know only a smile, or only a frown—but they will not move from one to the other like the shifting of balance in a dance.

Christiandumb is the *kingdom of man* that has mastered the smile or the frown, but is simply dumb when it comes to speaking the truth.

The church is the body of Christ who knows why the human body blushes; for they are the ones who know the gravity of guilt and the reality of grace. The church has the answer to the question, "Whence shame?" Yet they can also say, "I am not ashamed of the gospel, because it is the power of God for the salvation of everyone who believes..." Romans 1:16).

In the Gospel is our identity, and the dissolution of shame and anxiety.

263. Why are we surprised by corruption in the church when nearly every New Testament book was a letter dealing with the corruption

in the church? There is a great misunderstanding flitting about in regard to what the church is.

I hear people say that they do not like *organized religion*—and by this they usually mean the Christian church. So I then wonder if they like chaotic religion better. Would they prefer truth to be anarchy and a scatter-shot frenzy; or ordered and purposed by design?

All religion is organized. But what I think they mean when they say they don't like organized religion is this: "I don't think that I would like anyone to hold me accountable for the things I say I believe." Or: "It is easier to be selfish by myself." Or, maybe: "I'd rather do it my way because then I can compromise truth on my own terms." It is darkly funny how people go about trying to find other people who "don't like organized religion" and in doing so they become an organization, that is, a group of people identified by shared interests, or purpose. If what people mean is that they don't like the Church to be run like a profit-concerned coffee company or mass-production factory, then they should say that they don't like the commercialization of God instead of decrying *organization*.

The true Church is an organized body; that is the way Christ set it up. Christ builds His Church. Now, to say that we don't like the selling of the body of Christ (and we know well what it is to sell a body) is different than saying we don't want the body to be organized. It is different to say that I don't want to be a prostitute then it is to say that I wish my body was put together more haphazardly. I am all for speaking out against the commercialization of the things of God, but I certainly would prefer an organized and functional body rather than a scattering of fingers, toes, and randomly tossed bones and entrails. The concept itself is gory—let alone the reality. We often do not understand the violence of our words.

A problem regularly felt but rarely cognized is that the church is often mechanized, a steely movement of bits and pieces that move together, but are not intrinsically related. The upshot of this mechanized church, church run like an assembly line or corporation, is the subtle *evangelization* of a deistic God—and in the places that God does not move, man has to take up arms, roll up sleeves, and get the job done himself—that is, market, manage, quantify and qualify.

The church ought to never be a dogmatic mechanization—it is an organic organization founded upon trust in the person of Christ Jesus.

264. "When Jesus came to the region of Caesarea Philippi, He asked His disciples, '*Who do you say the Son of Man is?*' They replied, 'Some say John the Baptist; others say Elijah; and still others, Jeremiah or one of the prophets.' '*But what about you?*' He asked. '*Who do you say I am?*' Simon Peter answered, '*You are the Christ, the Son of the living God.*' Jesus replied, '*Blessed are you Simon son of Jonah, for this was not revealed to you by man, but by my Father in heaven. And I tell you that you are Peter, and on this rock I will build my church (ekklesia), and the gates of Hades will not overcome it.*'" (Matthew 16:13-19).

"Those who are led by the Spirit of God are the sons of God" (Romans 8:14). The church is the community of individuals called by God ("*for this was not revealed to you by man, but by my Father in heaven*"), who tell of this call and the resonance of truth within them, who entrust themselves to their Creator.

The Church is those who live and move and have their being in Christ through His Spirit (Acts 17:28).

The church is not where we go to worship; rather, it is the living community we belong to. The Church is the *ekklesia*, *a public assembly of humanity*. The church is not a place, it is a *being*—it is the will of God moving through a community of humanity living in obedience that is love. The church is *what we do* only for it is the joyful expression of what we are—and this is founded upon *who's we are*.

The church is not a crowd of people, not a mere clock-working of individuals—this is a mechanization of true community. Rather it is the necessary synergy of individuals who live out of the same source—Jesus Christ. Those who live out of their own origin can never have true community, for they will all have disparate and opposite moving origins—themselves.

Yet the real church is made of individuals that all live and nourish from the same taproot—and in this they are intrinsically connected, truly in communion. This is why Christ said that "they will know you by your love and unity"- for this harmony can only come from the unifying factor of living from the same eternal life source, the same entrustment of their lives to ultimate reality—Jesus Christ. This is to say, they live from only one will—God's.

265 There exists both the *real* and *the unreal church*. The polarization of the real and unreal church is not defined by national boundaries, by economic status, by temple structures, or hard political lines—rather it is defined by the line that runs through the heart.

The Church is not like an apple orchard that sits across from a thistle field—it is an apple orchard with thistle throughout. There is no easy dichotomy. In other words, and in the words of Jesus—it is a wheat field scattered with tares. The authenticity of the Church is not marked by denominational lines or national boundaries, but by the line of obedience that runs through the human heart.

There are those who follow Christ and there are those who do not. This is not an indictment against the world—it is the illness within the church. Look within the Scriptures, test the history—there has always been a real and an unreal church: from Cain's lackadaisical offering, to the people pleasing priests of Judah, to the Levite who served Micah in the Book of Judges, to the Pharisees that called Christ a devil and a bastard—the most ancient of struggles has been between the real and unreal church.

Now, it is important to truly understand that this is not some denominational polemic. This is not a liberal vs. conservative issue; this is something far more insidious. It is about the heart of darkness that masks as the light of Christ. It is about a gospel that is almost good news…but most definitely not—and that is always bad news. It is about the human heart.

Because the church is an institution within time and space, by recourse of the fall, it will be tangled with the unreal church. Remember, evil is a distortion, a parasite, a derivation of good. This being the case, evil has, and until the earth is melted and re-forged by the glory of God, will be moving through the halls of church buildings great and small—and so the church is not a building or denomination; it cannot be.

The real church and unreal church are mottled, messily twined together until the reaping at the end of time.

Read Matthew 13:24-30 and 13:47-50 in joy, fear, and trembling.

A perfect church is an *a-perfect* church; an a-perfect church is a perfect church. What does this mean? This means that a church that does not see it is faulted by human nature is not functioning as it should and is therefore not what Christ intended—that is, complete reliance upon God to use the weaknesses of man. The church that knows it is a-perfect (not perfect) understands its dire and furious need to rely upon the grace and strength of God, for on its own it is broken—this is the church that Christ intended, a reliant church.

266. Affluence can be a barrier. Socrates once said that "contentment is true wealth, and riches artificial poverty." Jesus, in

superlative fashion, said that it was "easier for a camel to go through the eye of a needle than for a rich man to enter the kingdom of God" (Matthew 19:24). A barrier—a barrier to what? The acknowledgement of our need.

God is not against money, God is not for money; what God is interested in is us loving Him and our neighbor more than money.

Jesus spoke often about money not because he was interested in our finances, but because he was interested in our hearts. Jesus is not against money, this is a false dichotomy—He is against mammon, that is, the false god of financial security one entrusts themselves to.

Christ spoke often about money not because he was finance oriented like we want to map onto his divinity, but because money is the great idol that we believe is sovereign. It was not because Christ was financially motivated, rather, it was because humanity was entrusting themselves to a worldly security.

Who has the gold to buy back our souls? Only He who holds the mountains and all the gold in them. Only He who could turn gold pieces into the blood of atonement.

The greater miracle is not a camel being thread through a needle; the greater miracle is the human heart acknowledging its dependence upon God. If this is the case why are we more often awed by an ostentatious miracle rather than the miracle of a stony heart turned soft by God's holy wind?

267. Let us be reminded that the despair of secular existentialism (dreary humanistic thought) has flowed out of the affluent cafes of Paris and other richly adorned cities; it has come from the wealthy more often than from the underprivileged. Why is this?

The suicidal poetry of American suburbanite teens comes as they write about a godless land in the fragrant air and the steam of fresh coffee grounds—meanwhile footing the bill with their parent's credit card. There is a reason we call it being spoiled—it spoils us. Riches are dangerous because they have a buffering effect; they keep us from the realization that we truly do need God. They keep us from realizing the monster under our skin by way of the pretty distractions without. We should not be proud of being spoiled. When we are spoiled we are ruined without knowing it. We must know that we are ruined and that we need a Savior. Money keeps us from seeing we are ruined.

On the other side, much of the world's greatest (God revealing) literature and songs have come from the underprivileged, financially busted, and heavily oppressed. From slavery came many of the great hymns and from these came the shining jewel of Gospel music (we should be reminded that rock music was born from Gospel music, so was blues which fathered jazz). From the career-less and bankrupt came many novels of floating hope and inspiration. Why is this?

Through the blurry eyes of suffering we see clearer—for we see we need a Savior.

We can see further from the heights of a bended knee than we can from the pinnacle of worldly success.

Why, if affluence is so often a distorter of reality, a deception that keeps us from seeing the truth, have many often pursued it and considered its acquirement an acid test for being faithful to God? Or worse yet, a test of His faithfulness to us?

Christ promised us neither riches nor poverty—but He promised eternal life, and offense by the world. He gave no divine fiat for all humanity to give their money away. For if He did, someone would merely inherit the curse that another promptly got rid of—is this Jesus' way, blessing one by cursing another? He gave no principle that financial prosperity is an acid test for faithfulness and righteous living.

Such money based "acid tests" of modern Christianity—*the faithful are prosperous or the faithful are ascetic*—are not indicators of truth! Rather, they are more like tests made up by theologians testing the effect of acid on their theologies. They are not Biblical and they cause us to stumble, to be self encased, as if we were really in a purple haze. We live in this haze because we trust our inclinations over Jesus' words: "Those who love me will obey me."

The World likes to change definitions; it has changed *success* and *faithfulness* from *obedience*, from *entrusting oneself to The Father Son and Holy Spirit*, to the accumulation of material goods and rising financial numbers.

268. The Western church is both thin and decadent; it is as the thin-wasted cows that haunted the Pharaoh's dream that was interpreted by Joseph. It is the skinny cow, wasting away as it consumes more of what it deems necessary to advance its kingdom; cannibalistic, it is growing anemic as it feeds upon the closing doors of other churches, as it feeds upon scattered people who are not led by the Word of God. Gorging itself upon all things *Christian*, but squeezing itself into a phantom. This is not the true church—for the body of Christ will thrive—even amidst a disembodied church that calls itself the Body of Christ. In each generation the true Body of Christ has risen victoriously over the specter of an unreal church.

Take money away from the true church and you take away a tool from the hand, but the worker is still alive; take away money from the unreal church and you rip its very heart and its bones from within.

Many who claim to be the bride of Christ are thin but decadent Cows of Bashan. God wants not trends and fashions; He wants justice and mercy in the hearts and the hands of His people.

Freedom is not meant to lie upon ivory beds, but to work for the good of others. There is an oppression of omission.

Christiandumb has a one eyed prophet—"*Beware the sins you commit!*" The Christian church has a prophet with two eyes: "*Beware the ills of commission and omission!*"

269. The true church is the *communio sanctorum*—the communion of saints—those who live in the joy and fear of the Lord.

The church is the community of those who tremble in joy of the Gospel of God; it is those who, like the shimmering of sunlight on a wave-fractured lake, warm and illumine the world around them by directing and reflecting the light of another in a thousand different directions.

The church: the community of the broken/brilliant; the communion of fractured waves woven together as one blanket of light born by the sun.

~Moral Treasons~

270. Externalism, legalism, moralism, and religion. These are the sad synonyms of our existence. Can you hear them? Listen: sssm, sssm, ssssm—thud. This is the sound of wood being sawed, of cross beams being driven together. These four words should be acknowledged and used interchangeably—they are what necessitated the crucifixion of Christ. They are the *moral* treason.

Moralism is the white rot—it is that which grows and feigns life, but is the strangler of life. So church, why do you evangelize by driving forth moralism, by broadcasting externalism? This is not evangelism; it is the making of sons of hell.

Religion is the movement of moralism. Moralism is different than morality. Moralism is a belief, an ideology, a way of framing the world in which we live; yet morality is the outworking of a belief—the fruit of the root. True Christianity is not moralism, but it certainly is moral.

Moralism says, "You can do it." Christianity says, "You cannot do it; you are incapable of righting the wrong, you cannot cross from treason to trust—Jesus must do it." Here the Christian faith shows its rationality: it is impossible to do the impossible.

Legalism is self-salvation. Self-salvation is incoherent in the framework of truth. One cannot be a hero to oneself—it is contrary to the definition of *hero*, of *savior*. Moralism is the hallmark of absurdity—of course it is; it is the treason of truth.

When we are seduced by moralism and its various styles of theology, sooner or later the hollow core will show itself through a crack in the mask. (Entropy has a way of revealing God's truth.) We can either become entrenched in the lie and plaster the crack over with our own form of deceptive plaster (we are very resourceful when it comes to self-deception), or we can continue to poke our fingers through the papier-mâché. The exposure of the hollow will either reinforce the Gospel (the now obvious, vacuous sinful nature of humanity and its need for redemption by grace) or it will embitter us against the church.

It is no great mystery why so many turn away from the church. The fallout of *the disillusioned* has exploded from a religion of moralism (this is a tautology, *religion of moralism*), not a union with Christ.

271. Christiandumb is a Xerox of a Xerox; a religion that is spoken of in and between the lines of the famous T.S. Eliot poem, *The Hollow Men*; a religion that has "*shape without form, shade without color.*" It is not the kingdom of heaven, but a twilight kingdom with sermons of straw, of tumid and bland water; followers not of Christ, but followers of the winds of culture that "behave as the wind behaves." It is a religion of staved scarecrows rather than passionate reformers carrying crosses of sacrifice. It is about scaring crows—but not about peaceful doves. It is of "head pieces filled with straw," not heads filled with passionate thought and inspired intelligence. It looks like what it is not—it is not what it looks like.

As followers of Christ, should we not pray for all illusions to crumble at the feet of truth—especially those illusions that are within the church?

If we cover up corruption in the church rather than sweep it clean and expose it honestly to the air, how can we bear the Word of God? How can we be an ambassador for truth and not deal truthfully within the body of Christ? If we let corruption reside in the church, let it linger and hide because we don't want a scandal, don't want another black eye, we will fall under the weight of God's Word.

We are either stumbled by God's Word or we are crushed by its weight. Better the nearsighted judgment of the world than the perfect judgment of God. We must respect God more than we respect man.

272. The greatest debunker of external religions and of the puffed-up self-righteous was, to the surprise of many, Jesus Christ. A great portion of the Gospels are the telling of Jesus deconstructing external religion. He was cleaning cups from the inside—and in doing so the outside was then cleaned. The fact that this sounds so strange to us is a pinching truth, a pricking wake up call to us—the externalists.

Let us not forget who coined the term *hypocrite*. It was Jesus who used this word of the Roman stage meaning *actor,* and applied it to the movements of religion. It is an ugly inversion that followers of Christ should be called hypocrites when the one they follow was the one who called out hypocrites. Let us not forget, that if we are hypocrites we are not following Jesus.

273. Beware the moralists! We, the moralists, who call up a sin list that is heavy-handed on the externals: drinking, smoking, sex. It is easy to smell the nicotine ghost or the sweet hops of beer it is easy to see the swollen belly of impatient sex. But what of gossip's nearly invisible, quick, forked tongue? What of the slow burn of envy? What of the translucent heat of disobedience? What of the monotonous tundra-wind of selfishness? What of quiet bitterness that pools like rancid water in hidden places? What of the hulking emptiness of unbelief under a smile? Beware the externalists! The legalists! Beware of us!

An irony: an externalist is one whose sins are covert.

Moralism holds reason captive, for the heart is fast forgotten.

Religion is the amnesia; externalism, moralism, and legalism are the arduous zzz's of our sleeping identity.

Here we see moralism rear its manicured medusa head: Do not say "Oh my G-d"! Do not even write it for this is what God's third commandment means! Could this be true? Yes—in part. But there is a greater offense that gives this one weight.

Might I say that the use of the names God and Jesus as exclamations or expletives might not be what the second commandment is *all* about? I do not deny that they are a portion of the truth, but the greater truth should not be marginalized; the greater sin should not be forgotten. Might the third commandment be about religion? Just maybe the commandment is about talking vacuously of God, or making Jesus, who is the very image of the invisible God a mere trinket or motto, and never realizing the relationship. Maybe it is about the hypocrisy of calling oneself a follower of Christ yet never following a single thing He says or does. Maybe it means that we are not to call Him our best friend if we deny Him in every other breath and backstabbing thought. Maybe it means trivializing the name of God by correlating Him as an accomplice in our selfish actions. Maybe it means claiming Christ but never carrying the cross. I tell you, it is far easier to not say *Jesus* or *God* in an expletive manner than it is to respect the reality of God with our entire lives. It is self placating and easier to not say these simple "bad formulas of syllables" than it is to glorify the name of God by living in accordance with His reality.

This commandment is not about bleeping out a word that will burn the ears as if the syllables themselves were cinders, but about bleeping out a treasonous heart that will burn us from the inside out, cementing itself in rebellion against The Creator.

The word vain comes from the Latin word *vanus*. So literally, when we use His name in vain we are making it empty, reaming it out, making ourselves His judge and calling Him less than the ultimate reality. Using God's name in vain is to live a life out of our own broken origin rather than entrusting ourselves to reality.

When the first truth of the commandment is observed, the expletives and exclamations would stop authentically. We must focus on the source—the heart. The mouth is merely a tributary of the heart; the waters of the heart will always flow over the lips.

274. Legalism makes an internal impossibility an external simplicity. It makes righteousness a wage not a gift.

The word *Pharisee* has come to mean something that repulses us; something pale and obviously sick. We are quick to cry Pharisee and wield a pointing finger. Yet, rarely do we see that they are the most like us—the image is spitting. But, instead, we loftily compare ourselves to mighty King David, tan and muscle bound (not the sinning David of course); to wise Solomon, head above others; to Saintly Stephen, suffering in innocence. Why do we not compare ourselves to those who are remembered as a brood of vipers? Isn't the fact that we rarely see our scaly skin rather Pharisaical?

Sin is obvious through windows, but obscure in a mirror.

Legalism is the illusion that grace is attainable. It is the lowering of God's standards. It says "Be perfect like man is perfect" rather than Christ's seminal "Be perfect as your Father who is in heaven is perfect" (Matthew 5:48). Legalism takes the horizon and draws it as a line in the sand to be adeptly stepped over. Legalism takes the stars of Orion, unbinds them, and places them in our hands to arrange them as we please. Legalism takes what God alone can do and debases it. Legalism is slapping the face of reality.

To lower God's standards moralism will shift focus from quality to quantity, from motive to motion—it is a quantification of Christ. Moralism can be counted—*I have never done this, I did this twice, I am a virgin, I go to that building twice a week, I have never smoked.* The trajectory of the heart is not counted by its pulse, but evidenced in its warmth and actions. A tyrannical heart can have the same counted pulse as a saint.

Moralism subverts the entire purpose of the Bible. The Scriptures were written to attest to Christ. From Genesis, when humanity was created in God's image, to the Lion-Christ in Revelation, the entire record was to foreshadow Christ, to reveal Christ, and to reflect on Christ. Christ is the scarlet arc that sweeps through the Biblical account. He is the marrow through the whole bone of narrative. He is the cohesion of the testaments, the keystone that holds the arch of the doorway in place and the alpha and omega stones upon which it stands. He is the radiance of God's glory. Moralism attempts to dim God's radiance; when we understand this we can see why it is the favored tool of the deceiver.
Moralism subverts the purpose of the Bible by taking the weight of redemption off of Christ and placing it onto something else—mainly the frail shoulders of man.

The shoulders of men are strong—but the strongest shoulder stutters, and is crushed like dry paper by the weight of God's lightest whisper. Man cannot carry the burden of redemption. Man alone cannot bear the glory that is God's due.

275. Legalism is bizarre. Is it not strange that God who created the universe, who created man from clay, who has filled the oceans with whale to krill, the fields with locus to leopards, gets upset when a human drinks a glass of aging grape juice just because it has sat around for awhile, or tithes something other than ten percent on a given week, or eats some ceviche with shrimp and lobster, or lifts a baby stroller on the Sabbath, or goes to the mountains to sing hymns on rare occasion rather than go to Sunday morning service? Legalism places *evil* and *good* on the things of creation and not on the obedience to God in regard to such things. It places authority in the creation and the creature rather than the Creator. It mistakes obedience for idolatry, idolatry for obedience. Legalism is faith in idolatry—faith in creation—faith in man rather than God!

Legalism turns God into an arms dealer of volatile, arbitrary do's and don'ts. This is the pale God that religion has fabricated, scanned, and faxed to the world; and the world thinks this is the God of the Bible.

Nothing in God is arbitrary—all He does is purposed because He Himself is our purpose. All He does is meaningful; God seeks the heart of men, not mint and cumin (spices tithed by the Pharisees). God seeks compassion, not a rote sacrifice. What the Word of God commands (not what the traditions of men command) are for the good of humanity, for fertilizing the soil of the heart so that there may be eternal growth and eternal relationship with God. Moralism turns deep seated realities into trivialities. The moralist lives from the frayed edges, and never knows the substance of the center.

Externalism is a deep internal problem—it seeps from a sour and unregenerate heart.

276. I've heard of Indian Yogis, *holy men*, burying their heads in the dirt and doing holy handstands for hours in order to commune with God. I've heard of them saying they were "the closest to God they have ever been," while they were sticking out of the ground like a thin ostrich in a loin cloth. Is there a better illustration of how upside down we are when it comes to right relationship with God?

Let us remember it is not only Yogis breathing sand and twiddling their toes in the sky that are upside down—how many of those who call themselves Christians have buried their heads in the sand and have felt closest to God when they are neck deep in some ascetic task, when they are drowning in moralistic ground fill?

Now here we see the rationality of Christianity—God wants us to breathe His air not His sand. He wants our toes to walk His earth, not to beat at His heavens. It seems that He wants us to love Him as a bride loves her groom; not do monkey tricks, not live our spiritual life as if we were earning our *trainer's* favor with each tumble, and paying our way to heaven with quarters thrown into our red fez of religion.

277. The external and temporal world cannot bear the weight we assign it. When we dismiss eternity its weight falls upon temporal things—and they cannot hold. Both we and these things crack, and the despair within spills through.

Moralism is simply the matrix of rules that we have knotted together, judged as right, out of our own authority. Though these rules may intersect with the Word of God, there is still a phoniness to them that is flagrant—a papier-mâché-like quality that comes from the dusty hands of man trying to rework the eternal truth of God.

The un-churched world is right in rejecting moralism. Moralism is nothing more but hidden anarchy of the heart—and deadly, for it is poison that dresses like nectar. The great rejecter of moralism is the one most often rejected because of moralism—Jesus Christ.

Christianity has morality; it has morals; but its ethical code is not the source, rather, it is like the shine that comes from the burn of the sun.

278. Moralism lies to us. It whispers into our wanting ear that sin is outside of us, separate, and able to be quarantined. If we can just separate ourselves from polluting sources! Moralism, in all its machinations undermines the Bible and shouts with industrial strength, with hissing steam, that sin is something separate from us. It tells us that sin is like a foreign viral agent rather than a congenital condition. It is something by sheer means of the hands, of the feet, of the eyes that can be held at bay. If we only are diligent in taking the right spiritual minerals and vitamins, if we do not visit the sick wards, the lazar houses of the world, if we eat rightly and wash our hands with certain rhythms and rote movements then we will be safe from that outside agent called sin.

Moralism straps us down—our head, our feet, our hands, our eyelids, our tongues—to a cold autopsy table. It manacles us to our sin by misdiagnosing the root of sin, and therefore keeps us from moving freely. It chains us to a smaller and smaller world—fencing ourselves ever inward, and closing us off from the wide open spaces of joy.

It is not life by the Spirit it is life by the machine—an iron lung that lets us falsely breathe, but not roam the country side and experience life. It is a living prison, a strapped-down life. Life by the Spirit is a warm and moist lung that works within us, that lets us run from the sea to the summits with the freedom of a right heart.

Externalism, legalism, moralism, and religion—they are the sounds of an iron lung. Listen to the machines noises: lsss, lsss, lsss—and when it clamps down and dies—**RELIGION**!

Legalism keeps us from breathing the breath of God in stale places—for fear that we may smell a little musty. It keeps us from bearing the white-glow a dark room needs—for fear someone will see us in the shadows. It keeps us from irrigating wastelands and keeps us from planting seeds into the muddy earth—for fear that our hands might get dirty.

Externalism keeps Christians in circles rather than in expanding crosses. It makes subcultures rather than cultivating the great Kingdom of Heaven. It makes a friend a source of pollution rather than a receiver of God's promise; it makes a bar a poisonous well rather than crowd of thirsting men and women; it imbues a secular college campus with more power than the truth of the Gospel; it makes a rock song the source of our discontent; it makes a man or woman on the television the source of lust; it makes Jesus look questionable when He was with a prostitute or a tax man; it makes a man in a silk tie look wealthy; it makes a man in a cardboard box look worthless; it makes wealth look like faithfulness; it makes the cross look like foolishness.

Legalism reverses the order of reality: It says *obedience before acceptance*. The Gospel of Jesus Christ is the inverse of religion: It says *acceptance before obedience*. Legalism says, "Be like god and you will be forgiven." The Gospel says, "God will forgive you if you trust in Him."

279. The brood of vipers has four names: Externalism, legalism, moralism, religion. You can hear them hiss then strike: isssm, isssm, isssm—***Religion***!

Start to use these words interchangeably—they are of the same breed; yet religion is the manifestation, the bite of these poisonous ideologies.

Externalism, legalism, moralism and religion—these are the brood and their bite, born from the serpent of humanism. Remember the call of the serpent, "You too can be as gods." This is the great treason of existence.

The serpent is the bearer of humanism—is it no wonder that many world religions hold the snake up high in a holy role; a position of guardian and teacher; a bearer of protection and regeneration! Yet Christianity alone curses the serpent! Religion holds the serpent high, for Humanism—the serpent—is the father of religion.

Do you recall the bronze serpent that Moses held up? "And the Lord sent fiery serpents among the people, and they bit the people; and much people of Israel died. Therefore the people came to Moses, and said, We have sinned, for we have spoken against the Lord, and against thee; pray unto the Lord, that he take away the serpents from us. And Moses prayed for the people. And the Lord said unto Moses, Make thee a fiery serpent, and set it upon a pole: and it shall come to pass, that every one that is bitten, when he looketh upon it, shall live. And Moses made a serpent of brass, and put it upon a pole, and it came to pass, that if a serpent had bitten any man, when he beheld the serpent of brass, he lived" (Book of Numbers 21:6-9).

What does all this weirdness mean, and why did it happen? Why were the people bitten by fiery serpents? Because after God had delivered them from slavery "they spoke against God and Moses, and said 'Why have you brought us out of Egypt to die in the desert?'" They simply and absurdly did not trust him! They judge him here in the desert just as they did in the shade of the tree of the knowledge of good and evil!

God made a good world and set man in it to rule—then they set themselves over their benevolent Creator. God freed the people from slavery and was guiding them to the promised land—then they doubted Him, and judged Him of doing them ill! They trusted in their own selves and not the trustworthy God!

So why the brass serpent on the staff? Because the only cure for their cold condition was to look upon their sin of self-trust. Why the serpent though? To remind them of the sin of humanism, of idolatry of the self that brought sin into the world, that sent man packing from the garden and found them in slavery!

The serpent was not the antidote—but the cure was to acknowledge their sin of idolatry, of self-trust which is humanism. The cure was to see the sin and trust God alone!

It was for this reason, for the great treason of our existence that Christ was to be lifted up, and made a curse for us—to kill and redeem the heart of humanism! "And as Moses lifted up the serpent in the wilderness, even so must the Son of man be lifted up: That whosoever believeth in him should not perish, but have eternal life" (John 3:14-15).

Christ became a human in order to rid us of humanism—oh the brilliance of God!

~The Spectacle~

280. The world of religion is full of many bizarre things—for its tent is staked to *the spectacle*.

Circuses are bizarre things. I am troubled by circuses. There is an air to them of something sinister, something ominous bulging under a thick canvas veil. Something that seems funny and jovial, but soon slips into something sordid, something dark—and because it seemed jovial at first, it becomes even darker when exposed.

When I was younger I was not quite sure what disturbed me about circuses. I have never had an affinity for clowns—I never found them funny or amusing; I found them more obnoxious than anything, and always felt that they were best at home on black velvet, painted as crying.

It is not that I am not amazed by the technical skill and discipline of trapeze artists and other acrobats. It is not that I think circus professionals are creepy people. It is not that I am a buzz kill or a killjoy. But there was something substantial and nameless that clawed at me. It was not that greasy feeling you get when you are on carnival rides in dusty summer heat after eating cheaply buttered popcorn. For a while I thought that the disturbance was simply the emptiness of spending fast money on a tawdry show or short-lived roller coaster.

I also thought it may be because I saw the movie version of Ray Bradbury's classic book *Something Wicked this Way Comes* which scared me as a little boy. Yet this was not it either. But I have come to know what it is that troubles me so. At the heart of the circus is something very disturbing. Let me explain how this riddle came to light.

Circuses are similar to places of worship. I should qualify this—circuses are similar to most places of worship. There is a center ring, a sanctuary of sorts where the people go for a short time of entertainment, then leave and return to *everyday* life. There is an expectance of miracle and magic. There is a ring leader, a charismatic barker who addresses the crowd and works adeptly on their emotions, shoving them all about into moments of wonder and awe. There are side shows such as the bearded lady, leopard boy, the hall of mirrors, youth group, the local cranky prophet, study groups, and choir rehearsals. There are sales pitches, there are costumes, there are bleachers and pews hovering around all around a spectacle. There is a show. It is a compartmentalized show to watch and then walk away from. There are painted smiles that give the illusion of joy—but when you get close you see they are just clowning. There are costs for admission and costs for missions. There are superstars and adoring fans. There is more limelight than sunlight. There are runaways and there are business men. There are humans being applauded for their obvious skill—children of merit, worthy of admission costs. There is talent, there is treachery. There is marketing, projected earnings, and there are elephant-size pretenses under the big top. There is authenticity, but there is smoke among the mirrors.

The church (that is, *the nominal church* or *Christendom*) is very similar to the "Greatest Show on Earth." But we do not have to wait for the heat of summer to rise for the circus to come to town; each Sunday we can watch the show—or be a part of it—paint our faces.

Now I come to the dark heart of the circus that makes me feel oily and unpleasant, as if there were chameleons under my skin. It is the taming of the lion. The lion, that alluring main attraction that has been tamed and caged, has never exhilarated me. It is a lukewarm, insipid something that comes over me—it is the recognition that the Lion has been tamed, and is neither lion nor lamb, but a mastered once-king. This is more troubling than a joint-bending rubber band boy, than a grimacing clown, or a gaggle of those clowns trying to cram themselves into a toy car, all the while joke-punching each other over such an absurd idea.

The heart of the Circus is a sad absurdity—the heart of religion is a circus, painted smiling with distractions.

The circus and the nominal church have both tamed the lion. The crowds come to see the mastered, but safely-dangerous king of the wild. We pay our admission to watch a man stick his head into the jowls of the *wild lion*; to watch the majestic king hop over theological chairs, dance on holy rolling barrels and let costumed monkeys jump on his back. We applaud and leave, feeling somehow victorious but not transformed, just invigorated in our ways.

Something in us feels powerful in that we have gazed upon the wild and survived—that we have bested the beast—or bested the Sovereign Lord.

This is how the church became a circus, by the taming of The Lion, by subjugating The Lion to the power of man; by seeing if we could stick our head in His mouth to prove ourselves His master. This is not only how the church became a circus, but how the fall of humanity broke upon the world—to conquer God and taste the fruit of autonomy!

281. The primary motion of the spectacle is to attract an audience. This is a twisting of an original good. Before the fall mankind always had an audience, a benevolent audience of one—of God approving of man in his creaturely state. But this divine audience has been replaced by the cannibalizing audience of man.

The spectacle twists that original intention of an *audience*, a gaze that said "it is very good," into a need for numbers of men and women as a surrogate sense of worth. If there is no audience then there is no spectacle, no thronging over some oddity. It is the gawking of humanity that makes for a spectacle. It was sin that created *the spectacle*.

What makes a spectacle is its absurdity and incoherence; think of a leopard-spotted man or a mermaid—there are natural boundaries crossed, *incoherence,* and a distortion in "what should be." It is something contrary to what is considered the norm. This is why so many spectacles are, in the end, found out to be frauds (merely tattooed men or women with a prosthetic tail). And in the end, this is why religion will be found out as a fraud (a prosthetic righteousness, a pseudo relationship with the divine).

It is man separated from his true origin—his Creator— that makes for the spectacle of religion. Religion is an incoherence in reality; that is, it is fraud, for it is the denial of the true God. This being said, when the Christian church is a spectacle, it is not the Christian church.

A spectacle delivers amusement, not joy; and it always makes a voyeur, not a man of action or compassion. The spectacle amuses and preaches vain moralism; but the beauty of truth bears joy and grace.

Is it not an irony that the church, which was ravaged by the spectacle of the coliseum, has often become such a spectacle itself, now ravaging the Word of God? If we are to learn from history a lesson of the coliseum, it is that success comes not by the crowds of *the spectacle,* but by the obedient few who are children of the King. The coliseum is now only a skeletal frame of a tourist site— the church is a living organism that will outlast the deepest foundations of the earth.

A spectacle is that which is memorable for its appearance—but not for actuality. The modern church (I mean the church of the Western world) has in large part been enchanted by *the spectacle*— and has become a church of appearance rather than a church of action. It has become a church of putting forth lofty ideology, but with hands rarely calloused or bleeding by obedience.

Because it has become *the spectacle*, aligned with man's self-origin rather than Creator God, it has become captivated with pleasing crowds. Yet true Christianity's goal is one—though, like a prism's light, is refracted in myriad ways—its aim is to praise the worth of God alone.

But be careful here! Do not to make an error of moralism and say that now only the small numbers show faithfulness! The church must grow—and it should have great numbers, for every number represents a human soul that Christ lived and died for. Numbers, many or few, are never an acid test for obedience to the will of God.

282. The focus on numbers is the symptom of idolatry—idolatry not of numbers, but of man. We need to see the tie between numbers and unbelief in God that elevates the role of humanity. The lauding of numbers are the necessary upshot of idolatry. We must see that: *The quantified church comes from qualifying Humanism*; or *The quanitifed Christ comes from the qualifying humanist*. Remember where humanism was first spoken—"you too can be as God knowing good and evil" (Genesis 3:5).

Are not numbers an appeal to the opinions of men?

Here is the number theory of *the spectacle*. If it works, it is good, it is of God. How do we know if it works? Because the numbers of humanity are drawn to it—what do the numbers matter? They tell us the voice of the majority, the voice of man! So in the end, it is the voice of man that gets to decide what is right and wrong—no longer the Word of God. It is the voice of fallen man, man who has eaten of the fruit of the knowledge of good and evil. The numbers game was born of idolatry, born of the entrustment of one's own voice over the voice of the Creator.

Numbers as indicators, as facts of history, as mathematical realities are no more evil than a hammer; but when the numbers are the thrust of an ideology, a way to decide what is truth, then the hammer meant to swing and build the church to God's glory is now a hammer swung at God himself to build the fame of men.

283. There is much ado made about windfalls. Yet there should also be a voice concerned with watersheds. What I mean by this is that popularity must not trump the perfectly pointed message of Good News.

Numbers (ministerial job security) must not be more valuable than the Pneuma (the Holy Spirit). Christ had multitudes following Him, chasing Him, calling His name and ready to crown Him king. When He died there were tens of thousands faithful to him—No! When he died there were only approximately 120 left. Why? Have we ever asked ourselves why the watershed? It is because His teachings were hard, were hated.

In John chapter 6 many followers left Jesus because of His *hard teachings* (impossible teachings) on who He was, on what it meant to follow Him. Where are the hard teachings of Christianity? We must ask ourselves how honest and pure is the Gospel we are preaching if no one feels it is too hard, too radical, too lofty to reach with our own hands.

We ought to wonder about the purity of the Gospel we preach if we are tolerated by a world that hates the Gospel. The masses follow the money trail, the easy road, the cool option. The masses do not line up to hand their life over for crucifixion.

Are we a watershed or a windfall Christian? Let us feel the water in one hand and the wind in the other. Here is a tension that is much avoided—for we would rather be popular than wet with the drowning waters of eternal life. It is usually a voice from the desert that speaks of watersheds—a voice in the wilderness.

284. The Gospel is good news because it is too hard, too radical and demanding—and therefore we need its grace to cover its

demands. Jesus embraces those who say, "This is impossible for man!"

To follow Jesus means *Gethsemane*—means *Golgotha*. It means the cross, the tomb, and then the ivory scars of victory. To deny these is to deny Christ.

Another warning: Those who seek out the fat wallets and bulging purses, those who talk more, shall we say, *sweetly* and *devoutly* to those with Rolexes, those who "in the name of God and His service" learn to milk children of God like cows, those who learn how to get free things—what you get free is at the cost of truth and grace! What you get free is costing you right relationship with God and man. What you get free is spiritual plundering.

Many *Christians* are like pirates with a cross on their flag (they have taken the skull off because it is better for business that way). Do not aim yourself at the fat cats that come through the door. Am I against cheerful giving? Am I against donation and support—no! But I am against suave robbery in the name of Christ. One cannot schmooze God no matter how magnetic one's sanguine personality is. Do not become *"judges with evil thoughts" (James 2:4)*.

The miracle we should (truly) long for is not a pyrotechnic display, not some supernatural ability to impress the masses, not a twenty dollar bill multiplied like loaves of bread; but the miracle of repentance, the marvel of belief, and the wonder of regeneration. The miracle of trusting in Christ—that is what ought to make us applaud. Now this is not a miracle that turns a difficult life into an easy one; rather, it is a miracle that turns a dead man into a living one. The miracle comes not in the elimination of difficulties, but in the exaltation of God through the difficulties. In fact, it is a miracle that sets our face against the chapping wind; one that multiplies many hardships, one that increases our share of flak.

A living man faces more obstacles and difficulties in the world than does a man in the grave. The miracle of regeneration sets us up firm against the world, but firm in Christ.

For an example of the "mistaking of the miraculous" one should turn to the book of Jonah. What is the miracle in the book of Jonah? Say it with me—the swallowing and spitting out of Jonah by the big fish; right? No—wrong. This is not the big miracle; this is just a vehicle to get to the good part. The big miracle is the grace of God that sparks hearts to repent. The real miracle that ticks off grumpy Jonah and shows God's character is the repentance of the wicked hearts of the Ninevites—the hearts of humanity.

285. Jesus was not always nice—but He was always loving. When we think Christianity means merely being nice, wearing an uninterrupted smile, we are more interested in ourselves than we are of others; we are more driven by popularity then purity. Jesus was driven by grace and truth, not by turning religious tricks to draw the masses. Jesus was not a man of the perpetual smile, but He was and is the heart of perpetual love.

His teachings were hard, but His yoke was easy (but notice, it is still a yoke and not a yacht). It is work—the glorious work of the Kingdom of Heaven! This is not a contradiction, but a sweet paradox. His teachings were impossible for mere flesh and bone; but they were possible for God to do with flesh and bone. An easy yoke born of hard teachings should not sound strange to us—if it does we are unfamiliar with the melodies of grace.

I have often heard it said that "God is a gentleman." God is gentle at times, yes. He has hands of velvet and gives light touches; but God is not a gentleman.

God is good. A gentleman is a social construct, a man who plays by the societal rules, one who won't make a fuss, or spark an issue to crisis. Yet God breaks man's rules as He does what is right. God causes stirs and storms; He sparks our hearts in a moment of crisis—and each is good for all He does is good. A gentleman is often dishonest in order to stay gentle. A gentleman is one who compromises truth for image. God can never be dishonest. The Bible does not know God as a gentleman; it speaks of the good God. We should be thankful for this. God is often gentle because He is good. He is not good because He is often gentle.

If everyone loves us—then can we love God? If we have never had a confrontation, do we stand for truth? If we can stay in silence then has God spoken to us? If we can so easily stay cool about the idolatry about us, then has God's word kindled a fire within our bones?

There is nothing more offensive than the polite *Christian* who "washes his hands of blood" as not to be *uncivil*. In being polite the Christian often becomes the barbarian who clubs truth to death with his smile. In being polite, we often stand idle, watching truth be violated.

286. There has been a conflation of truth, the revelation of the Word of God, with the power and process of democracy. The problem is democracy only works if it is held in check by and founded upon truth, an overarching standard. Democracy can never dictate truth—when democracy is used to decide truth, it is no longer democracy, but tyranny.

The problem with numbers is that the world is fallen and the voting apparatus of the human heart is fallen. So if one appeals to the masses, if one hangs upon the verdict of the *vox populi*, one merely hangs upon the distorted opinion of man, of the fallen condition—but not upon truth. Democracy is not meant to establish truth, but truth is meant to direct democracy. And so it follows: democracy in a world without truth is only the game of power and money, image and illusion.

Most Christianity has no Lion and no Lamb—only some mutated form, some bleat-growling chimera that was never meant to be.

This mutant is an unholy compromise born when the church forgets how to hold in dynamic tension the mighty Lion of the Lord with the sacrificial Lamb of salvation. The compromise has made a less than serving, less than mighty God. It has made a God that can be bumped slightly off center so humanity can take center and make up for the weaknesses of the near immobile freak of half-lamb and half-lion.

Church should not be a circus. Now this certainly does not mean the church should not be a place of joy and laughter.
The church of the spectacle produces spectator *Christians*. Spectator *Christians* is an absurd term—for a follower of Christ is not a spectator, but one in the service, and in action for the King. To think a Christian to be a spectator is simply bizarre.

287. *The Bizarre*

I. The Wind at the Door

Who comes here?
    What feet kick up the dust from the East?
The dry thunder fires, flickers, fumes
    Overhead, like our thoughts of glossed discontent,
Smeared— still—sterile.
Our thoughts of the night before
Bury deep, and tell
Of the shadows of being, of shadows
That fell on the wall and on the floor.
Our thoughts now
Like a broken bell's hollow
        Only whistling in the wind—
The tongue and hammer gone.
Here, where bronze used to sound,
There was a strong melody
That reached the fisherman's shore—
But, then too, silent of the news, there were white washed tombs;

For all is not new.
Today cars roll in thin gold,
Rich suits and plum dresses stroll—
Speaking to each other in clips and worn symbols;
The wingtips only stride the ground,
(Bare toes not touching down as though
by the muggy heat of some burning bush),
And seek rest from the wind in the white temples
Of mortal architects, carvers of marble men.
En masse they come
Crook-necked at the thunder—
Brows bent and squinting
    Under the half-light, and on into their chambers.
The time has come and
They don't mind if they're late
    Or early…as long as they're seen;
And for that they hate the wind,
For its unseen hands mess their hair

The Choir (to modern music):
"Leave us be, Leave us be!
Don't trouble us, cruel weather, strange elements, in our worship;
Don't grumble at us from beyond the solid walls
    Sheltering us from the wind—
Keeping at bay the hard things—
    The storms our children shouldn't know,
The shadows we can't bear to see
    Least *they* be tempted…
Let us be uninterrupted, let us be un-plagued,
Let us be the plush, the untouched
    By the mud the rain makes,
The darkening of the street,
And those it calls familiar—
Darklings, those who are dangers to our homes
    And penned, quantized schedules."

The Stranger leaves no shadow
And comes to be seen.
Light that speaks of the torn fiber of men—
Who comes here?
   Who comes to be the questioner?

To speak in our dreams of souls wasted thin and tall?
The wind comes to speak;
   Not to answer what has already been answered
At the crossroads of time,
But to call.

The Choir:
"Leave us be. It is so.
It is so-so;
Leave us…
…God, from whom all blessings flow;
Praise him, all creatures here below;
Praise him above, ye heavenly host;
Praise father, son, and holy ghost."

Then the cars roll on, roll to, on they roll to houses,
Though never home, roll on
Roll to work
And beyond
On the streets that lead to the dead lights, yellow buzz
   of offices, to the resorts at the edge of the sea;
They lead to the fancy places, the colonnades,
The restaurant houses, the drone of green neon,
The movie shows.
And thoughts without fire,
Words without hope,
   Like bones without sockets,
Prattle and show the wasted efforts of nights
In the hands of men—
Judging by the fruits of a tree without any roots.
But the nights, they move on in metropolitan flair,

Laden by the songs of the singers
—The cries for God linger
In the warm tonic air
Of the throats of the brothers and sisters
Of the Choir.
Of the night.
Of the silence of redemption.
—The bread is not in the mouths of the hungry;
And those of the rite are drunk on selfish wine
  And wanton with the bread.

"For we are tired of the taste of bread
For we are satisfied
    In the feasts we have made—and now enjoy the sweet cake."

And the wind moves

The Stranger speaks:
"Who are you who bewilder my children?
Who are you to sing songs with crooked mouths and darting eyes…
Feigning your praying?
Why do you not ask questions?
To whom do you lift praises?—you dress in fashion—
Lift a smile—proud of the feelings you have of your ways?
Who do you think is watching you?
  Ask *who* is watching you.
More than men watch you—though here
You are consumed by mortal gaze and can no longer see.
Praise when you are naked, alone, broken.
Can you not praise in the shade of your home?
Would your anger and worship would stress the sickness?
When the dissonance is seen in an instant?
Is your closet too rattled with bones?
Call them bones! Call them disjoint!
Unwounded—and you cannot worship!

Could you not face such a show?
The terror of an honest mirror!
Is this why you enjoy the shows of men?
Is your doubt so shallow it is only pleased
        With a small pocket tight-full of cash?

With a hip pocket swollen by easy friends?
Is your faith so fragile a statement can break it?
Would you spur a friend if they could shake you into waking?
Face you with your unknown thirst?
Would you remain gentle if they gave you some ash?—
And would you be all "saintly" smiles
If they wiped your dry forehead
And found no oil
   And called you out—called you to take account?
Held you up to the truth like an envelope to a light bulb
        Only to find harsh words and dark letters inside?

I say
You are like wax fruit—
You shine-tempt souls and are in perfect form.
    You cause mouths to drool;
But you are poison to the tongue who would taste you!
Eating upon you forever, but further from sating,
Never supplying good.
You choke the widest throat;
    You clog the seeker's belly!
Be sincere! Know your thirst.

Ask the question
To whom the blessings, whom the curse?
Blessed is he, who stands in the wind—
For he will know the ways of the Lord
Who holds the roots of the temple of the world,
Who supports the vault of the sky!
Ask for the wind.
   Ask for the unknown fire
To lick your souls with the oil of love a-prism.

Blessed is He who recognizes The Stranger
In an easy land. Where atrophy is draped within the soul
Like fallen curtains re-hung, untouched and forgotten.
For how will you know yourself if you do not know The Stranger?
The face that haunts you?
Because of the curves and the lines that speak of pattern
Though un-caged and of prime origin?
The face of origin that haunts you.

And
What is the way to the place
    Where the lightning is dispersed,
Or the place where the east winds
    Are scattered over the earth?

I, the Stranger, ask you:
Who cuts a channel for the torrents of rain,
    And a path for the thunder heads
To water a land where no men live,
    A desert with no one in it? Yet I am in it! Know it! Have broken it!
And hold its whipping reigns in hand?
Who has unlatched the vault of heaven
To satisfy a curled and fractured wasteland
Bending to the sky for what it knows I alone can give?"

The Choir (to an ancient dirge):
"These are hard sayings. This is our church.
Don't burden the laborers.
Leave us be,
        To do *our* work."

II. The Numbers Sermon

Leaders Voice from the Stage:
```
"The work has sped up; the work has grown quick.
There is no time for time.  We must better plan—
Find a better phrase! —
```

Economize, and help ourselves help ourselves.
Much information has shown
That it is not enough—
The percentages have grown.
We need more progress, newer ways;
For tomorrow is gold! With each second
Today has grown gray,
Ready to slip into the tired past and be of no use.
The time for patience has been spent.
Quick,
Be swift our inheritance is thick!
These are the number hours.
These are the days of great mass.
Numbers, not names.
We can't count names.
We will forget them and lose our pace!"
Numbers not words—the word?
What word is better than a heavy number?
    Thunder.
"Faster. Our time is short.
Quickly—grow!
Where's the reports!?"
Thunder
"Now!-before the others gain
The support
We need to show!"
Thunder.
"Build—the storm is coming.
We must be strong."
Thunder.
"We must jump
Trends
Before the numbers go!"
Thunder.
What is wrong?
What's the hook?
Switch the bait!
Thunder!
"Add the colored lights;
Change the marquee board!
The people are bored!
Hurry!
Hurry!"
Thunder!
          Glow.
     "Don't go..."
It is so.

III. The Steward's Song

The Stranger (in strong voice):
"Build—But not with bricks
Your spirals to the sky!
Grow—but not in sickness.
Turn the seed; turn the fruit—
Stop tearing the kernel from the earth—
Don't be lax in its keep!
Your hook is of the salesman—
   Your rod—limp opinion;
     It is not the crook of the one who tends sheep!
 You Hireling! Your motive is cold!
Why plant if you will not care for its growth?
   Do not boast about what you have put into the ground;
Stop doing the work of *your* father...

Now
Turn around!
Turn around and see the twisted and mottled field
You have sewn,
    You have abandoned!
You have anxiously seeded—then run on,
Like a frantic shaking hands, a politic—
No breath to take a name.
If you do not see them, you do not see me!
I am in your wake and you leave me famished!
You leave my belly to bloat—
My lips licking flies!
—Ohh, the ones I love on stony plot!
You have given no support; you have crushed the infants' heads—
You lay weights upon my tender reeds!
You desiccant! You dry sprouts for your own profit!
You throw empty words—like saltwater to swig—
A sudden satisfaction,
Burned with each drink;
   A raging consumption
Of your deadly waters—

A hook in the nose of an already wrecked man.
Who are you to mete out gray moisture?
Can you tip the water jars
When the dust becomes hard
    And the clods of earth stick together
In great cracked pieces?

Now
Turn around and see,
See the Lord your God—
For if you move on in haste
(From fertile fields, thin soil
  Above stone, ground elder knotted turf)
You are no different than your age—
You abort the children of my hand!
Show your father by your fruit.
You would not do these things if you knew my Name!
Tell me, what is my name?

Be careful, for you judge yourselves.
Be wise, for you judge the ones I love"

~

*   Who is this who comes,*
Whose feet kick up dust over our heads?
Who riddles us with an answer?
Answers we fast hate, our anger breaks white,
For these answers question our ways we've made—
Our blind forays into light.
For us
There is no relief in the violet eve,
When the hair is combed long, when the A/C comes on;
The windows are shut still
For the wind will rattle the blinds
And ruin the rest of man.

Fathers sleep next to mothers who plead-dream
Of a man that would listen to them—
Children wrestle with the echoes of stinging words
And learn a god of cruel design—
Imprints of angry fathers—
And they learn how to smile until no one is looking
And then hit something.
And man dreams he is not a man,
But an animal or a god.
The heart cannot escape the heat of day.
It knows no peace
Even though there are those who say "Peace, peace."
And pass the offering—
And week passes to week—
    And pieces to smaller pieces.

The Choir:
"Leave us, leave us!
For this is hard. These are our homes;
This is our church!
We do not know this voice. Do not
    Disrupt our peace, our work
—You have come to hinder us!
This is a bizarre
Gospel that does not fit our land—
    Our dreams, our debt load, our plans.
What kind of devil comes in a storm?
What kind of monster wants entry to our homes?
Even our inner rooms?
    We are those with white fences, white hands!
We have order. We have our place.
We have our ways.
No one tears down what our fathers have made!
This runs too deep!
These are holy things.
It is so, it is so."

The thunder moving,
Unheard under the applause of men.

The stranger has trod,
Has kicked up dust in the west—has moved—
The dry fire over head
   Murmurs rumors
Of the time of the test—
When knowledge was want for wisdom,
When happiness was want for hope,
When words were want for the Word
And the ground groaned for want of the storm
That man would not bear.

In the hearts under the thunder,
In the churches beneath the arid flashes of sky,
In the home under the eve,
Upon the space within,
   Between the shadow and the spark
There is the mark of The Stranger—
And in the blowing of the wind
An alien notion
Of another kingdom whispers
"Obedience—and this is love."

Religion is born of discontent, mothered by anxiety and angst; it is an attempt to overcome boredom, to hide from ourselves the reality of our condition. The Gospel of God lays all this bare, shows us to be existentially naked, and in need of God the Creator. *The spectacle* clothes us in distraction—yet Jesus hung naked upon a cross. We are saved by Christ alone.

~Media Fools~

288. To what can we compare modern media? It is like the flashing blade of a naïve knight marching into battle. Yet the danger lies not in the blade's sharp point or cutting edge—its danger is in its reflective polish, its surface of mirror in which the knight catches a brief glimpse, stops his forward march, and gazes at himself indefinitely, forsaking his errand and endangering the lives of those in the village he is to protect. The blade's danger is in the distraction of catching a glimpse of ourselves and the following obsession of self-deception and omniscience that are the workings of narcissism—therefore the danger lies in the knight; not in the steel that was sharpened by the hands of man.

289. Man loves to look upon himself—but hides from himself in the same action. We both hate and love mirrors; we avoid them and fill our houses with them. Many forms of media are looking glasses that allow us to gaze indefinitely at ourselves, without ever acknowledging we are looking at ourselves. This is one of the wonders of television—knowing this, is it no wonder that when the images fade to black glass, and there we are seeing our image reflected in it, that we get up and walk away? For it is no longer amusing. We are no longer distracted from ourselves.

Man hides the truth that haunts him; not under a stone, nor in a vault, but by a life in pieces, a myriad of fractures. We hide our fatal wound not by putting a bandage over it, but by shattering the whole body so the mortal wound is not seen amidst the mess of other lacerations, scrapes, and bruises.

Humanity tears things apart not because we are looking for something, but because we are hiding something in the disarray. In the fray, in the shrapnel and pieces, we seek to bury the truth. The more fractures and distortions the better! We believe we can hide amidst the distraction of the disruption, escape amidst the angled cracks and shadows. But standing in an open place, a *uni*verse, a unified reality, our fatal disunion will be seen. Nothing is as horrible as standing in an open place.

Trying to hide from God will eventually work itself out into the wholesale attempt to annihilate everything. Suicide is how one destroys everything (it is an insult to all existence and to its Maker). But we must remember that there are many ways to kill oneself. Obviously there is the physical death of the body; yet there is also the overlooked but commonplace suicide of the soul that is an attempt to destroy all the universe—and it attempts the annihilation by a gun to the head of *coherence*, a bottle of pills down the throat of *continuity*, a noose to *unity*.

There is much done in the name of creativity, amusement, and dream-chasing that is simply the suicide of the soul. Such suicide of the soul is not because we think so little of ourselves (it may manifest that way upon the surface), but the gross truth beneath is that we think too highly of ourselves, higher of our self than all existence, and so we feel justified in dashing it all to pieces!

Humanity, in the name of distraction has seen to it that the world is compartmentalized, disjointed, and de-contextualized. Amusement is the cultural acceptance of this compartmentalization, this attempted flight from God.

290. The television is the great de-contextualizer of the modern world: sound bites, talking heads, emphasis on disunited images, commercial breaks, news flashes, smiling news reporters telling of genocide and "now from our sponsor—*Happy Fun Theme Parks!*" And for this de-contextualization it is loved universally.

If there is no context, no ultimate narrative, and everything has its own context, if everything is its own little contained bit, then there can be no contradictions. Stop here! If all is self contained, then we can vaporize that stubborn reminder of a standard—the annoying dissonance of contradiction!

A contradiction is a set of mutually exclusive statements *within the same context*. This is why we tear reality into separate pieces, this is why tensions are severed—so there can be no ultimate context that would show us as wanting. Reality, the universe of God, is a unified meta-narrative—it *will* reveal contradictions, it *will* reveal an overarching moral code, a standard, and for this there will be consequences of both joy and weeping and gnashing.

It is the Christian who lives in tension, in trust of a world unified under the Creator God; it is the un-entrusted that tear tensions apart to make way for their incoherent worldviews. God created the universe of order, reason and the Beautiful Standard; man tears and gnaws, trying to make his own multiverse, his own shattered-verse.

291. Do not smash your television—smash your desire to be God. Smash your envy of the only one who is perfect. If we kill our televisions we have done nothing but given ourselves an excuse to buy a better, higher definition television (or be secretly envious of those who have the latest technology).

We must not lay an axe to the root of the Technicolor tree—this is only a misdiagnosis that will keep one from true healing, and like the many-headed hydra of myth, for each Technicolor tree we axe, two more sprout from the cable in the ground. It is a hopeless proposition to conquer media without shattering the pride of the human heart. It is man's heart that has put the hollowing images on the screen; it is man's self-addicted heart that pulls and consumes the images off the screen. The only way to stand against the prattle and buzz is to bow to God and stop bowing to ourselves.

I am not a *neo-luddite*. That is, I am not against technology nor do I long for a simpler life from a certain number of years ago. It is not the *existence* of television, but its *centrality* that is bleeding us, drying us up like cracked desert mud. The medium of television is not one mere entertainment in a world of many other things; rather, it is the central lens that turns all things into entertainment. This is the sin.

292. What is entertainment—it is what loosely holds are troubled selves together; it is the amusing of our souls. *Amuse* means to distract, to divert from serious issues. We are not meant for amusement, but for joy. This does not negate fun or humor, but it breaks past the mediocrity of amusement. Because we tear things apart, yet feel a need for unity (for we were made in the image of God), we incessantly chase amusement—it allows for our contradictions to remain unchallenged, for it attempts to distract us from our fractures.

Watch T.V., but watch yourself. Fifteen minutes of fame will often throw eternity to the wind. Better a benevolent audience of one then a cannibalizing audience of millions.

Hollywood comes at us with a beautiful knife—and we welcome the kill. We welcome white-noise, we invite the prismatic hurricane of images—it keeps us from our self and lets us *live* vicariously. It keeps us distracted, and for this we will throw our money onto its altar—our altar.

Do not easily dismiss videogames. Man has always tried to be his own origin—to create a virtual reality. We will see the industry of *gaming* boom and grow demographically wider as the technology allows for more realistic environments and greater control. Truth—that cares! What we care about is being caught up in our own drama of self-origin and self-salvation. What can feed the drive of the self-originated soul more than a virtual world with the parameters at our finger tips?

What is it about a storm that makes people seem friendlier? Is it that man bonds with man to survive and help each other stand against the elements on account of love for fellow man? Or is it that there is now a buffer between strangers, friends, family, and lovers—a great distracter between them that allows them to talk, but remain dislocated? A common enemy to face and focus upon, rather than deal with the existential tempests of trust and origin? "So, how about that weather…"

293. I am not against television or a video game anymore than I am against electricity. I am for the lighting of a darkened room yet not for the electrocution of a child. I am not against hammers—I am for the building of shelter yet not for the smashing of a skull. Yet I am against the selfish heart of man; I am for the renewing of the heart of man.

What I mean to say is that certain mediums have certain bents and certain limits. We must realize that we have made the medium of entertainment our central medium—and run all life through it, stamping amusement and entertainment onto everything that is squeezed through its cables and screens. To entertain is fine, but to make everything entertainment is the darkest form of perversity possible.

The moralist burns televisions, protests electricity, and bans hammers. How useless are these misguided energies! They only diminish and dehumanize, and leave us unsheltered and in the dark. They only make us angry at the God of our salvation.

But what of Jesus telling us to poke out our eye or cut off our hand that we may not sin? The Spirit here is twistedly missed—and see, He does not say destroy the technology or gift of nature that fed you, but destroy *the part of you* which was used for evil. If a moralist would take this wisdom to the extreme they would chop themselves into unintelligible pieces until all that is left is a disembodied heart—so let us first start with the heart, then we can keep our creative fingers and the blessing of sight. We should have the fountainhead cleaned so all the land is fed with crystal spring water. We cannot clean the fountainhead—that takes a miracle. Grace is a miracle.

294. Let us remember this one word when we are dealing with television, with the internet, with videogames, with the light field of fame: *distraction*.

Distraction is the key to popularity.

Modern media is an unending chase, an incessant hunt, a constant dump of images and moving sound that are designed to enthrall and distract. This is why television is loved. Television distracts us. Television can never satisfy—it is the essence of its form—it can only egg on and tease; it is a virtual carrot that can never be eaten.

Television can never satisfy—ah, now this is why we love it! *But why would you say this; this can't be right. Don't we love it because it satisfies something within us?* No. We love it because it is a constant feed that keeps us preoccupied and ever agitated. We love it precisely because it cannot be obtained and found familiar; it cannot be found boring and found to leave us quiet in our boredom once we have been *satisfied* with it. For when the program is over, there is simply another amusement piped in, and there are a myriad of channels that we can jitter back and forth amongst—so even no one channel becomes boring!

Boredom is a sign of the needful state of our souls. Boredom is an advocate for the reality of God, and an indicator of man's dire situation.

The satisfaction that the world desires is to *remain in chase*.

Truly, television only satisfies our desire to stay unsatisfied and keeps up the frenetic hunt so we don't have to listen to the still small voice within. We love it because we use it to forget the discontent of our existence, the anxiety of our origin. We use it to gag the whisper of *good tension* within us that drives us towards self-knowledge of our God-need, and we replace it with the ill anxiety of keeping up with the Joneses and covering up our disease.

We are addicted to unreality. Television is like a blanket that is too small on a cold night. You are ever shifting, moving it here and there, warming one spot while another goes cold—it is a constant moving but never finding of rest.

Rocks thrown constantly into a pond will keep it moving, rippling, and keep the calm from ever forming and revealing a true reflection. I do not believe we are ever conscious of this when we turn on our favorite program(s), but somewhere within our winding souls we are afraid of what the calm surface will reveal—so we throw rocks and call it entertainment.

Television is addictive because it can never satisfy. Isn't this the sickness of all addictions?

Distraction is a dialect of *the lie*. The bulk of deception is distraction. Think of an illusionist, a magician: distraction, smoke and mirrors—they are devices to keep us from the truth. The deceiver is also the distracter. The entertainer is often the deceiver.

Television can educate; but television can never satisfy. Television is a modern marvel and a mirror of the human soul. We can never be satisfied with our selves no matter how novel we seem; our soul's hunger calls for more than our own narcissism.

I was born into a generation and culture that might as well of had RCA cables grafted into our veins. I too like good movies—television and silver screen. I own a television. Much grace has come to the world through the television. I would no more initiate a ban on television than I would a ban on phones or pacemakers.

295. The greatest temptation of modern media is not the pet-list of sins or the lust of the eyes. Some would lay claim that the problem is one or two channels or one or two sexualized programs or websites; this is a misdiagnosis of the problem. Such content is a huge problem and I do not minimize it. Yet, it is the wide array of

channels, of networks, of satellites, of websites, that stimulates the greatest and most devious temptation…

The greatest and most dangerous snare is the sin of the pride of life. The hidden dagger behind the media machine is the desire for omniscience and to conquer the world—to be as God. Television and the internet offer virtual omniscience and power; with them we are given access and gaze beyond human powers. It is the lust for godhood that really addicts us to the media feed. With power and far flung access at our fingertips we feel divine. Television and the internet have been used as a magnifying glass for humanism; they are the go-to tool for our own idolatry.

We are addicted to television because we are addicted to ourselves, and as self-made gods we must tear apart the world to maintain our delusion. This partially explains our excitement at what is entropic, what is violent, and degenerate—yet we want it with a dose of sparkle!

Television offers brokenness in vivid Technicolor; the sin of the heart in digital surround sound 5.1. Don't be surprised by the coupling of beauty with evil, of ingenuity and illness; this is how it has been from the start, for Eve saw that "the fruit was pleasing to the eye, and also desirable for gaining wisdom" (Genesis 3). The fruit offered promising things. Beauty is not evil, but evil does come in the form(s) of beauty—after all, evil is deception, and we are distracted by the beauty of the blur of images.

296. The wise man reads the media like the seasons; he reads the light field for glories of God and evidences of man's fallen state; he then untwists it, uses it, points to it, to speak of what is within the human heart and beautiful remedy of the incarnation of Christ. The wise man does not disengage, but he evangelizes the media by his very presence of service and humility.

We make a mistake when we blind ourselves to the eventual translation of mere ideas to mean actualities. As light runs in front of sound, ideas herald action; the ideas purveyed by media are the flash, but soon the thunder will inevitably shake us! We are drawn to the sparkle-flash, but we cower under the thunder when it makes its way to everyday us. There are consequences to the character of our entertainment, to where our media stream flows.

Modern man reclines in armchairs, listening to talking heads discuss this and that in arguments that tout rationality, data, numbers, and news—and in these motions of rationalization, he has lost the obvious to the absurd, has lost the foundation for all dialogue and meaning. In the noise, the weight of sheer existence is tossed aside as God is forgotten, true choice/action has become the will-o-wisp of opinion, and truth becomes a mere object that is grabbed at to be possessed rather than submitted to.

The media is a *talking about* that is an assault on reality; but Christianity is a *living through* and acknowledgement of true existence. Modern media is the inane conversation that debates the existence of the man in the room, and for that, it thins our existence into an apparition, a civilized madness, and a (s)hell of a life.

~Humility of History~

297. The Cross is taller than it is long. Though we are to value our neighbor, to extend love, compassion, and mercy laterally to humanity, we must always value God more than the respect of man. We must follow God no matter what it costs us in the world of man, in the culture that we live. Yet, we must not forsake our brothers, for in doing so we forsake God.

We cannot relate rightly to God if we relate wrongly to humanity. The tension of the cross calls us to seek the Kingdom of Heaven first, to respect God above all; but one cannot do this without loving humanity. The cross is taller than it is long—but because it is tall it can be long. If we tear this tension apart, we will offend God by lifting up man, or we will disrespect humanity and therefore not be followers of God.

History is penultimately the story of mankind—it is ultimately the story of God.

298. There are two divergent modes of thought: one that validates based on antiquity and one that validates based on novelty. The Bible says it is neither old age nor chronological newness that validates; rather, it is the truth that validates. Tradition is not correct because it happens to be ancient; innovation is not correct because it happens to be shiny and new—each is only correct as it is in agreement with God's will.

Followers of God ought to be innovative and risk taking, starting new life—those that go forth—just as Abraham was innovative, just as Moses went, just as Christ was pioneering. Yet followers must also remember their history and their traditions which are the firewalls against the many empty philosophies and corruptions of each age. Tradition and innovation: here is a tension rarely held! Here is a war hotly waged!

Without the concave optics of history we are blinded by our own age, by our flatness in *knowing what it means to be human.*

Church history, national history and world history are all sidelined by a false and fashionable view that the future is better than the past. We are chronological snobs that say our age is the best and our tomorrow will be better than the day we were handed; as if we were the alchemists who were great enough to make into gold the lead handed to us by dead ancestors and senile elders!

How are we to gain bearing in the great scope of time and space when all we know is the millisecond in which we live, care only about the culture within arm's reach? When we know nothing of the last minute of existence; nothing of the truth told in the long wind of history that has traced the globe?

299. History is essential to Christianity; it is entwined with space and time. God created history—it was commissioned to be written when the voice of God called from the mysterious burning bush. History and freedom come together. The commissioning of recorded history came with the commissioning of the freedom of God's people. It was Moses who was sent to say "Let my People Go!" it was Moses who was to write the history books.

We are freed from our myopic and inward drawn views by the graces of History. Never forget. Remember. We must remember that God has called us to remember.

The horse and its rider have been thrown into the sea—we must remember our history. We must write it down; we must sing it; we must put it on canvas. The purpose of looking upon and learning from history is not to give us ideas about how to be stronger—no it is to show us that we must die to be strong! It is to show us the reality of the human condition and the holiness of God--the vapor and the Rock!

We learn of God like we learn of other persons— through story, through time—for He is not an idea that is spoken of in abstraction.

When we forsake the Biblical record, when we ignore the history of the church, we fall prey to deceptions that God has used the hand of history to unmask; we lose sight of God's will and the great glories He has given us to dwell upon, to play in our mind's theater.

300. We would do well to have the scope of Stephen and the scope of Paul. Their scope extended beyond their own age; through revelation their scope reached into the ancient past and into the fulfillment of all time. They understood the story arc that was centered upon Jesus. They had found their place in the story of God—this is what it means to live.

The world does not have a Godly scope; for this reason up goes the cry "life is not fair; there is no justice!" Justice is a matter of scope; we cannot assess what is just without correct perspective of scope.

Without entrusting ourselves to a standard, justice is only opinion.

Imagine with me an easy scene: A man and his wife are watching a crime thriller of a movie. It is a movie with a horrible atrocity—imagine this movie in black and white with the extreme angles and ambiguity of *film noir*. Somewhere in the middle of the movie the criminal is taken into police custody, but is soon let off to roam about in the shadows. Now the husband gets angry and mouths, "This is not fair, this is not justice! It should not be this way—that criminal has gotten away with his crime!" The wife, being very wise, says "But you have not finished the movie; you cannot call it unfair if you have not seen the end." The wife understands that justice is a matter of scope—the husband has ignored scope and become frustrated by a *middle event*.

If we, in our now limited sight cry that life is unfair, it is because we have ignored the scope of history that lies within the scope of eternity. The moment we may be within seems unjust and is unjust temporarily—but existence is under the care of a good God and it will find resolve in His perfect being.

The tyranny of the heart is that it gets what it wants—separation from God, or intimacy.

The slow scope is not cruelty—no! It is the opposite—love; for we are all guilty and God's timing is grace.

Better justice to be eternal and overarching rather than temporary and instant. This is grace.

The faithless heart has no true bearing for justice. One cannot claim "*Justice!*" if one cannot claim "*God!*" If no God, then one can only claim "*meaninglessness…*"—and it is meaningless to do so.

Followers of Christ, those who trust the Creator and Savior, they alone know of a justice that is not free floating and knocking about, a justice that is not whim. Justice presupposes a standard and a standard tells of a Creator.

The scope of Stephen and the scope of Paul got them killed. The world vies against the scope of justice that the Gospel brings. The scope of history bears the witness of God—and the world would like to bury the witness of God because it shows them wanting; that is why it buried Stephen and Paul, and now tries to bury the importance of history in general. History is evidence of who we are.

What is dubbed "Consumer Christianity" simply *does not have time for history*—and for that it is of the kingdom of man. Henry Ford spoke for the unreal church when he said 'history is bunk." Moses spoke for the real Church when He said "remember".

"Does not have time for history"—the phrase itself is self-refuting.

301. We have forgotten how the prophets were treated—have we not?

When one has to explain that Christianity is an offense—then how far from the truth have we fallen!

Christianity is an offense because it shatters all the kingdoms of men. It does not come from heaven to be a resident, to hold a plot of ground within the walls of man-made castles. No! It comes to raze them to the ground in a word, making little of man's greatest efforts with a simple breath. It comes us its own kingdom, not one to be incorporated into the kingdom of man.

The Kingdom of Heaven Inc. No—the kingdom of heaven is never incorporated; yet many have tried to buy it, and incorporate it into the cubicles of man. Man incorporates what is of man—Heaven is an antithetical Kingdom and is at odds with the will of man.

Hah! To be a Christian means to claim self-contradiction, and then contradict the self. To be self ruled is to not acknowledge self-contradiction, yet to be a contradiction. Self rule then rules out knowing the self.

Self rule is mere illusion. It is a kingdom with no subjects, a chimera, a tyrannical fantasy that screams itself into a wisp! It is a kingdom that builds grandiose castles that are wiped away by a mere sneeze; no more substantial than a vapor.

302. Moses, the man bronze-faced for being in the very presence of the Lord often reminded the people of Israel to remember, to recall their history.

To the Lion | 339

"Only be careful, and watch yourselves closely so that you do not forget the things your eyes have seen or let them slip from your heart as long as you live. Teach them to your children and to their children after them. Remember the

day you stood before the Lord your God at Horeb, when He said to me, 'Assemble the people before me to hear my words so that they may learn to revere me as long as they live in the land and may teach them to their children" (Deut 4:9-10).

"Remember how the Lord your God led you all the way in the desert these forty years to humble you and to test you in order to know what was in your heart, whether or not you would keep His commands" (Deut 8:2-3).

The Meekest man on earth was a man who told of the importance of history.

By Jesus' own lips: "the meek will inherit the earth."

History is a priceless gem stone; it is a witness to the reality of human nature; it is a hard and real gathering of evidence, of facets that reveal we are dusty and loved, that we are bound to fail unless we remember that God has chosen us, not because we are great, but because He is great.

History is the sea that sways with the life of God and drowns the pride of man. It is an irrefutable witness to the frailty of our hands and the shortness of our breath.

History is a chronological cat scan that shows us our disease, and reveals the healer's ability.

This is the two-fold lesson of history: man is grass and God is good.

The timeline of history is a long wick that has burned with the love of God, and has revealed the soot and ash of humanity. History shows us the glory of God—it shows us the darkness of man without God.

If we live short-sighted, we will build monuments to the prophets of yesterday but murder the prophets of our age. A shallow history will dig mass graves.

303. Friedrich Nietzsche once said that he would "only believe in a God that danced." He looked at history through a fractured lens; he missed the obvious, and then mistook it for the monstrous. Through the fractures he saw God as lumbering and spastic—and declared that this could not be God! But he was amiss for these refractions of his heart!

History is the retelling of the waltz that God initiated with man, the foxtrot, and the sweeping slow dances that have since followed. The scriptures are the drama of the great dance; its stumbles, its stutter steps, and its graceful arcs.

Melodies were written to remember God; music is born from our need to remember; music is born from our need for God. When we sing a melody it is because we need God. It is the creature that sings: man, the angels, the cosmos—and it is God who is ultimately sung about! For though man can curse with his tongue, song and tongue were made from him—and their sheer movements are involuntary praise to Him.

Nietzsche said that "What doesn't kill (destroy) us makes us stronger"; but he was wrong. In truth it is the hard opposite: what kills us makes us strong. In the realm of the spirit, what kills us— that is, what kills our pride, our self-dependence, our illusions, and our selfish insanity is what makes us stronger. For we are only strong when we rely upon God; until then, until we die in that baptism of faith and honesty, we are the weak play acting as the strong.

Nietzsche also said that "There cannot be a God because if there were one, I could not believe that I was not He." Again, his brilliance is upside down, his wisdom profoundly dark. Rather, the truth is that there must be a God because *we do believe that we are He.*

There is a God, and so we believe that there isn't—and we place ourselves in His stead by judging so. If there were no God, why then do we constantly try to usurp Him, and desire to become the center of worship and the conqueror of the world?

304. Let us be discontent with this world—but not discontent with our God. In this tension one can cry that life now seems unfair, but God will, and is meting out Justice. This tension is the truth that we are within a great plan that ends well, but that we are now time bound somewhere in the turbulent middle.

Though we are time bound we have been given the surety of history's resolve by the Scriptures and life of Christ. This tension opens the door to the fight for injustice as it allows for us to have a peace with God that gives us the strength to stand against the injustices, the chaos of the world and the arrows that beset us. The peace *with* God bears the great weapon to wield against injustice: peace *of* God.

Only with God do we have the love that enables us to fight the monstrosities of the world and not become a monster our self. If we do not have true love, the love that comes from God, then we are only smacking a cymbal when we cry for justice (for the naked cry for justice is selfish). Godless cries for justice multiply the injustice. Godless cries for justice are only fresh tyrannies.

We must look into the eye of our enemy if we are to face him—but to do this without Christ as our taproot into deep righteousness, then we will be drawn into, grafted into that which we fight.

Jesus is the Alpha and Omega—the beginning and the end. These are not just pretty words—these are the reality of the words *justice* and *grace*. These are the words that give backing to God's command "do not fear."

If God is sovereign *and* good, what then can we fear? Then, even the tears of our nightmares turn into the seeds of the city of Heaven.

If God is sovereign and good, then what we fear will be ourselves—ah, but we do!

Psychology and technology will never save us. Only the holy can save us; only the God of reason and wonder, the marvelous *Ancient of Days* that inspires poetry to express the inexpressible; only that love which comes to love the unlovable can save us. Only the down-to-earth poetry of the incarnation can save us—only the love that suffers in our stead.

History shows that it is entropy that currently rules over the earth and not progress as the modern man asserts. It is *dystopia* that we are living in and falling towards, not *utopia* that we are climbing to. The land of the "good man", the myth of "*Mankind the Good*" exists, literally, *nowhere, no-place*. Utopia means "no place". But "God the Good"—that is reality, and He is everywhere.

305. Science's concern and ultimate end is to tell of secondary causes; it can go no further than this. A wonderful mystery is the first cause. God is the first cause. Only He can reveal the first cause—*the why, the who*, and *to what end?* This is the jurisdiction of history.

Our origin is a matter of history. No doubt, science and biology are very much a part of this history, undergirding what we call time and moving like the gears of a wonderful clock beneath, but the study of origin leans not on biology, but on history.

I come from a zygote and a sperm—yes—but I know my origin from history, from lineage, from real places, from personal names, and from people moving about in this realm of time. History is revealed to us, given to us by those gone before. History is a revelation. Who we are is to be found in revelation, our origin in story, not in an autopsy of a cell. The beauty of biology, cellular autopsies and the wondrous finds of archaeology are not these things themselves, but the story they buttress, the history of existence they lend flourish and depth to.

Our meaning, our purpose, is given to us by the Word—the revealed history of the Bible—and it is verified by Jesus Christ. Jesus the miracle worker, the riser from the dead, the perfect teacher, Jesus the wounded healer, Jesus our God—He attested to the reality of the scriptures; He revealed the revelation as true.

History: it is revealed to us. God could have given us an ancient chart of the elements, some chemical formulas and molecular symbols of hydrogen, dust, and etc. to speak of our origin. Many act as though this would have been a better way—that a 'real god' would have shown a more sophisticated way of communicating the beginning of life, something other than *story*. But this is only silliness to be tossed aside by clear thinking. God bless the mapping of the human genome, but never let it replace the story of our ancestors or replace our family tree.

As T.S. Eliot said, "In my beginning is my end. In my end is my beginning." In our origin we find meaning. If we are wrong about our origin, if we live in the aftershock of a wrong worldview here at the very start, then we will not understand our meaning and not live in our purpose. Everything will suffer from a misperceived origin. Others will suffer from *our* misperceived beginning.

To know the Savior one must know of the Creator; to know the Savior is to know the Creator!

306. Trust is never inert—it is only action (inward and outward action) but never a mere idea! This is why one's fruits reveal the roots.

When Christianity is only a realm of ideas, its sterility is overcome only by *new ideas*; and this chase of "innovative thought" will inevitably alter the Gospel message. The key here is to be pioneering, so the very nature of this system will bend the truth of the Gospel for the truth is the same yesterday, today, and tomorrow—*and that just will not do! We must have novel ideas!* Rubbish! Novel is only an attempt to do away with the Ancient of Days! To erase the Alpha so we can make our own Omega.

But, ah! The eloquence of action! Action in truth's name is never sterile and is always fertile; it is ever present and never old hat for action is that which is present.

The Gospel's power is not mere innovation, but the efficacy of the truth. Salvation is more than a synapse, it is incarnation.

Now, a wonderful irony comes in that only in knowing the *Ancient of Days*, the infinite *Alpha and Omega*, can the finite creature ever experience new wonders! In seeking what is new and in spurning *He that does not change*, man can only walk in an ancient rut littered with apple cores and bones.

~The Poiema~

307. There are two movements of art: one artist seeks to create his own universe upon canvas, within poetry, with his ascending notes; the other artist seeks to speak of the unity of all there is.

The artist worships God in acknowledging His design and boundaries; the humanist artist worships himself, seeks not to communicate truth, but seeks to express his god-likeness, his ability to create worlds and then fill them with the praises of people.

The artist acknowledges that God is worthy of all attention, and does this by sacrificing to create. The humanist artist will sacrifice oceans; will collapse mountains into dust, as long as it will make him feel god-like in the procuring of the attentions of men.

The humanist artist curves in upon himself, collapses everything into his world; *the artist* opens up the wonders of God, magnifies the beauty of the Creator.

There are two types of poet: *The Poet of Christ* and the *Poet of Men*. The Poet of Christ is he whose words are marked by inwardness—that is they are bound to his deepest being. His active words demand love and for that demand action; and in the demand of truth, the desire to do so is born. His words are the synapse of the real and ideal; they are a diamond shot through with light—sound and precious.

The Poet of Men is he whose words bleed for only a few. His words speak of love's right for preference, love's right to exclude; they are the words of man's dubious desires that demand to be fulfilled. They are an endless chase, the seeking of an idyllic and non-existent youth, they are the delusion of nostalgia, and the ghost of vain hopes; they are a will-o-wisp chased into a bog—transient and phantom. They are words that run men aground, leave the stranded.

308. In Christianity there has been a softening of language like the softening of an undisciplined belly; it is unhealthy, and the heart suffers under the weight. The softening of language comes with a softening of orthodoxy, an anemia of teaching, and our tendency to divide and reduce. The softening comes from laziness and desiring the path of least resistance—this is not the way of passion! Not the way of the cross!

There has been a slope-sliding loss of beautiful language to express the Gospel. We live in a world dominated by average prose; a world that tags poetry as pretentious language, a waste of time and disconnected from reality. We live in an age that derogates prophetic prose as "purple prose" or romantic mush.

The crowd wants a quick, succinct, and easily understood explanation—no fertile words, no mysterious meter. Pragmatism and the desire for economy have flattened language because they have flat-lined the truth of the Gospel.

It is the desire to control that has flattened language. Faith makes language fertile; but pride has steamrolled language into Kansas asphalt. This is dangerous! When we flatten language we also flatten ideas—we flatten our cognition, our ways of acknowledging reality. No wonder God is not a mystery and a marvel to many people—it is no wonder (literally, no wonder) when the church, more often than not, communicates God as a cold, lifeless, instruction manual or mutual fund report. One files mutual fund reports into steel cabinets; yet one takes poetry and piercing prose with them all day, feeling it in their chest, carrying it in their mind.

Our words should be soft only in that they are like feathers, not like some saccharine pudding. Our words should be hard, like diamond, so listeners and readers can turn them about, and learn from the forming prisms.

Our words should not be irrational—poetry is not irrational. Our words must be rational but should not be the language of rationalism. Again, *rationalism* is man starting with himself and trying to consume the cosmos with his mouth and mind!

309. Poetry is rational, yet the diametric opposite of rationalism. Rationalism pushes man into insanity—or, rationalism is the flailing of the insane soul—both! For it is the snake eating its own tail, the self-consuming serpent clenching itself smaller, thinner, and less substantial in more violent shrugs inward.

What is a word, but an acknowledgement of reality? Whether true or untrue, it is a reference to and therefore an acknowledgement of reality.

What is a word but an attempt to communicate, an attempt to relate? Language is born of relationship. What then does flat-lined language tell us?

Was not the Bible written in poetry, in song, in artistic form? In part, yes—so why do we communicate it all as though it were a monochrome tax form? Now, it is not language that brings God to life, but it is God that brings language to life!

Doesn't a renewed heart want to spend time dwelling on and communicating the wonders of this mighty God? If so, why do most of us speak about God with tofu, washed-out words with not a tremble of excitement in our voice? Should not pastors often sound like poets? The world's poets should try to imitate the pastors and priests of God!—but they do not, and for good reason! So much of preaching and passing on of the Gospel is void of any creative bright blood!

When the church's pulpit is unsympathetic with the poetic mysteries of God, the creativity that rises out of passion out of the agonizing soul, then God raises up musicians and writers, poets and artists to prophesy, to shatter glazed gazes, to herald the awe and holiness of God. Holiness is no tax time newsletter; it is a raging funeral pyre of self-origin in word, melody, or canvas. God comes in fire. Poetry is a sacrifice of the flesh; God came as Jesus Christ—the speaker of parables!

Talk about economy of words! The Bible was written mostly by a desert dwelling people to whom too many words was a matter of life and death in the Sinai heat! Their words were chosen carefully—yet still the Hebrew writers of Scripture spoke in a language of fertile poetry!

God is poetic. If He was not, then He would not have spoken to Moses through a burning bush on a mountainside. If He was not, then David's lyre would have been mute. If He was not, then Christ would not have spoken in poetic parallel, in crafted parables that turned on a diamond center. If He was not, then His *Word* would not have carved the valleys and hollowed the sea basins of the forming earth; he would not have made the deep dark oceans lined with white waves, like the black and white of script on paper praising the Creator!

Prophets speak with words that burn from the same origin of the fire-bush that spoke to Moses. The mere words of God are greater than man—dancing, burning, and alive and growing! They are more real than us, more sane than us, and they will move through us as sunbeams chase their own laughter clean through a shadow.

God shows Himself as poetic to us because He is greater than we know, more beautiful than we know, and more purposed and loving than we can interpret and read. Even if we had a thousand eyes, a thousand ears...

God is poetic—this is Scriptural. God called reborn humanity His *poems*. "For we are God's workmanship, created in Christ Jesus, to do good works," Paul wrote in Ephesians. The word workmanship in Greek is *poiema*; it is the source of the word poem.

God is the divine wordsmith and we as followers of Christ are being crafted into metaphors, symbols, and intentional rhythms to express God's ideas, to speak beauty into the universe. God creatively spoke existence into being, and one day He will sing over us (Genesis 1; Zephaniah 3:17).

Acknowledging that we are God's poems, His workmanship, is the antithesis to the proud heart. To be a poem of God makes us the crafted, not the writer who calls forth the world. All true poetry acknowledges this—that we were made in His image, and not He in ours.

I speak that God is poetic, but what I mean is that poetry is of God, a gift of his hand. Its artistry and craftsmanship are benevolent echoes of the creative and redeeming God.

As with any good gift, we can twist words to spit them at the giver. We as humans can hide behind flowery language, build massive castles of polysyllabic, collegiate words; or we can pretend we are perfectly pragmatic and be tightly economic in our words. Both of which can be the semantics of pride.

Should we not use the lushest language we are capable of, *and* that which expresses His matter-of-fact ways to tell of His wonders?

His simplest beauty is beyond our most expressive genius. When we love something we praise it. When we are in love frozen-codfish of words are not enough—for in us lives a reality that must be expressed! When the heart is lush with God, then lush are the lips that speak His praise! The world will call this foolishness. Then be fools with beautiful tongues!

To those who believe words to be of second rate importance, was it not the changing of languages that stopped mighty man in building his tower to the throne of God? God changed their words and he changed their physical, time-space lives.

310. There is an upside down belief that has come down to us from certain philosophic roots. From the Greek worldview that made gods of men and men of gods comes the belief that the poet is touched by madness. We nod our heads to this. It is standard to look at the poet, or the genius, or the creative person with a furrowed gaze and shake of the head. We tend to think that there must be a screw loose, a few whole-notes missing from the melody of those who stray from the status quo.

It is an embedded belief (much like an infected splinter) in our culture that to be the creative one, the intense poet, or the brilliant mathematician, that they must be receding into insanity as their super-brilliance glows. This is a false belief; it is an upside down belief from a worldview that made gods in man's image. This topsy-turvy view makes the dark things of this world as lights; it credits good to evil, and banality to good. This belief in itself is a form of insanity.

This lie credits the beauty of creativity, the wonder of genius, and the wisdom of the poet who is in love with God, to the un-Godly things of corruption and derivation. It is not the madness, the destructive tendencies of sin and guilt, the psychoses or neuroses of fallen man that make for brilliant creativity. It is all the very opposite. The arts are from and for God! It is the poet for God who has tasted reality and is going sane amidst an insane world. It is the genius and the creative ones that have seen the walls of the sanitarium and know there is a better life beyond them.

The Scriptural idea of poetry and of the artistic "burn" is that it is one way in which we bear the image of God; it is a gift from God that is meant for the glorification of God—it is a touch of sanity and reality. Madness is of men; but reality, the glory of sanity, is of God.

Art comes not from madness, but finding order, proportion, and purpose amidst the insanity that has swarmed us like August humidity. True art is a move to our origin; it is the echo of the

Word of God streaming a bullion banner between day and night; the echo of the divine drawing of a silver line between the tide and the shore.

But note, and you must note this or you will greatly misunderstand my point about the poetic nature of God. Poetic does not mean gaudy, exasperating, snobbish, or archaic words glued together by thee's or thou's. It does not mean words all jumbled and cryptic to merely express the confused self. It does not mean obtuse or bohemian. Poetry can be simple, short, long, or complex; modern or medieval; regal or rustic. So what does poetic mean?

Poetic means deliberate—that is supra-conscious, ordered and intentionally crafted; poetic means fertile—that is born from a living heart of love; glorying—that is acknowledging what is glorious and worthy; and passionate—that is costly, sacrificial, and in the end, sweet. Poetry is that which moves to speak of our origin—the personal yet infinite. Poetry is intimate; it breaks itself open to communicate, to be personal and fight machination, and it reaches beyond its own grasp—calling upon the infinite, praising the God who is without end. This poetry is not merely written—but it is lived. Poetry is written both on paper and in the dirt—lines upon paper and lines upon flesh.

Do not confuse pompous with poetic; arrogance with artistic. Pomposity and arrogance are the outflow of a deceived heart. They are the cologne of the person in love with their own insanity. Never, never do our words fool the God who has given us our tongue and who reads our hearts as letters.

311. The modern church must become aware of a danger—a zombie haunts the bride's corridors! I have seen this zombie many times—a pretty zombie all dressed in fashion. Distance deceives, and so one doesn't know the danger until one is close and the zombie-mouth is opened, and only must and moans fall out.

There is an absurd illusion of communication that is spread about the Christian subculture like the black plague. This black plague is Christianspeak. It is like the black plague, yet the symptoms are seen not in the speaker (save malaise) but the one who hears the infection being spoken and spread—the symptoms being headache, nausea, vomiting, and a general malaise.

Sadly, much of Christendom spits about Christianspeak, a specialized language that often means nothing, but is carried swiftly along by a mediocre shell of religiosity. It is quite dead, to be sure, and animated by some spell or lie.

I believe the pandemic of Christianspeak exists because we truly have nothing of real importance to say because of anemic teaching and relativistic preaching. There is a whole lexicon used, that if we were to force the moment to crisis by asking the speaker *what that certain phrase meant*, they would only end up spinning off other vague phrases that reveal they do not know what they are talking about in the slightest. Eventually, they would exasperate themselves; get frustrated with you, and walk away muttering, "...I'll pray for you."

It is easy to shrug off issues in loaded language; it is easy to look caring or intelligent by invoking the fitting Christianspeak. There are entire colleges devoted to teaching students the lexicon of Christianspeak, and nothing more.

Just as there are dead metaphors, the subculture of the church often communicates with what are "undead symbols" or "undead semantics"—they are not so much dead and silent, but dead and acting as if they are alive—so, undead they are. We have gads of these verbal zombies moaning about the halls of churches and living rooms of Bible studies; and unfortunately, haunting the passages of most inspirational books published—a real sadness of mine.

There is nothing quite as unsettling as finding a *highly recommended* Christian book to be gagged full of tritely spun Christianspeak—

and after finishing such a read, feeling rather queasy as when one gets zealous at a summer fair and eats the whole stick of neon cotton candy on a hot afternoon.

Think about the symbol of or the many expressions we speak in regard to the cross of Christ—"just lay it at the foot of the cross" we say glibly, and of course, meaning only, "don't worry about, it's no big deal!" The cross in general has become an undead symbol of mercy—undead because we have drained it of reason and revelation, for we have often thought that justice was set aside by mercy here on the cross. This is a symbolic zombie for sure, dead to reality but animated by smiley Christian-speak! For on the cross justice and mercy met. God did not grant mercy without fulfilling justice—for that was the necessity and the purpose of the cross!

Love—here is another zombie of Christianspeak. "Love your neighbor," it is moaned dustily. But what is meant is simply to smile at them in passing or refrain from choking them when they disagree with your theology. Yet rarely does it mean obedience to Christ, and living sacrificially for the ones that one would rather… *avoid.*

312. Moving along with this nice little theme of zombies, undead, and the like, Christianspeak is vampiric. I it revels in obscurity (therefore the look of horror when you ask someone "what does that mean?"), is pale and draining (speaking but not saying in accordance with reality, and exhausting resources and fatiguing the people we try to tell the Good News), and romantic in a macabre way—for we elevate and are seduced by obtuse Christian-sounding mottoes as mystical mantras. We think there is something supernatural in the way we annunciate and string together certain things—we are attracted to the musicality, mysticality, and power of such.

Such Christianspeak serves to preserve our pride by setting a Mason-Dixon divide of spirituality between us and them, as well as setting up a pride-based hierarchy even within the body of Christ.

This is to say that it serves as an agent of corruption in the loving of the world and the church.

In the end, Christianspeak seems to be a symptom of the modern view of truth, the modern epistemology in which reason and faith are ripped apart and placed in airtight compartments. Who would dare ask us to explain our faith reasonably—who would dare ask us to explicate some poetry that is the expression of a personal faith? Really, all this moaning, purple, and gravely-animated language is the upshot of attempting to find God in a "mystical something" rather than knowing Him where faith and reason meet.

It is easier to say, "Well, I'll pray for you" than it is to know where to look for an answer in the Scripture, or to say, "You can stay at my place when the foreclosure hits…" Christianspeak is the tongue of apathy.

Surely this is not to invalidate the real "I'll pray for you!" and other language that used to be tethered to reality, and for many, still is. Yet, we must learn that to speak without an *inwardness* is to speak with violence against reality.

~On Being 'At One'~

313. Just as one without eyes cannot appreciate the molten gold and streaming greens of a sunset, one cannot perceive the central beauty of either the Old Testament or the New Testament without having an understanding of what *righteousness* is.

Righteousness is conformity to primary reality. It is living *originally*, in accord with our true origin, with our Creator. It is becoming "at one with reality". "Atonement!" is, though disguised in many ways, the unrelenting cry that aches our bones, our hearts, and our minds. At one-ment!

314. Why does the on-looking world despise the self-righteous? Because the upward thrust of repressed reality *will* find expression—and it calls us to acknowledge the absurdity of being self-*authoring*. The world thinks it is a knock against Christianity to condemn the self-righteous—hah! It is quite the opposite! The true Christian is the only one who is not self-righteous, but righteous through the Creator and Savior—Jesus Christ.

To be self-righteous simply means conformed to one's own derivative origin; to be one's own standard. Self-righteous = self-originating.

Man sinned; he did not entrust himself to God. By un-trusting his Creator, man shattered the righteousness that is the trust, the mediation of man to God.

"This is His name whereby he shall be called, The Lord our Righteousness" (Jeremiah 23:6). Jesus the Mediator is our righteousness. Jesus is reality, the conformity of man to God, and the mediary in which we can again be in accord with God who is the truth.

315. Justice—when the Old Testament speaks of justice it uses the word *tsedeq* which is also used for *righteousness*. The word *tsidkenu* of

Jehovah Tsidkenu (the Lord our Righteousness) is a variation of *tsedeq*.

How is justice righteousness? Justice is what God demands because He is good—justice is the conformity to the reality that God made and then called good; justice is the entrustment of oneself to God the Creator.

Social justice that does not dry up like a puddle of spilled water *must be* the outworking of true justice—righteousness—the entrustment of oneself to reality. That is, it must be by faith alone, evidenced in obedience to Christ. Justice by any other means will collapse in upon itself and soon wield cruelty, for it is founded upon man's flittering opinion. One man's justice is another's tyranny.

How are we to "let justice roll down like living waters" as the prophet Amos says? What this means is that we as creatures are not to damn (spelling intended) up the way things ought to be. We are not to contort the order of reality spoken by God.

We cannot do justice unless it is done by Christ, unless Christ mediates it through us. We cannot be righteous, we cannot trust in God who is ultimate reality unless it is through Jesus—the Lord our Righteousness.

The Lord our Righteousness: The Lord our Origin/Creator/Ultimate Reality.

316. Jesus Christ: He is the negative and positive charge that sparks the light, and is the lightning rod to absorb the strike: He is the lighting rod of trust. He is our righteousness because He starts our heart to throb in rhythm with reality.

Truth is exclusive by definition. Christ is the Truth. Christ then is exclusive. This is not prejudice or metaphysical bigotry; this is not man set over man, rather, it is God set over man, good set over evil, reality set over phantom rumors.

The only way to the Father is through Christ—the only way to live in accordance with reality is to trust reality. This is beautifully simple! "I am the way, and the truth, and the life. No one comes to the Father except through me. If you know me, you will know my Father also" (John 14:6-7). This is not egoism or a vain philosophy, but this is ultimate realism.

"He has showed you, O man, what is good. And what does the Lord require of you? To act justly and to love mercy and to walk humbly with your God" (Micah 6:8). How are we to act justly and to love mercy unless it is done by Christ, unless Christ mediates such things through us—for the law has shown us to have failed? As in Genesis, here we see that God has revealed what is good ("He has showed you, O man")—it was not needed for man to say what is good or evil when it was revealed by the Creator. What God says, is.

What is justice? Living in accordance with our true origin.

There is no justice without faith, without entrustment to the Creator God who gave all a good purpose. We are not meant to violate, to murder, to hate; we are not meant to gang rape the earth, to horde treasures in vaults while others are empty handed and belly-bloated; we are not meant to treat a human as an animal, an animal as a human; we are not meant to live in deception; we are not meant to be God; and God is not to be looked upon as though He were a man; Justice is upholding the order of creation. Justice is trusting the way God crafted shalom; it is as simple as "the way things ought to be."

If there is no God, then there is no "ought to be" and there is no justice for all is equal—rape, love, charity, torture.

This correlation of *justice* and *righteousness* shows us the great continuity between the Old and New Testament: the God of wrath that made mountain tops into the likes of Vesuvius is the same God that touched humanity with a velvet hand, and who hung upon a cross bleeding. The God who gave sweet grace to nations and men in the desert of Sinai is the same God who called out "you brood of vipers!" and also overturned silver-tongued tables in the temple court. The wrath and mercy of God always move together—they are the concurrent light and heat of love. Is God never not Himself?

The marrow that runs all the bone of Scripture is *righteousness*. It is Jesus Christ.

"Oh my people, what have I done to you?
    In what have I wearied you? Answer Me!
For I brought you up from the land of Egypt,
    and redeemed you from the house of bondage;
and I sent before you Moses,
    Aaron, and Miriam.
O my people, remember what Balak king of Moab devised,
    and what Balaam son of Beor answered him,
and what happened from Shittim to Gilgal,
    that you may know the righteousness of the Lord" (Micah 6:3-5).

Is this not God telling man to remember the divine acts, the gifts of the great exodus and the establishment of peace that were each a movement to restore man to entrusting his Creator? The stories of men tell the glories of God! He is to be trusted.

"Brothers, think of what you were when you were called. Not many of you were wise by human standards; not many were influential; not many were of noble birth. But God chose the foolish things of the world to shame the wise; God chose the weak things of the world to shame the strong. He chose the lowly things of this world and the despised things—and the things that are not—to nullify the things that are, so that no one may boast before

Him. It is because of Him that you are in Christ Jesus, who has become for us wisdom from God—that is, *our righteousness*, holiness, and redemption. Therefore, as it is written: 'Let him who boasts boast in the Lord'" (1 Cor. 1:26-31).

317. Wisdom—what is it? It is living, acting, in accordance with the truth; it is skill at living. How does one acquire such wisdom—seeking through ancient vellum and papyrus texts! No—trusting in God! Wisdom starts in faith.

"The fear of the LORD is the beginning of wisdom: a good understanding have all they that do His commandments: His praise endures forever" (Psalm 111:10).

Christ is made our wisdom—Christ is our skill in living! The ground has just shaken! I must take off my shoes! Christ is our skill at living! He must do the commandments for us—for we are unable! Now through him—we are able!

Christ *is* our righteousness! Are you so cold! This should stir the embers in our bones!

"If any of you lacks wisdom, let him ask of God, who gives to all liberally and without reproach, and it will be given to him" (James 1:5).

Righteousness is not the keeping of a law; it is the pivotal relationship. This is because ultimate reality is a person, not an abstraction. Righteousness is trust in a person; trust in the one who set this whole universe spinning, who anchored it within his love!

318. "Then the word of the Lord came to him: 'This man will not be your heir, but a son coming from your own body will be your heir.' He took him outside and said, 'Look up at the heavens and count the stars—if indeed you can count them.' Then he said to

him, 'So shall your offspring be.' Abram believed the Lord, and He credited it to him as righteousness" (Genesis 15:4-6).

Now consider the writings of Paul: "Consider Abraham: 'He believed God and it was credited to him as righteousness.' Understand then, that those who believe [entrust] are the children of Abraham. The Scripture foresaw that God would justify Gentiles by faith, and announced the Gospel in advance to Abraham: 'All nations will be blessed through you.' So those who have faith are blessed along with Abraham, the man of faith....Clearly no one is justified before God by the law, because, 'The just [the righteous] will live by faith'" (Galatians 3:6-11).

He goes on: "Christ redeemed us from the curse of the law by becoming a curse for us, for it is written, 'Cursed is everyone who is hung on a tree.' He redeemed us in order that the blessing given to Abraham might come to the Gentiles through Christ Jesus, so that by faith we might receive the promise of the Spirit" (Galatians 3:7-14).

The curse of the law was not the law itself, but man's inability to reach its golden mark. Christ is *sashed* in the golden mark of the law, dressed in the purity of innocence that it demands.

Romans 4:17 reveals the object of Abram's faith was *the God that called into being that which doesn't exist*—Creator God; also, *the God who gives life to the dead*—Father God who resurrected His Son, the Savior, Christ Jesus. Abraham had faith in God the Creator to be his Savior—he did not entrust his origin or salvation to himself as Adam did. The righteousness of God, *of Christ*, was credited to Abraham. This is the death toll for religion.

319. Abraham is the Father of faith for he bowed to God twice—to the Creator, and to the Savior who makes the dead living; for Abraham looked forward to the day of Christ.

Atonement is the action of love tearing the veil that separates man from God—righteous violence! It is the costly love that binds together, that unites, that melts divorced hearts and forges them in accord. It is the undoing of a false tension and the re-weaving of shalom.

Atonement is the hammer strike that metes out the heat of justice to a world in winter's hold; the prying light of mercy to scale-covered eyes.

Atonement is the friction that bears righteousness; it is grace broken over humanity by the incarnation, crucifixion, resurrection, and ascension of Jesus Christ.

When Jesus says "Be perfect like your father is perfect" He is not instituting an extended ladder of achievement, but is shattering all ladders of achieving righteousness. In one breath Jesus has just pronounced the unified theory of everything—God alone, *Deo Sola*. One cannot be perfect alone; if one exists, then one is in dependence upon the goodness of God. One cannot be perfect like the Father—but one must be like the Father. So Christ has just shared with the world a resounding declaration of the necessity of Grace. In that swift utterance He shattered all hopes of moralism! One cannot attain what needs to be attained. God alone provides salvation—the gray drizzle of moralism the denial of this bright hope.

When we are seen by God we must be seen under the covering of Christ—If Christ is our covering we will be seen with an alien righteousness, a righteousness not our own, but now clothing us as though it was our own. Perfection comes when we are known to be flawed—when we bow to Christ and we are wrapped in the arms of righteousness. We are released from the earth of our sins like a sapphire from the belly of a dark mountain—we can now shine in the sun. Only in Christ are we our true selves.

"Abram believed the Lord, and He credited it to him as righteousness" (Genesis 15:4-6). The pivot is trust; it has always been trust, from Adam to Abraham, from David to Paul—from Paul to you.

It is rightly placed trust that soothes the existential ache. It is the misappropriation of trust that separates us from ourselves and mocks life by making it a bawdy masquerade.

~The Naked Ache~

320. To what can we compare the human condition? We are like the keepers of a great secret; a secret so powerful that it could change everything—and for that, it was kept even from *the keepers*. *The keepers'* apparatus for protection was an endless parade to divert and entertain, to keep them away from this *secret*, in which they might look into if the carnival came to an end. The greatest fear was the end of the parade, so *the keepers'* greatest passion was the maintaining of the distraction.

And so it was, that with distraction being the lofty goal, there was little concern about what the parade wore or just how it writhed through the streets—its one concern was not to remember—and this self-amnesia took all shapes. The parade was all things with abandon: a black parade, a burlesque, a homely thing, a pornographic stride, a macabre procession, a camo-clad military march, a fantasy pageant, a spectacle of religious vestments, a pragmatic drive, a creeping of apathy, the sway of black tattoos and waterfalls of blue ink, the steady progression of papier-mâché faces. All was allowed among these keepers of the secret—except to remember that one word that would reveal the secret beneath. This is the masquerade.

321. *Nakedness* is the sign of alienation, and *covering* the sign of intimacy. In nakedness, we stand alone as though we were all that was in existence; yet lovers in intimacy are covered with each other, and the children of God are covered by the love of Christ.

When one shames another, they strip them. Tyrants are always fond of stripping their adversaries. Nakedness speaks not of one man's shame, but the disunion of all men, the distortion in relationships.

Sin is alienation. There are four limbs to the fallen and naked body: alienation from the self; alienation from one's neighbor; alienation from God; alienation from reality. It was the break from

God that caused the estrangement of these other three—like a heart wrecked by a heart attack, the limbs then went cold and the vibrant mind faded to grey matter.

322. Alienated from God, masks become necessary. We must hide ourselves from others in order to maintain civilization, in order to not destroy each other or to not collapse violently inwards. Secrets are the necessary binds of the *civilization of man* that is separated from the *Kingdom of God*. The civilization of man functions by shadows; the Kingdom of God lives by light that moves though all things. Secrets are the straps that hold masks to faces.

Secrets are a defense measure; without them the civilization of man would fall apart in trauma. This is why man is clothed—to stave off the disintegration of coming to truly know ourselves and the multitudes of others that pass us by in the streets. Masks become the props that are needed to manipulate ourselves and our neighbors.

But to know God one must stand naked again and spurn the masks necessary for living in man's world. God called out, "Where are you…" This was not a question, but a call to man to stand before God as creature, and to acknowledge the reason and order of creation.

The heart was cast in the forge of reality, breathed to life by the Word of truth—so there is a love/hate, push/pull dynamic in the crafting of and strapping on of masks. We hate that they are necessary, and they are necessary by means of our own designs and desires. We hate that they are designed by our hate—so we hide them from ourselves.

Why the masks—because of the terror that is beneath—because of the empty black space of no countenance. We do not have a face; we are not known as a true being until we are a creature of God, invested with a face by the glory of God—given an identity when the light of the Word destroys the darkness that claims itself to be "God!"

Our own pride, the very darkness of our vacant-face, is the mask-maker; it is the great mimicker, the inauthentic architect. God clothed Adam and Eve to point towards the face of Christ—yet we mask ourselves because we desire to create our own identity. As long as we have a mask, we have no face.

Do not push this on Hollywood alone. Do not *otherize* this. No, it is us—all of us. It is in Tinsel Town and Mundania; in the giant towers of the city and along the streets of suburban sprawl. It is the superstar and the homeless—both who might numb their wounds with a bottle. It is the doctor who parades in degrees, the housewife who parades with compulsive neatness, the nerd who protects his heart with his brain, the athlete who finds acceptance in strength, the priest who carnivals in tradition, the laborer and his sweat, the professor, the child, the aged, the broker, the broke, the fraternity brother, the absent father, the stylish, the square, the virgin, the pimped.

One of the favorite masks of man: The crowd.

We all find poses and postures to conceal the cracks. We turn our tricks to silence our troubles. We dress up and parade to stave off boredom—boredom, that great silent creaking that speaks of our true condition.

323. There are powerful *evidences* for God in the dissonances of our existence: anxiety, despair and boredom. These dissonances reveal a standard of existence; a dissonance is defined from a standard. Moralism is the amplifier of anxiety; and again, anxiety is the cognition of knowing we are less than what we are meant to be; it is our sub-surface fear of judgment, and our desire for embrace.

Despair is the denial of who we are—the *denied* discord of the disunited self. Boredom is the fear of recognizing our despair and anxiety. These exist because there is a good God, and we are not He, though we long to have His throne. These are back-handed gifts of God—they are spiritual nerves that tell us something is wrong. They spike fire in our system; they shoot impulses that cry, "No! Not this way! No more masks!"

Boredom is the silent scream we cannot bear to hear. If we trace its quiet line, we will be overwhelmed by shame.

Beneath boredom is a great fault line of shame. We cover our shame wildly, elegantly, and creatively. This long black parade started with the simple cover of fig leaves. And like the fig leaves, the cover of our ostentatious costumes won't do. There is one who sees us. We need a more severe covering—one that cost love and life.

324. Nakedness is the expression of self-origin, of creature claiming to be Creator—the denial of the true Creator; and so, it is to see oneself as god. Yet this is why we cover ourselves, because we believe we are gods, yet our nakedness, our creature-ness reveals that we are not gods. Nakedness speaks of both our former glory and our devastating sin. We were once dressed in the regalia of *relationship with God…*

We are ashamed of being known, of being fully exposed. Don't let the popular hobby of exposing human flesh fool you! The nude, too, have inner landscapes to hide. They may use a manicured and naked body as their rebellious variance of costume—as a pink camouflaged wall to keep real intimacy from occurring, to keep real self-revelation at a great distance; but they too fear exposure that they cannot control. We may let others see our toned body, but rarely do we let others see into our emaciated nature, or read the handwritten pages of our soul.

God clothes us. God did not send Adam and Eve east of Eden bare skinned to the wind to further shame them. With grace, He clothed them with the world's first sacrifice. He covered them and said, "Again, when the time is fulfilled, I will be your covering, I will be your garment of righteousness! I will be the lover that covers you again with glory!"

From first to last, God has offered grace. He clothed *the shamed* with the skin of an innocent; their clothes a perpetual reminder of their shame; their clothes a perpetual reminder of God's grace and who we are meant to be; their clothes a foretelling of Jesus. Instantly, upon the heels of utter rejection, God in His unfathomable goodness gave grace!

The great shame of our nature is that we are less than we are meant to be.

325. *All these words about nakedness—they are only symbolic, mythic, not applicable or seen in my daily life!* This is far from true. The well-known philosopher Jean-Paul Sartre didn't like that He was *revealed* to God. He resisted the idea of an omniscient God who could always see him. He refused to believe in God because he felt it was demeaning to be utterly seen by the Creator.

Sartre did not want to be seen. He called this danger of being seen *the gaze*. He saw *the gaze* of others as a source of shame for the self. He even called the gaze of others *hell*. In his famous play called *No Exit*, he frames it like this: "So this is hell. I'd never have believed it. You remember all that we were told about the torture chambers, the fire and brimstone, the 'burning marl.' Old wives' tales! There's no need for red-hot pokers. Hell is—other people!"

Sartre believed that we perceive others perceiving us, and the act of such perception (the gaze) objectifies us—steals our true freedom of being, makes us less, and alienates us. In response, we see the other as superior to us, and therefore we try to show ourselves as superior to them. Therefore, warfare of social interactions ensues over the power for freedom and identity control.

As Sartre shows, in the most banal motions of life we experience shivers of the *naked truth*. Think of it; you are walking down a street, into a store, and you come to the realization that a stranger is staring you down. The stare, the gaze of another person makes us feel exposed, violated. Something about the stare involuntarily dredges up an ancient pride—along with its fists of frustration, teeth of anger, tremor of anxiety, and shadow of shame.

It is as if the gazing person knows us in a secret way, a compromising way that might leak our hidden thoughts and closet actions to the civilized world—as if their stare is truly all knowing.

Reasonably, their stare doesn't leak out our inner life; but like a magnet, the stare draws the iron shards of our heart together so we notice them in a red-hot instant. We become aware of our *less-than-intended state*. For this reason, the simplicity of a stare and the complexity of shame witnesses to the truth of God's Word. Have you never felt guilty just from another's glance? Even the glance of a stranger?

We hate the stare because it reminds us of our condition we try so laboriously to suppress.

Yet, to be known by God is the great glory of humanity—not the dehumanization of it! It is the greatness for which we were born, not the despair we find in life.

The despair we find in life is the threat of being uncovered while hiding ourselves from God's gaze. To be found by God is to look into the reality of our great shame—the pride which initiated the shame, which only spirals wider, and for that, it will not seek to acknowledge the shame—the acknowledgement that would be its healing!

Despair is a life on the run from reality—the self spiraling further from itself.

326. Our inability to reveal ourselves shows our inability to love—our inability to glorify God. This does not mean we should unbuckle and get naked physically. It does mean that we ought to throw down our pretenses and get naked with God. It means we expose ourselves as the shamed one we are so that we may be remade again with a good heart—dressed in beauty that is the righteous clothing of Christ.

This simply means we are set free from our shame by the un-shame of another who is acting as our proxy. It means someone gave us His flak jacket, and then took a volley of bullets made especially for our heart. We are set free from shame, and we have been found innocent and good under the robe of Christ.

Atonement is what transmutes the gaze of God from a torture to a treasure immeasurable; from the glare of a persecutor to the desired look of a lover. His look was always love.

The greatest of all fears is that Jesus may one day say, "I never knew you." Is it any wonder that Dante rendered all his figures in Hell naked? He did this because it was inspired by the Bible—the unredeemed are naked, exposed for what they are; the redeemed robed in righteousness—they have become more than god-pretending creatures.

It is common to think that salvation comes in us knowing God (here is a devious subtlety in words that allows us to remain hidden while God is exposed), but this is not what Jesus says. Salvation comes when God knows us, when we shed the pride of fig leaves, of carnival costumes, and open our shame to God: "I am a wayward creature. You made me from your very breath—yet I have spit at you…forgive me."

Salvation comes in humility; when we reveal ourselves to God then we are known by Him. So let us stop hiding from Him. Let us stop hiding from Him by retreating into the shadows of the world, or into the darker shadows of the religions of men.

This is important to understand: It is not because God was unsure of our nature and needed us to reveal what we were concealing; but rather, it is because God knew our nature and so He wanted us to confess, to acknowledge the reality of our grasp at godhood; to open ourselves to Him in trust, that He may clean and heal the fatal wound. He wants us to live in reality.

Those who admit their nakedness will be clothed. Those who deny their soul-nudity will remain naked and anxious. "Blessed are those whose lawless deeds have been forgiven, and whose sins have been covered" (Romans 4:7).

327. When we go to The Lion, His claws tear the melancholy from us as spring strips away the winter's hold. It is crushing to the mortal man, this joy that rips away the grey haunt of our brooding nature that has exponentially shrunken our world.

When we go to The Lion we become more real for we are found more joyful. We are more joyful because that is the weight of reality, the glory of God. We must remember that there is brilliant laughter in heaven, and when its light breaks through the silent clay of our ears, our wispy hearts and minds will be enlarged, becoming more and more real—like the wooden Pinocchio becoming a real boy; or like an idea being fleshed out in action.

A human is enlarged, realized, and made manifest by the joy of the Lord—by the faith, hope, and love that is the veracity of life. Sadness comes and goes like a summer rain; grief comes like a whirlwind then leaves; but behind these temporal disturbances there is an eternal secret, a constant blazing sun—a brilliant and winged reality called joy. Our essence is no longer a languid shadow or paper mask, but a vitalized be-ing.

The *eighth deadly sin* is sadness—it is the echo within the self of being from God, but attempting to live without him. It is the residue and shiver of *not being who we are meant to be*. Sadness should always be painted naked, shivering.

328. We masque in opposites; we are inclined to both writhe in the dust and to fly straight into the sun. Why pursue heaven and hell? Why revel in the dark *and* the light. Is it because we do not know the difference between? If so, then how wanting is the soul not to know heaven from hell!

How is it that we seek *and* shun *both* horror and beauty? What is it about the soul that trembles at both what is appealing and what is appalling? It is the odd, but perfectly cut stone called Christianity that answers the oddity and irregularity of our nature. It tells us why we dress up in the bone and canvas wings of a devil, or wear the feathers of a cherub. It tells us why we are drawn to and afraid of nakedness.

If we have never been terrified by what's inside, then we have not acknowledged the stringent light of grace. The gratitude that springs from grace is the overthrow of this terror—the overthrow of the anxiety of ill-born origin.

Salvation not only redeems us from external entropies and dark influences, but the greater overthrow is of the disunited-self. We need to be saved from ourselves. Anxiety is the buzz, the white noise, that when translated, says over and over again, "Save me—from myself!"

329. What is the remedy to do away with my automatic masks that do not seek my permission, that do not hold back in rising up?

Worship!—the acceptance of reality! The praise of God is the remedy to posing; worship is aligning oneself with reality; it is the antidote to the epidemic of the mannequins—it is what makes us real at last. Worship is the garment that stills the shiver of sadness.

God help me! For I need no help in worshipping—though I need help worshipping that which is true! You who are good!

Help me to worship the one who dressed all the world in splendor, yet hung shamefully naked upon a cross, exposed and humiliated, while I played games for His garments!

Think upon it; there they were, those Roman soldiers gambling over the clothing of Christ, throwing bone dice, when over their heads hung Christ who was at that very moment carrying their shame in order that they may be clothed in His righteousness. The irony pierces like a whaling arm—like a spear to the belly!

The naked ache because they have shaded themselves under icy garments and dark-sided masks of self-design, rather than stand in the sun and fire of the mantle of God. They ache because they have frozen from the bones outward—they no longer are tied to the dynamic warmth of their origin. They are *the broken*, but unwilling to be beautiful.

330. "Woe to the rebellious children, says the Lord, that take counsel, but not of me; and that cover with a covering, but not of my spirit, that they may add sin to sin" (Isaiah 30:1).

"Bless the Lord, O my soul. O Lord my God, thou art very great; thou art clothed with honor and majesty. Who covers thyself with light as with a garment: who stretches out the heavens like a curtain" (Psalm 104:1-2).

One of the many tensions of our existence is the desire to be exposed and known; yet we feel the deep impulse to shield and hide. We desire intimacy, but hate what the honesty it demands will surely expose.

An irony: The self-consumed have no true self to consume because they deny the infinite! For this they will know no rest, only an eternal ache, and an un-sated hunger.

What is it to be naked? To have a disunity of the self; to have despair creep into the soul and start its prying, its wedging apart of the self. Nakedness is the dissonance of the fallen self; the existence out of joint!

Repentance is the acknowledgement of our despair.

We are becoming who we are meant to be when we acknowledge that we are naked, that we are impotent—and that we need God to be ourselves.

To be clothed in Christ we must call out, "Look, I am an *emperor* with no clothes! How foolish I have been!"

~ Rest/Paradox~

331. The Gospel abhors mediocrity. The tension of holding good things together does *not* speak of compromise; it is not half this or half that. To hold goods together one must trust, and to *half-trust* is not to trust at all. One cannot have *half-faith*. The half-measure will prove to be no-measure, and will be thrown into the ash pit, will be vomited away. Were we not warned by Christ about being lukewarm—either hot or cold?

One can have small faith, but small (*little, young, etc*) is not half. It is said, "Lord, I believe; help my unbelief!" not, "I half-believe, help my half-belief become belief!" To cut in half is to compromise, it is to make for murder, for monsters, for messes—but not trust.

Tension is a condition of *either/or*—a condition of the antithetical nature of reality. And for that it comes from Shalom, a perfect existence, a peace and a standard—it comes from The Absolute. This means that one does not hold evil *and* good in tension and call it good! No! For one must choose either good or evil. And the taproot of all is the good God who created, and said "It is good...it is very good."

The world is not dualistic—it is not born out of equal evil and good! It was born of good alone—this is why we can say there is right and wrong, good and evil. This is why there is true peace, and why the heart can find existential rest.

This is why we must trust God—for He is the good. To trust anything over God is to compromise the truth, to wage war against Him; for there is either our good origin, or our spurning of that good origin.

One must say "I love the world and hate God," or "I love God and hate the world." God exists or he does not—one must choose one or the other. It is because of the either/or nature of reality that I can say, "we must hold in tension the good gifts of God!"

Any tension, any *both/and* that is held, presupposes the either/or antithetical nature of existence—and this relies upon a God who it The Absolute. This is to say that reality is not contradictory. God is God—Sovereign and good.

Truly, we live in a unified *uni*verse; that is why it is called such; and it is the place of man to have a unified will to obey God. To be double-minded is to live in contradiction, to tear at reality, and to doubt God—to be His enemy.

Let me show you a battlefield: Here it is, full of motion, full of writhing and loud pounding. It is formed of slopes and curves, with troughs laden with blood. There are inroads, out-roads and byways—and it all rests upon a golden plain called desire. It is the human heart. It is the heart, the seat of desires, the throne of the will where choice is made. *To love God and hate the world* or to *hate God and love the world*: this is the Great War that has birthed all wars; it is this antithesis that's marks our destiny. Now, we must act! Choose! God or man—Gospel or religion!

332. Religion is amusement; that is why the honest person sees it as such; that is why it has been loitering since the thud of the fall; that is why it is universal. Religion is a diversion, the great universal distracter of mankind.

To what can we compare religion? Religion is like the person who tries to hide in the shadow of a great giant, and says to their shaded self, "I am too close for him to see me! If I just trace his movements I will stay hidden!" But they are soon crushed under the heel of one who was looking to *help them*—for the giant was not great only in size, but was a good giant all along.

Religion will inevitably bear twins: despair and anxiety. It bears these twins—one sulking and one screaming—because it asks us to divorce the heart from the mind, faith from reason. This is because religion, all the way to its deepest root, its unfounded taproot, is irrational. (And remember, religion is moralism and moralism is nothing more than a self-salvation project—the idolatry of man.) Religion is irrational because it denies the reality of the human condition—we cannot breach the man-God gap no matter how busy our hands, no matter how meditative our stance.

Religion is institutionalized anxiety; organized despair. There is no rest in its elegant bed chambers. But the Gospel of God, ah!— There is true peace!

A Christian's tension is not anxiety. Anxiety is like paper tossed and boxed in the wind. A Christian's tension is surety; it is standing strong, like a deep rooted oak tree, against the winds that once whipped us about like tissue paper. The Christian's tension is resistance.

The *religious* live lives of self-reliance and rebellion; the follower of Jesus lives a life of dependence *and* resistance. Trust—this is the pivot, this is the hinge—do we trust Jesus Christ? Only when we trust Christ can we truly resist the world.

Why do we, somewhere deep within, think religion will work? It is because the Creator must be the Savior; and since we live out of self-origin and are the *self-made*, then we could also be the savior. The Christian trusts God as both Creator *and* Savior; those untrusting of God, by antithesis, entrust themselves as both creator and savior.

Our works of self-salvation reveal who we believe the Creator is.

When religion divides the intended unity of the human being, the mind sulks because it can find no answers, and the heart screams because its finds no rest. In religion the mind is an amnesiac and the heart an insomniac.

Religion is irrational for it is a man-originated kingdom— a virtual reality. Man, being the center of *his own universe*, cannot then coherently call God the center or his origin (though religion asks him to) —for it is not rationally based upon his deepest religious presuppositions. Man cannot worship the creator if man is trying to be his own savior.

Such incoherence drives the soul crazy, and forces one to abandon faith for reason, reason for faith, or to live incoherently by compartmentalizing them (Sunday, faith. Monday through Friday, reason).

Religion asks the heart to betray the mind, and the mind to commit treason.

The divide of mind and heart is not of God—it is of the religious man.

Religion is the expression of a soul in unrest; a seasick pushing towards and pulling away from the truth. It is unreasonable striving; the cutting of the ocean with a knife.

The Gospel synchronizes the mind and the heart—it holds them together by the true magnet of their origin—God the Creator. In this union of God and man, and of man with himself, there is peace and rest.

333. So let the Christian go to The Lion, stand in the warmth of His countenance! Let His claws swipe away your soul-disguise; shatter the plaster of your mask! Let us reveal ourselves in humility, for this is true love, because only then do we acknowledge the reality of God by revealing the fractures of *the fall*. Revealing our nature is glorifying God; His strength is made perfect in our weakness. In confessing our fractures we confess our need for our Creator; we acknowledge the intended order of creation and no longer strain to make and keep masks.

In the confession of our fractures we reveal the reality of the Creator and our need for the Savior—we bend both knees to

Jesus—and when we bow, our mask falls off. An even greater wonder is when we rise with Him His radiance gives us a face.

The only way to rise above the Coliseum of the world is to go to The Lion. We are to stand amidst the horde of distorted masks as well as live before the *face of God, coram Deo*, and resign the absurdity that we ourselves are Caesar, that we ourselves are god. We are to go and to let the ivory teeth of The Lion sink into the soul's marrow so we may be born again to bear His beauty.

To be pierced by the gift of love is to rest in His mane; to be defended by His strength—wild and pure.

The maw and claws of love change us. Love is not a velvet pillow we sleep on, it is a thick mane we die peacefully in.

334. Seek not martyrdom—that is vanity; seek to live a Christ centered life; to trust Jesus. The pursuit of martyrdom will betray the truth by trusting in a self-seeking fame; the pursuit of Jesus Christ will find us in the will and glory of God.

Seek not balance. A concentrated effort only on "theological balance" will lead to vertigo and too much *self-consciousness*—it will birth an ugly idolatry that at first glance looked like a beautiful baby. Rather, we should focus on obeying Jesus. This brings balance and a focus on truth rather than the self.

We should disobey ourselves, and obey God. "Those who love me will obey me," Jesus said. Without obedience faith is a mere musing, an anaesthetizing daydream. We must remember that "the work of the Lord is this, to believe in the one He has sent." Trust without action is not trust, but a lie set atop unbelief.

335. *Teleological* means "in regard to the end". If we live *teleological* then we will also live fully in the moment. We must remember that God's glory is the end of everything—the beginning of everything. When God is the end that we have in mind and in heart, then all

that is in the moment of living will be the radiance of God—that is, we will live Godly in the present if we have a true understanding of what it means to live for the glory of God.

The Kingdom of God is at hand/the Kingdom is coming! It is both.

Those who live in the past are consumed by despair; those who live in the future are worn phantom-thin by anxiety; but those who live in the present live in trust and rest. In a beautiful irony, it is the person who lives in the present that has the greatest hope for the future. Obedience is always now; obedience bears peace.

If we live *teleologically*, if we live as if the glory of God is our ultimate end, then we will live God-centered; for God can only be our end if He is our means. This is what it means to be faithful, this is what it means to obey: to live for the Glory of God through the mediation of Christ.

336. We are to live in tension, to live amidst paradox, because an *idea of God* can be substituted for God. As we have seen, a Christian is one who does not live in idolatry but rather entrusts themselves to reality. We are not to live in the idolatry of having God figured out, set in an easy box. We are not to stamp Him into *an idea* that we can copyright; that we claim and brandish, wield or withhold. If we do not live in the paradox of God-ward trust, if we do not rest in the tension of living in Christ and dying to our self, then our *God* is only *an idea*— and therefore only an idol.

If our God is an idea then He is an idol. He must be beyond opinion. Orthodoxy must be paradoxical.

337. The Christian in tension finds rest in God alone.

The unrest of our existence is only healed in the replanting of our existence in its true origin. Rest comes when we are no longer an in-between creature strung between the heavens, grasping at a throne that is not ours, yet with feet rooted in the earth as a creature.

Rest comes when we are a creature fulfilling its purpose: ruling over creation and bowing before the Creator. We are to be at home in a righteousness that is not our own; in a universe that is not held together by our efforts; in a place of stewardship—here the heart can rest.

The heart can rest when it is in the hands of the living God who has come through death; the God who has walked the same dusty trails we now walk. This is the rest that surpasses human understanding. And what a rest this is for the mind! It no longer has to destroy itself by seeking to put the heavens within itself! It no longer has to try to be what it was never meant to be.

338. The Christian in tension is one who beholds, as Paul says, "the goodness *and* severity of the Lord" (Romans 11:22). These two cannot be divorced. Think here of gravity; it is both good and severe. Gravity can break your thigh bones when you believe you can fly on your own, when you try to walk on the sky. Yet gravity is wonderful, beautiful—it allows for all life on this planet, and keeps us anchored from spiraling out into the cold of space; it is what allows us to walk on the earth and swim in the sea. To live in accordance with gravity's reality is good; the ramifications of denying gravity are severe.

The Christian in tension is one at peace with God *and* at odds with the *world*. The *world* is that multifarious system of selfish thought and heart that is upside down and inward driven; it is the flashy, but sterile kingdom of pride. If we are friends with the *world*, then we are the enemies of God.

Yet we must understand—this does not mean we do not love humanity or the creation! By no means! This does not mean we are not friends with those who do not know Christ; this does not mean we act brashly and treat people like marked enemies. What this means is that we cannot love the system, the poison of the fallen world, and yet love the opposite kingdom—the rule of love and ultimate reality. So Christianity is odd to the *world*. It does not capitulate; it is countercultural.

339. Jesus said, "My yoke is easy, my burden is light" (Matthew 11:30). Only with faith in Christ do we carry a yoke of rest, a burden that fulfills and satisfies. Jesus is the Lord of the Sabbath—He is the Lord of rest.

The fourth commandment of the Beautiful Standard (to honor the Sabbath) has pointed to Jesus all along! For thousands of years it has stood as a breaker to shatter the hollow vessels of *the idol of identity through work* and the *idol of self-salvation through works*. It has stood as a warning to our paper sailing ships of effort that we have used to lay siege to the island of paradise. It has stood as a warning that nothing gives us ultimate meaning but Jesus Christ alone; and that only those who acknowledge they are broken and incapable are those who find way to the beautiful isle.

None have entered heaven by laying siege to its open gates. None have loved God who have tried to plunder His love.

340. Earlier, it was said that irony is the difference between *the real* and *the ideal*; between *the is* and *the ought*. Here is a great and beautiful irony: Jesus is both *the real* and *the ideal*. He is the expression of reality, the radiance of God; He is perfection. He is man; He is God.

This is a tension that many attempt to do away with. "Man or God?" they say. No! Man *and* God; Man/God! Jesus was fully man and fully God. This is how He can satisfy his own perfect wrath, yet still dispense grace. One cannot be a Christian and do away with this beautiful tension.

Prayer helps us live a life that is in the tension of Shalom's weave. Prayer is the medium of trust.

Prayer is a dependent child speaking to their father—humility highlighting glory. The only power that is not an illusion is the power of dependence upon the ruler of the cosmos— Abba, Father, Creator God.

In all things we must pray; that is, in all things we must be dependent upon God, dependent upon the truth to save us from the lies and our wraith-like actions that shrivel us thin. God crowns the humble with salvation.

341. In the universe there are two possible routes to freedom. One is to crucify God; the other is the crucifixion of God. One dead ends and the other is life's beginning. Humanity seeks freedom by killing God, by cutting the bonds of any celestial rule, by severing any embrace of our origin. But by killing God in our hearts we are only enslaved to death, and the wide world of freedom we sought has become a sharp, suffocating pinpoint. True freedom only comes through the crucifixion of God and its radiating grace.

Only in bowing can we stand upright as human beings. Only under God are we as free as the skies above.

We should note the irony that when the pride of humanity wants to be free from a sovereign God, it wants to "be as free as the skies above"—but the skies above are all subject to the benevolent laws of God's reign. This is comic!

So even in raging war against God, man cannot conceive of an analogy that doesn't depend upon the ruling love of God! There is no sweet metaphor for human autonomy that is apt, because everything is already ruled by the beautiful law of God. All the sweet language of freedom will inevitably point back to God. How beautiful this is—all of man's punch-drunk rage cannot topple over God's love.

All man's kicking and cursing at the ocean or sky will never allow him to hold the universe together—he will only tear at the truth until he trusts the God who holds it together. Man's paradox: he will only know God when he is no longer god. He will only taste the heavens when he is baptized in God's sea.

~The Lamb/The Lion~

342. The just *and* the justifier—Jesus was both at the top of their energies.

The judge becoming the judged: does this not echo the revelation of man being created in the image of God? This is the song of the incarnation; it is the Lamb laying Himself down before the Lion of justice; it is God becoming man to make anew the race of men He made in His image! In this we find the meaning of joy—to be loved by the beautiful Creator and be made anew that we may know Him.

Only joy can awaken the amnesiac. Only the beauty of Glory can tell us the name we have been working for, but unable to earn. Only the beauty of Glory can overcome the violence that bore the amnesia. Joy is a grace—owed to no one—but poured through Christ.

343. Why theology? Why these words and this invested time? Why wrestle through all of this? This is for the fray, the *living through*—not merely armchair musings. It is for joy! And joy is consummated in action, not mere ideas!

Theology is *for* right worship; used any other way and it becomes toxic. It is not the mere love for learning, but the learning about our true love; it is not mainly functional, but it is mainly relational. Theology is for the reorienting of the mind, the dispossessing of ill-affections for holy heart-desires. Theology is not for setting ourselves above others; it is about seeing ourselves under God and within Christ, dependent upon the Holy Spirit.

Why could we not rightly call true theology *theomance?*—for, like an epic romance, it is the story of a hero, of glory, of the broken, of a journey, of trials, and of aching love. God is our hero; God is our champion; God is our God and the Bible is the story of His relationship with His bride—*theomance*. Our story is the paramount love story. The Scriptures are the history of love.

Theology is that haunting ground where romance meets reality, where we find that the *real* and *ideal* meet and kiss. It is the half shaded woods of longing where we see brilliant splays of light, and yet we see there is that which we cannot see in this hour, in this place. Yet the shadows are not irrational, for we know they are the silhouettes of leaves; and beyond our reach, beyond the borders of the grove is the platinum sun that makes sense of both the living light and shifting shadows.

344. All must be tempered by love. Love moves like a hunter; love lays low like a lamb. Love is no rag doll—for it stands *and* it kneels. Real love is an unbearable thing to an upside-down world. Love is what makes living in the upside-down world bearable, and what turns it right-side-up. But not any *love* will turn the topsy-turvy world around; not an impersonal force, not a flabby sentimental notion—no, only the costly love of the personal and infinite Creator; only the love that is good enough to sacrifice itself for the weak and wicked. Only the love that became flesh, died, lived again, and ascended to fill us with His Spirit can overcome and invert the perverted world.

Love is not maudlin, but a martyr—a witness to the truth.

Watch for counterfeit love. Much *love* is not love; it is simply a tool cast in a selfish die—a hammer, a sword, a wrench, a lever to manipulate. We must not be fooled by smiles or easy gestures. Why are we quickly fooled by easy gestures? It is because we desperately ache for authentic love.

We must not be fooled by hearts on sleeves. For if the heart is on the sleeve, it is either a false heart, or we are looking upon a dead person in a most gruesome way. The heart belongs in the chest, living and beating—it is no cufflink, no adornment. Love is foundational, not a decoration as it is so often defined.

Great are the books and the words that speak of love; greater is the Book and the Word that speaks of love's first cause, the love that birthed love—we love because He first loved us (1 John 4:19).

Our capacity for love is our response to His sweet glory.

345. In a world of immense irony, it is reasonable that the cure is called the disease, and the disease is called the cure; love is called the hate and hate is called the love. When true Christianity is accused of causing society's problems, we know then that it is the cure, the cure of Jesus Christ that sends the cancer writhing. So let us not fear persecution, for in it is the fuel in which to glorify God: the sticks in which to build the pyre of un-trust, the stones used to build a wonderful bridge.

Remember Telemachus, whose aim was to glorify God—so he found himself called to stop the popular butcher shop of the Roman Coliseum. As he sought for God's glory as the end of all things, it was God's radiant strength that worked in the moment allowing Telemachus to intervene in the Gladiators' brutal revelry that demeaned and minced the image of God in man. *This moment, for eternity! So God help me.*

We are not to simply mimic what Christ did, as though He were captain in a cosmic and crucial game of follow the leader. The only way to follow the leader who is Christ is to live through Him, let Him be the source of our actions. We are to trust Him, not trace His actions on our own shaky-hand strength! *For* God, *through* Jesus Christ, *by* the Holy Spirit!

346. We are first born broken, then reborn beautiful. We are first born as Caesars, then reborn as servants. This is the tragedy of the fall—it has dropped us all into the current of entropy and we swim with it—we are all born into its torrent of hubris. Then there is the wonder of the incarnation—God himself, in His mercy to us, set Himself into the violent flow of human history.

We are born with the tangle of these words embedded in our hearts: "*sicut erat Dei!*" This is Latin for "you will be as God!" This was that primeval temptation that Adam and Eve fell over, fragmenting their souls, breaking their bodies and the earth.

Yet when we are reborn, God writes anew in our hearts a wonderful script—it is the beautiful revolution: "Heavenly Father, thy will be done!" This is written on us in Christ's handwriting, in Christ blood!

347. *My will* or *Thy will?* This is the silly question that sits so gravely upon all our souls, eating ashes but trying to smile. Can a warring creature tackle over the infinite love of the Creator? Can the selfish desires of man set himself up as judge over the Creator? The question itself is bizarre.

But why talk of such spiritual warring? There is much peace today—isn't there? Christendom is spreading like a forest fire in Asia, Africa, and South America, and the Western world is inundated with churches that are distributing and preaching peace, prosperity, and healing…

…but what is that—a whisper that sounds as if it is coming steadily nearer? What does it say? The whispering is loud enough to make out: "Peace, peace!" And louder it becomes as the people cheer. "Peace, peace" ring the pulpits of men. It is a shout now, a yell, a war cry—a battle cry against the truth!! God forgive us!

In the Lord's service, Jeremiah spoke to the *priests and prophets* these biting words: "They dress the wound of my people as though it were not serious, 'Peace, peace,' they say, when there is no peace" (Jeremiah 6:14).

These *peace criers* were rebuked by the only one who could bring peace, and ironically, they kept peace at bay by not diagnosing the wound—the raging pride of humanity.

Do you think this fashion of men has died away? Today we are made popular and wealthy by dressing wounds in designer clothes, in thin images and silk fabrics—for bandages and salves are not sexy! They do not look appealing! But there is nothing more appalling than covering a cracked skull with a hat to hide, or treating the severing of a finger with the cover of a lacy glove. In these fashion statements there is not peace—only pieces of men and women stitched loosely together.

Peace comes not by external adornments and circumstances, but the posture of the heart: bending to the healer, for we are mortally wounded.

In Jesus there is a peace that surpasses all understanding—that surpasses even the kingdom of man's understanding of success and serenity (Read Philippians 4:4-7).

348. The honest man sees that the world is attracted to violence done against man. At this point, after this journey of learning, it seems there is a *why* to this ugliness; a *why* to the popularity of our hyper-violent movies; a *why* to our wars; a *why* to our innate violent desires. Why? Man is made in the image of God.

Violence done to man is violence done to God in proxy. It is, so to speak, a gross inversion of the crucifixion—man standing in as God's whipping boy.

There is an attraction to violence for the same reason there is religion—it is an attempt to do away with God, to dethrone Him with a kick or a slash, or a work or a rite. When we hate our brother it is because we hate the Father. When we kill our brother, it is because we long to kill the Father. This is why the Christians were bled and thrown under the lion's claws—by killing man they were killing the God they did not want to exist. This wasn't an intellectual move; no, it was a moral movement. It wasn't a conscious thought necessarily—but it was an ancient and dark undercurrent. It was man judging God and exalting himself. The fallen world has fallen on its head—it is upside down.

349. The Kingdom of Heaven is right-side up. Heaven is where the renown of the Lord is the very atmosphere we will breathe and the light we will see by. It is the complete and total reverence of God—and for that, it is the complete respect and love of every image bearer of God.

Respect—*respectus*: literally to *look again*; to *re-look at*. Heaven is where we see all for who they truly are: beautiful bearers of God image.

Heaven is full acknowledgement of reality. It is where all that is ought, *is*. It is the realm where there is no jaundiced lamp or humming neon buzzing like our anxiety, no dying yellow sun to collapse into a black hole; but where all is a glow, shot clean through by pearly radiance—a light that casts no shadow for it penetrates and perfects everything it graces.

"And there will no longer be night; and they will not have need of the light of a lamp nor the light of the sun, because the Lord God will illumine them; and they will reign forever and ever" (Revelation 22:5).

There will be a new heaven, a new earth, a New Jerusalem. What was lost in the garden at humanity's dawn will be restored and enjoyed in more intimate fashion, for the sacrifice of Christ and our adoption as sons sets us in a more glorious end than the Edenic beginning!

Humanity will again be in a garden and in perfect relationship with God—but when it comes to fruition it will be a glorious city of kin, an urban garden of God's people offering fragrant praises and colorful lives of joy.

Genesis tells of the garden established by God; Revelation tells of the tree of life, re-established, made again accessible to man through Jesus Christ. What was lost will be redeemed—it is coming: the restoration, redemption, and re-establishment.

What was lost will be found. The trajectory of history will find its mark: disunion will weave into peace and death's death will be feasted over—we will celebrate the victory over man's autonomy (the ill-eaten fruit) in the communion and feasting of man with God. Until then we remember the remedy and its cost—we remember the sacrifice of Christ in the elements of communion. Like Abel, we look upon our sin—and see it has cost us a life.

350. Jesus Christ—*the Lion and the Lamb*! There is perfect tension in the name—the timbre of it musical in its selflessness, daring in its love.

Jesus: the most humble—the brave one—humanity re-established!

The Lion of Judah is the Lord Jesus Christ. The name Judah means *praise*. The Lion of Praise! Is this not wonderfully odd—praise to the one who would kill the fleeing soul? Odd, but ultimately good! For it is the sickly and selfish gazelle of the soul that is overcome by perfect gold and ivory—overcome by the riches of the King! So let us praise the Lion that devours the wrath we have earned!

Let us praise Jesus Christ by obeying Him and making disciples for His glory. Let us acknowledge we are wounded hearts restored only by the grace of our King—the Lion of Judah, the Lamb who takes away the sins of the world!

351. When the melody of salvation rings in the human heart it sounds fiercely and beautifully, like bright bronze cast in a white-hot heat; it sounds like a warning bell *and* a wedding bell. The regeneration of the human heart is a wedding that annihilates darkness with just violence, with the beauty of God's healing light.

It is the hammer of hope that rings the bell of the human heart; yet this hammer also comes to shatter if that heart is wrapped in an idol.

Christianity is both a revolution *and* a reformation. It must be both. It is a quick surge of power shattering a marble heart; it is a slow and often unseen sea change done inch by sweet inch. It is a quick flashpoint *and* the slow burn of a wick melting a candle's body while shedding light.

The Lion's love can consume us in an instant; His precision-claws slowly cutting the cancer from our souls for years. In an instant the Lamb can gently absorb our fall; over a lifetime His wool can bandage our wounds, stopping the blood's flow and salving the pain. Suddenly, we are slowly coming to life. Suddenly we are adopted—slowly we are becoming children of our Father.

352. Truth can be known. If one does not believe this, then one is not a Christian. This is not my judgment—it is Christ's: "I am the way, and the truth, and the life. No one comes to the Father except through me. If you really knew me, you would know my Father as well. From now on, you do know Him and have seen Him" (John 14:6-7).

If one does not believe truth can be known, then one need not bother to read another word, another book, to think another thought. One cannot even use words such as *absurd* or *contradiction* because they are backhanded definers of truth. Every word ever written speaks of the absolute existence of truth; every argument ever foisted upon the mind that truth is unknowable supports the rationality of knowable truth and points to the ultimate reason: the *Logos*, Jesus Christ. God exists and He is known in the Lord Jesus Christ—He is the truth, and for this, He is the only way.

Why is there only one way? Because the truth is a person—and there is only one Jesus.

353. Humility and confidence: neither comes first—they are born together. They are born together when one is born of the Spirit and the Word; when one gains true humanity through living in Christ.

Be Humble and confident; know and remember, God has determined the time and place in which we live (Act 17:26). There is a wonderful hope that we live by, that we live towards! Our trajectory is Christ, our enabler and inviter—Jesus Christ!

"Seek the Lord your God, and when you do, you will come to know it was He who found you." Here again the hammer of hope hit my heart, and I find what was found before by one found by God! I am found thinking the very words of Augustine: "I should not have sought unless you had already found me." For when I thought that the Lion was in my crosshairs, I was surprised to feel a mane upon my cheek and the sting of a claw already in my heart.

Repentance is not the chasing after of God, not the hunting of Him as though He were a sprinting deer or some more wild game! Repentance is accepting that you have been found by God, and that you were running from Him as a fugitive. It is the breathtaking realization that we are lost, crooked, collapsed—and loved.

Repentance is when this reality presses upon us, surges through us and glows through our fractures. Yes, we are to ask, but the question has first set itself before us; yes, we are to seek, but it is the purpose of life that has come to us; yes, we are to knock, but it is the strange beckoning door that has appeared before us.

We must repent—change our minds, change the very forms and trajectory of our thoughts and our trust. The Beautiful Standard of God has shown us as distorted and dark, torqued and bent. We must trust in Jesus Christ, His life, death, burial, resurrection, and ascension. In Him is atonement, at-one-ment; in Him is reunion with God, our great origin.

354. In Jesus converge the hammer-stroke of the fall and the sweet release of new life; on the cross converge man's evil, God's love, meted forgiveness, and served justice.

The righteous live by faith; if we are to be made righteous it is through trust in Jesus Christ. "Therefore, since we have been justified through faith, we have peace with God through our Lord Jesus Christ, through whom we have gained access by faith into this grace in which we now stand" (Romans 5:1-2).

To fear god—and to be *reformed* at last! What joy! The fear of God is the love that quells human fear; a life in dependent love upon God dissipates fear. We are to fear God and to be unafraid of man. To fear *and* to be unafraid—this is a tension in the life of a follower of Jesus Christ. There is great bravery and humility in the reformed heart.

355. *We* cannot break the glacial contract of death we have signed— the covenant of our fatal wound—for we are suspended, and inert within it. Yet in Christ, we trust in our true and better origin—our redeemer—the author and sustainer of the New Contract, the New Covenant of life. Christ restores us to whom we were meant to be, and brings us back to our origin as a child of the living God.

Therefore hear the word of the Lord, you scoffers
  who rule this people in Jerusalem.
You boast, "We have entered into a covenant with death,
  with the grave we have made an agreement.
When an over whelming scourge sweeps by, it cannot touch us,
  for we have made a lie our refuge
and falsehood our hiding place."

So this is what the Sovereign Lord says:
  "See, I lay a stone in Zion, a tested stone,
a precious cornerstone for a sure foundation;
  the one who trusts will never be dismayed.

I will make justice the measuring line
  And righteousness the plumb line;
hail will sweep away your refuge, the lie,
  and water will overflow your hiding place.
Your covenant with death will be annulled;
  your agreement with the grave will not stand.
When the overwhelming scourge sweeps by,
  you will be beaten down by it.
As often as it comes it will carry you away;
  morning after morning, by day and by night,
It will sweep through" (Isaiah 28:14-19).

Like the Israelites who are here revealed as trusting in the Egyptians (whose religion was a "cult of the dead") to save them from the brutal Assyrian army rather than trusting in the Sovereign Lord, all humanity has vainly trusted in *man* and *religion* for their salvation.

To trust in man over God is to sin—and to incur death. But to trust in the *precious cornerstone* that is the *sure foundation*—to trust in Jesus Christ (see The Keystone chapter) is to live in peace and to never be dismayed; for to trust in Christ is to trust in the truth, in reality.

Man trusts in man—he will be devoured. Man trusts in God, in the cornerstone, in the foundation of all reality—he will live eternally. "The one who trusts will never be dismayed," for he lives in accordance with reality.

History played out the promises of God: Israel, the Northern Kingdom, trusted in man rather than God, and fell to the juggernaut of the Assyrian army. Israel trusted in the power of horses and weaponry—yet denied the very maker of the muscled horse, the originator of steel and blood. "Some trust in chariots and some in horses, but we trust in the name of the Lord our God" (Psalm 20:7).

356. God is nothing to us unless He is everything to us. If God is less than everything then He is merely a religion—an idol—and an idol is nothing. "We know that an idol is nothing at all in the world and that there is no God but one (1 Cor. 8:4).

"*We are gods!*" the world claims. "No! Not so! *We are God's!*"—this is the voice of truth. We belong to God; we are His creations.

Reality is greater than—yes—even the swollen ego of fractured man. Man cannot hold the world together—and so he must try to control it by compartmentalizing it, moralizing it, ritualizing it, rupturing it, and then moving the pieces about as he judges it all.

After he has slashed at God, then man takes to the unity of creation a sacred dagger of religion, or Occam's razor wielded with an atheist's hand.

We dissect the universe into thin slices because we distrust God who has said, "This is how it is!" We have crowned ourselves gods (because we have also dissected God and not found any life in the corpse we believed was His), but we are lousy *gods*, for neither our miters nor our microscopes can keep the world together.

Idolatry/humanism is like building a snowman on the careening ice of an avalanche; like building a house of cards on the spinning rocks of a rockslide.

Idolatry is not simply the imaginative stories of the Greeks, nor some pole danced around in a tribal fertility dance; but idolatry is religion, atheism, moralism, apathy and agnosticism. Idolatry is everything that has man as its center—it is *humanism*.

Idolatry is the absurd! It is the sad seed of all insanity.

The shadow of our idol is tied to our bent knees. Do you see? Idolatry is not just the bowing to a god, but the *being a god of false design. It is the absurdity of bowing to the self and chasing after the shadow in whatever form it takes*! Bowed to the self, life stretches out before us as only a shadow; we must turn and face the light that we have set our backs to.

With an ancient urgency come these words to us: "If you hear God's voice harden not your hearts—turn to God, for He has called you. Turn and live!" (Ezekiel 33:11)

357. In the beginning God created—but having fallen far from His words of "It is very good," the world lay in moan and wait to hear: *"tetelestai"* — *"it is finished!"* From the cross, God again looked upon His goodness, creation, and now salvation—and declared His worked finished. *Tetelestai*!

What passion! What great love is this?! May our souls not be languid in living out of our self, but set on fire by the wind and the Word. The wind comes mysteriously; the Word—we know His name, for it has divided all of time, and will trace a line of judgment through every human heart. May we bow to Him—a knee for the Creator, a knee for the Savior!

358. Christianity is no sphere of creeds, no triangle to be calculated, no square of social action, no mere line of history. Christianity is oddly angled, and cannot be called easily by *this* or *that*. What is this then, this *Christianity* that seems hard and supple, thin and thick, amorphous and absolutely defined, curved and sharp?

What is Christianity? The answer: not *what* but *who*. Christianity is Jesus Christ. It, this oddly angled thing called Christianity is *He*, the person of Christ and what He does—not us, and not what we do.

If we live "out of our self," if we live disunited from God who is Jesus Christ, then all we do will be against God even though it may be what we call *good* by man's judgment. *Moralism* and *religion* are the names of the entrustment of man over God—they are manifestations of the ancient temptation and the sin of origin: *humanism—idolatry.*

In Jesus, man no longer lives out of *his* knowledge of good and evil that divorces intended tensions, but out of the very existence of God that unifies creation; out of the eternal cistern from which the world was drawn.

In Jesus, man lives out of The Absolute.

From Jesus' wounds flows *Shalom*; not mere peace, but the harmony originally intended by and through Him—the concord of all that is good, the weaving together of the Creator and the frayed strands of man He loves. From His wounds comes the ordering of life and the holding together of all that He calls good.

359. By some wonderful mystery, I have come to the reasonable conclusion that it is wise to be a fool for Christ.

Now, with joy in fear and trembling: to The Lion—all the Christians to one Lion! For He has come and found you out! Found you out by the costly love of Jesus, by the offense of the cross, by the self-sacrifice of God the Lamb, and by the resurrection of Glory! "For of Him and through Him and to Him are all things, to whom be glory forever" (Romans 11:36).

"Behold, the Lion of the tribe of Judah, the Root of David, has triumphed. He is able to open the scroll and its seven seals. Then I saw the Lamb, looking as if it had been slain" (Revelation 5:5-6).

"You are worthy to take the scroll and to open its seals, because you were slain, and with your blood you purchased men for God from every tribe and language and people and nation. You have made them to be a kingdom of priests to serve our God and they will reign on earth" (9-10).

And then a multitude of euphoric beings—created beings whose presence alone would make us shudder in the chest and bones—began to bravely sing: "Worthy is the Lamb who was slain, to receive power and wealth and wisdom and strength and honor and glory and praise!" (5:12).

To the Lion by way of the Lamb…for love has love won.

~Appendix~

Paracletian

The light of day becomes the fire within;
In the hour changes the age.
Unto the dumb and heavy comes the tongue.
An assembly called to face one against many,
The twelve under roof met twelve in crowd-trodden street
To announce in divers tongues the cloven paraclete,
The very promise of protracted love!
At long last, the wound of Babel healed:
The irony of man *face down* over tower's height!
Of the *upward* gyre and the cursing tree!
At long last, the freedom of clay break
For the House of David's awaited seed—
The Lion awake,
Who has never and will not sleep.

He lives,
The obedient one with *all authority*—
Tread, tread the dark souls
Of dung and dusty feet, from sea to sea.
Walk the dusty middle lands
From an ill-repute village to the energy city.
Transmute your seed from lonely origin:
A man among the countless stars,
From barren sands with fire sprout,
To the kingdom it was long born to be.
Walk, walk to thy death upon your own cobblestones,
Drip your life to the labored rock, from the struck stone
Of the sacred city and its people that emit you out,
Drive you beyond the gate,
Denying you with spittle quivered chins.
Release trust in the stone that will save
In the breaking, but will crush the will
Of those in the coil of self trust.

Transmute ancient seed into comforting breath,
Breath of flat earthen bread
Sugared by the dark bouquet of vinegar wine,
Flavored again by the ferment of *death*.
And out of the dust what becomes?
Out of the agony what is the good?
Does one awake with a vestige of grapes
Still in the mouth? A remnant of love?
Does one awake to merely leave?
From earth to home without *hello*?
Leave us, the lonely, here all alone?
No residue of glory left on shoulders?
No monument in the heart?
But wait!
For the embalmers party came with a gap in their soul,
Yet they ran away with fear that the gap was sealed;
"Could it be? Could it be!
        Oh God!—could *you* be?"
In run, they wondered and knew;
Women with spice, now running with terrific hope.
Running—leaving behind the herbs to embalm
For all time.

So what of the absence that leaves one cold?
    It has been broken.
What of the light in ascension that makes the lovers run hard?
        It has been finished.
Now
Out of the void comes the light
A sun ray scattered, reflected, wide blown
Bearing the bridegroom's pattern on the languid
And semiliterate, the hiding, the hollow boned.
The presence of the Word, the pressure of ghost's form
Marking the men and the women in upper sweaty dorm.
Out of the dark come the words,
And the once huddling fisher's frame
Opened cracked lips to the cosmopolitan sea,

Opened release to the furled hand,
And to thousands, in a moment's eloquence, lipped the name
To show the One alive in recent absence,
To tug and pull from the writhing and ancient deep.

Like the cloven tongue,
One, yet half split in two,
The Christ Lion, within flesh, walks
The trails of dizzy earth, the darkened roads
As the emissary of help to the flat-busted widow,
The sore-broken and panhandling poor—
                The Lion walks,
          Walking amongst the field of reeds—
The impossibility alive!
As true as the bread and the wine
Are the recollection of God with man,
So is the ordinary flesh
And the blood of the wanting
The very temple courts of the most high
For the lamb has lain down in the trusting heart!
And this living day I hear tread the sweet dark souls
Of a wandering love trod sea to sea,
The peace of hand held out,
The creaking hand unfurled,
The season opening seed to breathe,
For when Christ awoke there was dust on his feet.

~Graces~

The composer has written many grace notes into my life. They have brought me much joy and love—and they are essential to the formation of this text.

Marla Joy: You are the elegant vessel through which God showed much of this to me! I love you, and I am faithfully yours; may I be to you like Christ is to the Church.

Pastor Tom Hovestol: You have inspired me with your words, and moreover, your life. Thank you for reflecting so clearly God's glory—for being a bearer of grace *and* truth.

Steve Stanton: Thank you for honesty and no apologies apologetics. I owe you much. Your hard work is appreciated and beautiful to behold; your friendship—a valued gift.

Stephen Reed: For a friendship like that of a brother, I am overjoyed! Thank you for your editor's eye, your service in the name of Christ, and a heart and mind that work in wonderful union.

The Teebkens: You have offered such trust and love—for these graces I thank you.

Mother and Father: Thank you for unfading love and your precious fear of the Lord—what higher gifts can be given? I am grateful. I am a blessed son.

Labor: I once called you ugly, but in revealing God you have become beautiful—thank you for your dust and ache that has taught my heart what it means to kneel.

The Lion and the Lamb—Jesus, My Lord and my God: You know my heart...*forgive me*, and *thank you*. Thank you...